CW01011260

THE
GUINNESS GUIDE
TO SUPERLATIVE
LONDON

Paul Murphy

DOMINE DIRIGE NOS

GUINNESS BOOKS

Editor: Beatrice Frei
Picture editor: Alex Goldberg
Maps: Peter Harper
Design and Layout: Eric Drewery

© Paul Murphy and Guinness Publishing Ltd, 1989

Published in Great Britain by Guinness Publishing Ltd,
33 London Road, Enfield, Middlesex

Typeset in Plantin
by Ace Filmsetting Ltd, Frome, Somerset
Colour origination by
Bright Arts, Hong Kong
Printed and bound in Italy by
New Interlitho SpA

'Guinness' is a registered trade mark of Guinness Superlatives Ltd

British Library Cataloguing in Publication Data
Murphy, Paul
    Guinness guide to superlative London.
    1. London—Visitors' guides
    I. Title
    914.21'04858

    ISBN 0-85112-461-5 (limp)
    ISBN 0-85112-384-8 (cased)

Illustrations on pages 2 and 3:
Bridge of size—a towering monument to Victorian engineering.
The Armorial Bearings of the City of London. The sword is that of St Paul, the City's
Patron Saint.

CONTENTS

ACKNOWLEDGEMENTS

This book is dedicated to Glenys, for first arousing my interest in London, for her contribution to 'Streetwise', and for her typing and tireless support with the *Guinness Guide to Superlative London*.

My special thanks go to William Forrester, an extraordinary London guide whose general editing, knowledgeable suggestions and help, in particular on tackling the 'big four' (the Tower, St Paul's, Westminster Abbey and the British Museum) have been invaluable. His energy, sense of humour and determination in getting around London, despite often having to use a wheelchair, is an inspiration to us all.

Finally, my thanks to the curators, press officers and information departments of London's museums, galleries and institutions for their help.

Picture Credits

HMS *Belfast*, Chapmans Photography—C. Dobson, Bruce Coleman, Hamleys, Matthew Hillier, Impact Photos, Lloyds of London, London Dungeon, Anne Marshall, Popperfoto, David Roberts, Spectrum Colour Library.

Paul Murphy has long been fascinated by the wealth of records, the unusual facts, the mind-boggling figures and all the amazing anecdotes that London has to offer and in 1986 quit his advertising agency job to invent and market his first London publication, Streetwise—the Official London Trivia Game. He has taken hundreds of English and American tourists around the capital as a walking tour guide and has co-written The Daily Telegraph Guide to London Docklands (1988).

INTRODUCTION

London is a city of outstanding achievements, fascinating facts and remarkable statistics. It is constantly changing and yet, in the famous 'Square Mile' (the original London), space-age buildings coexist alongside Victorian slum-land and the remains of a glorious Roman era.

It is this superlative variety, stretching back nearly 2000 years, that has shaped London and makes it one of the world's most interesting cities. However, this same variety can cause many visitors to London to feel almost punch-drunk when confronted with its surfeit of riches—The British Museum alone could occupy a week!

The Guinness Guide to Superlative London—whilst remaining a comprehensive guide—will concentrate on those aspects which we believe will most interest and best acquaint the visitor with London. Almost by definition the majority of the main attractions boast many superlatives, records and anecdotes, and around these the rich history and character of London will be unfurled. Of course there are London attractions without superlatives or records but which are still of great interest—these too will be featured.

The Guinness Guide to Superlative London is the first ever superlative guide book to the capital and is a unique way of discovering the tallest and shortest, the oldest and newest and the best (and worst) of London's attractions, its history and its personalities. Furthermore, although designed as a 'working guide' for tourists and Londoners alike, it is immensely readable in its own right. It makes few calls on the historical or architectural knowledge of the reader and can be 'dipped into' for light reading or reference purposes.

The main section of the Guide divides London's attractions by area, each forming a loose itinerary which may be fully or partly explored dependent on time, specific interests and stamina!

Whatever your interest in London and wherever it takes you, *The Guinness Guide to Superlative London* will act as your personal qualified guide, lacing the story of its sights with superlatives, records and anecdotes.

Notes to help you through the Guide

Museums, Galleries, Palaces, Houses

It is not the intention of the Guide to give an exhaustive list of every exhibit, but to feature those of outstanding or superlative interest to the average visitor. Most of the famous exhibits featured are on permanent exhibition. However, galleries and museums do rotate their displays so it is advisable to telephone in advance to ensure seeing a specific work.

Free up-to-date route-plans and information on temporary exhibitions are available at most major museums and galleries to complement the Guide.

Pubs, Wine Bars and Restaurants

Due to the subjective and often fashion-led nature of these types of establishments, the Guide will only feature a small selection of places that have been 'tried and tested' throughout the years and in our opinion are of 'special interest'. (All bars featured serve food, both lunchtime and evening, unless otherwise stated.) Of course it does not follow that a bar or restaurant of 'special interest' will serve the best beer, wine or food in town. In this respect the Guide does not give recommendations—but would refer you to the bibliography.

Itineraries and Planning

The different itineraries have been designed to cluster together attractions into small geographical areas which may be easily covered on foot. Some itineraries are completely detached e.g. Chelsea, but in other areas such as the City, where one square mile is divided into four separate itineraries, then inevitably they will merge together. The advice, therefore, when route planning is to consider not only what is in the same itinerary but also to look at adjacent itineraries

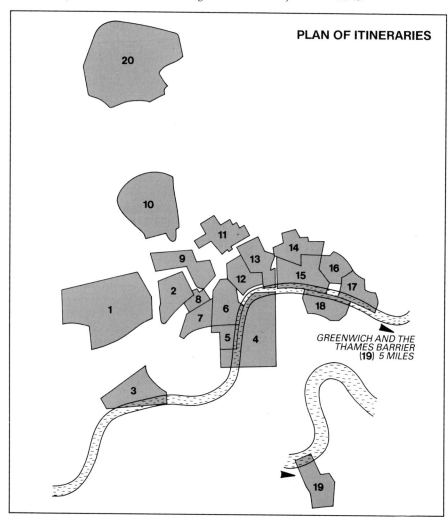

PLAN OF ITINERARIES

GREENWICH AND THE
THAMES BARRIER
(**19**) 5 MILES

PRACTICAL INFORMATION

Arriving in London

Fast trains and buses run frequently from Gatwick to Victoria Station (28 miles, 45 km) and Heathrow is linked directly to central London (15 miles, 24 km) by Underground ('tube').

Visitors without accommodation can receive assistance from the London Tourist Board's information offices at Gatwick, Heathrow or Victoria.

Money and banks

Currency 100p = £1. Gatwick and Heathrow have 24-hour banking and foreign exchange facilities. There are bureaux de change at major railway termini. Normal opening hours for High Street banks are 09.30–15.30 Mon–Fri (some suburban branches open on Saturday mornings).

Public telephones

These take either phone cards (which are sold by newsagents and Post Offices), cash (2p, 5p, 10p, 20p, 50p, £1) or credit cards (which are not so common). The cheaper rate for local calls is daily between 18.00 and 08.00 and all day at weekends, and for international calls between 20.00 and 08.00 and all day at weekends. Prefix London telephone numbers with 01 only when dialling from outside London.

Useful numbers

London Directory Enquiries   142
Directory Enquiries—outside London   192
US Directory Enquiries   153

British Operator (service difficulties and general enquiries)   100
International Operator   155
Emergency Services   999

Medical services

Medical Casualty Departments of major London hospitals will normally give emergency treatment day or night. For less urgent matters a local (or hotel) doctor may be contacted.

Chemist Boots, Piccadilly Circus, W.1. (Tel.: 01-734 6126). Open Mon–Sat 08.30 to 20.00 for prescriptions and medical items.

Public transport

The quickest and most efficient way of travelling within London is by Underground (see map). Avoid rush hours, 07.30–09.30 and 17.00–19.00, and remember the service closes down around midnight. London's red buses provide a slower sight-seeing alternative. There is also a network of special night buses that run throughout the night across London and into the suburbs. (All of them call at Trafalgar Square.) Various flat-fare types of Travelcard ticket may be purchased for Underground and buses—ask at any station for details or phone London Transport Information Office (01) 222 1234. There are travel information centres at the following stations: Heathrow (all arrivals terminals), Victoria, Piccadilly Circus, Oxford Circus, Euston, King's Cross, St James's Park.

There are some 13 000 officially licensed

9

taxi cabs in London. These are standard metered and their drivers are required to have passed a rigorous examination, learning 468 well-used routes within a 6-mile (9 km) radius of Charing Cross. Their availability is signalled by the illuminated 'For Hire' sign above the windscreen.

General tourist information

The main Tourist Information Centre is at Victoria Station. Other central London bureaux are at Harrods, the Tower of London (31 Mar–31 Oct), and Selfridges. There is a City Information Centre near St Paul's Underground station.

For general London tourist information ring (01) 730 3488 between 0900 and 1730. For information specifically on the City (the 'Square Mile') ring (01) 260 1456 or (01) 606 3030 between 09.00 and 17.00.

For Riverboat Information ring (01) 730 4812.

Opening times and details of admission

The specific opening times for each attraction featured in the Guide are given in the text. The following abbreviations apply:

O   Opening Times
BH   Bank Holidays (statutory public holidays)

The oldest, largest and most cosmopolitan city in Britain; '. . . there is in London all that life can afford' (Dr Samuel Johnson).

PH   Public Holidays

C   Particularly suitable for children

£/p Entrance charge for adults, £=£1 or
     more, p=less than £1 at the time of
     writing (no symbol means admission
     is free). Children usually half-price

T   Guided Tours for general public, £/p
     where charge is made

&   Accessible by wheelchair %=approxi-
     mate degree of accessibility inside
     multiple level buildings t=wheelchair
     toilet (no symbol means no special
     toilet)

V   Facilities for partially sighted and vis-
     ually handicapped people

H   Facilities for people with hearing
     difficulties

General note   Last admission is usually
half an hour before closing time. Most attractions are closed on 24, 25, 26 December, 1
January, Good Friday and May Day Bank
Holiday (first Monday in May). Where none
of the above information is given, the attraction is not open to the public (e.g.
Buckingham Palace).

**Special note on access for disabled
people**   It is always advisable to phone
ahead to request assistance, ascertain particular difficulties, check lift working etc.
Our wheelchair symbol does not imply international access standards but is intended to
indicate those places which we recommend
visiting. Unless stated otherwise there is flat
access into the building although this may
not be via the main entry. If in doubt telephone ahead or ask staff when there. For
more detailed information the definitive
guide book is Nicholson's *Access in London* or
telephone Artsline, the advice service for the
disabled in London (01) 388 2227/8 Mon–Fri
10.00–16.00; Sat 10.00–14.00.

General Restaurant Hours
Traditional restaurants will generally take
orders only between 12.30 and 14.30 and
19.00 and 22.30. However, there are many
restaurants now (particularly in areas such
as Chinatown and Covent Garden) which
serve throughout the day.

General Pub and Wine Bar Hours
Until August 1988 only two sessions were
licensed for the sale of alcohol, Mon–Sat
11.00–15.00 and 17.30–23.00, Sun 12.00–
14.00 and 19.00–22.30. The new licensing
law allows pubs and wine bars to serve alcohol from 11.00 to 23.00 without a break
Mon–Sat, 12.00–15.00 Sun. Not all bars take
advantage of the new extended hours however, therefore it is advisable to telephone in
advance if planning to visit a pub or bar outside of the old 'traditional' hours. Bars in the
City open at 17.00 for the evening session but
may close as early as 20.00 due to the City
'exodus'. Few bars in the City open at all at
the weekend.

General Shopping Hours
Normal hours are Mon–Sat 09.00–17.30 but
these can vary, with late night openings in
popular areas such as Oxford Street (Thurs),
Knightsbridge (Wed) and Covent Garden,
etc. Many smaller shops will also open late
and on Sundays.

General Church Hours
Most churches are open daily between 10.00
and 16.00 as well as for Sunday services.

Tipping

This is not obligatory and should never be
paid begrudgingly. However, where a good
standard of service has been provided in a
friendly spirit, and a service charge is not
incorporated into the bill, the customary tip
for taxi-drivers, waiters, etc. is around ten
per cent.

HISTORY

London chronology

54 BC	Julius Caesar invades Britain and crosses the Thames in the London area (no traces of settlement left behind)
AD 43	Establishment of London (Londinium) by army of Claudius
60/61	Boudicca (Boadicea) revolts against Roman rule in Britain, razes London and massacres its inhabitants
61–100	Imperial Roman city built
c. 190–200	Roman London Wall built. Population approximately 45 000–50 000
c. 300–400	London is renamed Augusta as mark of imperial favour
410	Roman troops withdraw from London and Britain
410 onwards	'Dark Ages': Little is known about London in this period
c. 600–700	London re-established as major city and trading port
851	Vikings invade, occupy and destroy much of London
886	King Alfred recaptures London and builds it up to become largest city in the kingdom
980	Vikings reoccupy London
c. 1014	King Ethelred II and King Olaf recapture London
c. 1050–1065	Edward the Confessor builds Westminster Abbey and Palace of Westminster
1066	Norman conquest. London surrenders to William I. City leaders negotiate rights with William the Conqueror. Population approximately 14 000–18 000
1189	Population approximately 20 000–25 000
1192	First Lord Mayor of London elected—Henry Fitz Ailwyn
1209	First stone London Bridge completed
1215	Magna Carta confirms the City's municipal autonomy
1265	Parliamentary beginnings, first meeting of 'Commons'
1280	Old St Paul's Cathedral completed
1348–9	Black Death (see entry)
1381	Wat Tyler leads Peasants' Revolt march on London. Tyler killed and peasants dispersed
1411	Construction of Guildhall begins
1500–1600	Dramatic growth in London commerce, established as major trading port
1535–40	Major disruption of London life due to monastic closures of the Dissolution
c. 1590	'Theatre-land' developed in Southwark, development of 'West End' of London

1605	Gunpowder Plot discovered at Houses of Parliament. Population approximately 225 000
1642	Charles I storms into House of Commons to arrest members (English Civil War starts)
1649	Charles I executed at Whitehall (end of English Civil War)
1650	Population approximately 350 000–400 000
1665	Great Plague (see entry)
1666	Great Fire of London (see entry)
1667 onwards	Rebuilding of London. St Paul's Cathedral begun 1675
1694	Bank of England founded
1750	Population approximately 650 000
1780	Gordon Riots, 2–13 June: minimum of 565 killed in the UK's worst ever riots in protest against repeal of anti-Catholic legislation
1801	First London census records: population of 1 117 290—world's most populous urban settlement. Population of City 128 000
1829	First London bus, Paddington to Bank. Metropolitan Police founded
1837	First railway in London, London Bridge to Greenwich
1834	Houses of Parliament burn down—rebuilding completed 1860s
1849	Cholera epidemic kills 14 000
1851	Great Exhibition
1858	'Great Stink' of stagnant Thames results in bill for creation of first sewerage system for London
1863	First underground railway opened (Metropolitan Line—Farringdon St to Edgware Rd)
1888	'Jack the Ripper' murders—thought to have killed at least five times between August and November. 'Jack's' identity never discovered
1889	First London local government coordinating body, the London County Council formed
1901	Population of Inner London over 4½ million, Greater London over 6½ million, City 37 709
1914–18	World War I: First air raid on London 31 May 1915 by Zeppelin, 7 dead, 35 injured. Total 670 killed in air raids
1939	Peak population of Greater London reached at 8 615 050
1939–45	Blitz and World War II (see entry)
1951	5–12 December, London fog plus smoke create world's worst ever smog disaster causing 2850 excess deaths
1956	Clean Air Act makes London Britain's first smokeless zone
1988	Population of Greater London 6 756 000

English and British monarchs

Reigns from Edward the Confessor to Queen Elizabeth II

Earlier Saxon and Danish monarchs are not listed here as, with the exception of Alfred the Great who ruled between 871 and 899, they are not mentioned in this Guide.

1042–66	Edward the Confessor
1066–87	William I (the Conqueror)
1087–1100	William II (Rufus)
1100–35	Henry I
1135–54	Stephen (Apr–Nov 1141, deposed by Queen Matilda)
1154–89	Henry II
1189–99	Richard I (the Lionheart)
1199–1216	John
1216–72	Henry III
1272–1307	Edward I
1307–27	Edward II
1327–77	Edward III
1377–99	Richard II
1399–1413	Henry IV
1413–22	Henry V
1422–61	Henry VI
1461–70	Edward IV
1470–1	Henry VI
1471–83	Edward IV
1483	Edward V
1483–5	Richard III
1485–1509	Henry VII
1509–47	Henry VIII
1547–53	Edward VI
1553	Jane Grey
1553–8	Mary I
1558–1603	Elizabeth I
1603–25	James I
1625–49	Charles I
1649–53	Commonwealth Council of State
1653–8	(Protector) Oliver Cromwell
1658–9	(Protector) Richard Cromwell
1660–85	Charles II
1685–8	James II
1689–94	William III and Mary II
1694–1702	William III
1702–14	Anne
1714–27	George I
1727–60	George II
1760–1820	George III
1820–30	George IV
1830–7	William IV
1837–1901	Victoria
1901–10	Edward VII
1910–36	George V
1936	Edward VIII
1936–52	George VI
1952–	Elizabeth II

The Black Death, 1348–9

The Black Death, a mixture of bubonic, pneumonic and septicaemic plague was the world's worst ever disaster of any kind. Between 1347 and 1351 it accounted for the lives of some 75 million across Eurasia, including 800 000 in the United Kingdom—around half the population. It reached England by June 1348 and by November it was rampant amongst the crowded insanitary streets of medieval London. Like the Great Plague it was transmitted by infected fleas on rats.

Details of the Black Death in London are scarce as compared to the Great Plague. There are no definitive historical accounts of conditions and the ecclesiastical records which might have provided accurate checks did not survive. In a time of minimum personal hygiene, no medical protection and nowhere to escape, however, the suffering would have been at least equal to that experienced during the Great Plague of 1665.

The epidemic raged in full fury for three to four months and by May the worst was over (see Great Plague for symptoms etc.).

Deaths occurred sporadically, however, for another two years. There are no accurate figures on the final toll and it may only be guessed at from snippets of information and the overall national picture. The population of London in 1348-9 has been variously estimated at between 45 000 and 75 000 and therefore estimates of around 25 000 to 30 000 deaths seem reasonable.

> The historian John Stow claims 50 000 buried at Smithfield alone but this must be discounted, given London's population at the time. It is claimed elsewhere, however, that 200 bodies were being buried there daily during the worst period from 2 February to 2 April and on that basis the plague-pit must hold at least 15 000 bodies, making it the largest of this period. A rare tombstone, commemorating victims of the Black Death, may be seen in the floor of the Great Cloister in Westminster Abbey. The tomb is said to hold 26 monks who died in 1349.

The Great Plague, 1665

The Great Plague was the second major bubonic plague epidemic to strike London. Exactly when it arrived and how many lives it claimed is unclear due to the inaccuracy of the Bills of Mortality, the parish fatality records; (see St Olave—Tower). The first official victim is considered to be Margaret Ponteous, buried at St Paul's, Covent Garden on 12 April 1665. Londoners knew the symptoms of black or inflamed rose-like blotches, swellings and sneezing only too well as sporadic deaths had occurred throughout the century. They had no idea, however, that the creatures which spread the plague were the rats which carried infected fleas. Tragically, cats and dogs were blamed and thousands were destroyed, so allowing the rats to multiply. Once plague was diagnosed in a house, the whole household was locked in and quarantined for 40 days, until recovery or death occurred. A red cross was painted on the door, with the ominous words 'Lord have mercy on us'.

Pudding Lane still aflame over three centuries on (see London Dungeon).

By mid-July the death toll was over 1000 per week. The richer members of society left the city, although poor refugees were often refused by the provinces and it is estimated that over 300 000 remained in London. Londoners who took to river boat accommodation survived best. Burial yards overflowed and huge plague-pits were dug. The author Daniel Defoe in his *Journal of the Plague Year* mentions over 1000 corpses thrown into a 'dreadful gulf' near the church at Aldgate. The virulence reached its peak in the third week of September when 8297 deaths were officially recorded. (The true figure would have been well in excess of 10 000.) The streets of London were becoming overgrown with grass and weeds only disturbed by the death carts and the drivers' plaintive cries of 'Bring out your dead'. By December many refugees were returning, although the King and court did not come back until 1 February 1666. The final official death toll was 68 596. The actual figure is estimated to be around 110 000.

No sooner had the City regained its bustle and made its mind up on how to prevent such an event ever recurring, than its festering alleyways were swept away in the Great Fire.

Two legacies of the Great Plague remain in the common language. The nursery rhyme 'Ring-a-ring o'Roses' refers to the symptoms described above ('a pocket full of posies' were bouquets carried to sweeten the air; this rhyme may be an even older folk memory of the Black Death) and the phrase, 'dead of night': the only time when it was permitted to bury victims.

The Great Fire of London, 1666

The Great Fire broke out in Pudding Lane from the shop of the King's baker, Thomas Farrinor, between 01.00–02.00 on Sunday 2 September 1666. It appears that he left a bundle of wood too near an oven which was still burning, and although he managed to escape with his family, his maid became the first casualty. It had been an exceptionally hot, dry summer and the tightly packed wooden houses allowed the fire, fanned by a strong wind, to spread rapidly. Samuel Pepys witnessed the confusion and went to Whitehall to warn the King, Charles II. The King took personal control and halted the progress of the fire by the systematic demolition of houses with gunpowder in order to create fire breaks.

It continued to burn until Thursday 6 September, however, before being finally halted. Five-sixths of the City area had been laid waste and the final catalogue of destruction included 13 200 houses, 89 parish churches, Old St Paul's Cathedral and numerous important historical buildings such as the Guildhall and most of the ancient halls of the City Livery Companies. Around 100 000 were made homeless but, due to the rapid evacuation of the area, only eight people were killed.

The final casualty was a Huguenot named Robert Hubert who 'confessed' to starting the fire deliberately. Although the fire almost certainly started accidentally and Hubert's story was blatantly absurd, he was nevertheless hanged as a convenient scapegoat.

Visionary rebuilding plans were submitted by Christopher Wren and others whilst London still smouldered. They were all defeated, however, not just by the resistance of freeholders to land pattern changes but because there was no money to pay for the schemes. The construction of the post-Fire City was therefore piecemeal and practical with brick and stone replacing the insanitary wooden medieval maze that had encouraged two disasters.

The Blitz and the Second World War, 1939–45

The word Blitz derives from the German Blitzkrieg, meaning lightning war. It was by no means confined to London, but to Londoners it has become synonymous with the bombing siege of the city from 7 September

St Paul's Cathedral, 29 December 1940, 'riding the sea of flames like a great ship'.

1940 to May 1941. During that first night, history's first 'fire-storm' occurred in the Surrey Docks at Southwark, killing 306 people. The bombers arrived for the next 56 nights, dropping some 18 000 tons of bombs causing 9500 deaths. The worst single attack happened the following year, on 10–11 May 1941, when 1436 died.

The area to be worst-hit by far was the East End of London due to its dockland importance.

However, far from killing the spirit of London, the hardship helped to cement unity as characterized, and to a large extent created, by Sir Winston Churchill's charismatic speeches, 'The people of London with one voice would say to Hitler "You do your worst and we will do our best"', (June 1941).

The most popular form of communal shelter were the underground stations and by the end of September 1940 around 177 000 people were using these. It is estimated, however, that around 60 per cent of Londoners took little or no shelter during the Blitz.

A final chapter of terror from above was provided by the V1 and V2 attacks during 1944–5. By March 1945, after the last air raid, the final death toll was over 15 000 and the devastation included 3½ million houses, damaged or destroyed.

The greatest architectural and historical losses include the complete destruction of the House of Commons and 19 halls of the City Livery Companies and severe damage to many City churches.

Much of the rebuilding of London did not begin until the late 1950s and early 1960s, due to lack of funds. When it did start, however, it was done in indecent haste, with an average of just 4 minutes per project spent on considering planning permission. Little time was devoted to getting the new to blend with the old and the legacy of such policies is characterized by the much derided Paternoster Square development around St Paul's Cathedral.

KENSINGTON, HYDE PARK AND KNIGHTSBRIDGE

The original manor of Kensington, dating back to 1086, developed into a rural market garden area in the 16th to 19th centuries until the spread of London established it as a pleasant country suburb for early commuters. The gentrification of the area was completed by royal patronage in 1689 when William III moved his court to the newly converted Kensington Palace. South Kensington is now synonymous with its priceless museums' collections, and is therefore one of the most concentrated repositories of knowledge in the world. This originated from a unique piece of civil planning, inspired by Prince Albert, which utilized profits made by the Great Exhibition of 1851 to ensure that 87 acres (35 ha) of land were dedicated to art and science institutes and training colleges.

Knightsbridge also dates back to the 11th century and owes its name to a bridge which crossed the now vanished river Westbourne.

Legend has it that two knights fought to the death on the bridge and during the 18th century it was witness to more violent confrontation with highwaymen.

It has since been developed into one of London's most exclusive residential and shopping areas where the greatest physical danger is probably being caught up in the first day of the famous Harrods' sale!

Kensington Palace   [1]

Kensington Palace began life as Nottingham House, purchased for £14 000 by William III in 1689 in order that the asthmatic King could live away from the polluted air and river of central London. Sir Christopher Wren was appointed to improve the house but his designs made no attempt at grandeur and even after his assistant, Nicholas Hawksmoor had designed the impressive

1. KENSINGTON, HYDE PARK AND KNIGHTSBRIDGE

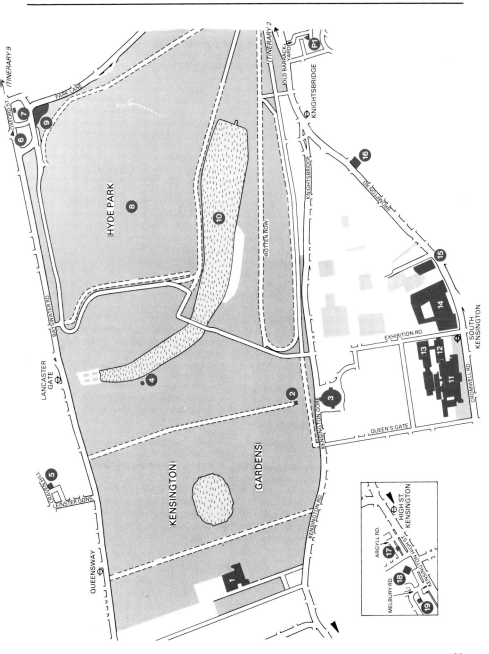

south front some years later, it was still known simply as Kensington House.

Queen Anne moved into the House in 1702, adding the 'stately Green House' which is now known as Queen Anne's Orangery. She was succeeded by George I who commissioned William Kent to decorate the new apartments. George II became the last reigning monarch to reside at Kensington and the Palace fell into a state of disrepair for the next half century. Edward, Duke of Kent (the father of Queen Victoria), moved in and commissioned James Wyatt to work on the Palace. The cost of the work, finished in 1812, was almost ruinous to the Duke, and he avoided his creditors by fleeing the country. He did return, however, for the Palace's most famous occasion, the birth of his daughter, the future Queen Victoria, on 24 May 1819. On 20 June 1837 Princess Victoria was awoken in the apartments with news of her accession to the throne and following her accession council she moved to Buckingham Palace. The apartments were later occupied by the Duke and Duchess of Teck and their daughter, the future Queen Mary, was born there in 1867. In the following decades, the Palace once again deteriorated and it was only due to Queen Victoria's personal intervention that it was saved from demolition. It was restored, however, on the understanding that the apartments were made public and these were opened by the Queen on her 80th birthday in 1899.

The Palace is still used by the Royal Family. It is the London residence of the Prince and Princess of Wales and Princess Margaret, who occupy private apartments on the west side behind the state rooms.

The Court Dress Collection

The ground floor is devoted to the history of Court dresses and uniforms, spanning 12 reigns back to the early 18th century. The most popular exhibit in the collection, already seen by millions of people on television, is the wedding dress worn by the Princess of Wales, 29 July 1981.

The State Apartments

Queen Mary's Gallery Unfortunately, few original fittings remain here, the most important are the gilt surrounds to the mirrors carved by Grinling Gibbons in 1691. The portrait paintings include Peter the Great, painted during the Tsar's visit to London in 1688 by Sir Godfrey Kneller.

Queen Mary's Drawing Room The most notable objects are the giltwood chandelier, probably English c. 1730 and a fine barometer c. 1695. The painting of the Infant Christ with St John the Baptist is by Van Dyck (1630s).

Queen Mary's Bedchamber The State bed originally belonged to James II. The most striking piece of furniture, however, is the elaborate mid-17th-century writing cabinet inlaid with semi-precious stones purchased by George IV.

The Privy Chamber The three Mortlake tapestries, depicting the seasons of the year, were probably woven for Charles I when Prince of Wales in 1623-4. The ceiling was painted by William Kent for a fee of £300 in 1723.

The Presence Chamber The elaborate fireplace overmantel finely carved in pearwood is attributed to Grinling Gibbons. The brilliantly coloured ceiling is by William Kent.

The King's Grand Staircase The 'illusionist gallery' created by Kent, which gives the impression of crowds thronging the staircase and peering down from a dome above (as they would have on court days) is regarded as his most outstanding decorative work. It is also a useful historical 'snap-shot' of the court of George I. At the top of the stairs are a Quaker and a curious character known as 'Peter the Wild Boy'. He was found living semi-wild on all fours in the woods of Hanover and brought to the court by the King. The wrought ironwork is by Jean Tijou.

The King's Gallery Measuring some 96 ft

(26 m) long, this is the largest and grandest of the apartments. At the centre of the hall is a splendid rare surviving wind-dial made for William III in 1694. The direction of the wind is indicated by a pointer connected to the wind-vane on the roof. The picture of the Madonna and Child is thought to date from 1583 by Annibale Caracci. The ceiling panels, depicting various mythological scenes, are by Kent. The most important works in the gallery are *Jupiter and Antiope* by Rubens c. 1614 and Van Dyck's *Cupid and Psyche*.

Duchess of Kent's Dressing Room The room's furnishings date from the mid-19th century. The gilt and silvered cabinet was a present from Queen Victoria to Prince Albert on his 37th birthday. The finely carved 17th-century German cradle was also bought by the Queen.

The Ante Room The showcase contains some of the toys used by Queen Victoria as a child. The doll's house is an early example of a child's doll's house actually used for play, as opposed to an adult's miniature model.

Queen Victoria's Bedroom Princess Victoria learnt that she was to be Queen here and 30 years later Queen Mary was born in this room. The ornate cot made in 1840 for Queen Victoria's first daughter was used for all of her nine children.

The King's Drawing Room The baroque-style ceiling painting (representing Jupiter appearing to Semele), for which Kent was paid £500 in 1723, is reckoned to be his most striking work in the Palace. The huge elaborately decorated clock in the middle of the room dates from 1743 and was worked on by master sculptors John Michael Rysbrack and Louis François Roubiliac.

The Council Chamber This room is now dedicated to the great international exhibitions which took place in the mid-Victorian period. The first and most famous of these was the Great Exhibition of 1851 held within sight of Kensington Palace (see Hyde Park).

Amongst the many elaborate items is a silver statuette of Lady Godiva given by Victoria to Albert as a 38th birthday present and a silver table fountain designed under the direction of Prince Albert in 1852.

The Cupola Room This was the principal state room of the Palace, decorated lavishly in 1722 by Kent, attempting to create an image of Roman grandeur.

The Orangery This is reckoned to have the finest architectural interior at the Palace. Wren was chief architect but it was mainly designed by Nicholas Hawksmoor and Sir John Vanbrugh in 1704. Carving by Grinling Gibbons features above the arches.

Kensington Gardens The extensive private grounds of the Palace, laid out in 1728 as one of the earliest English landscaped gardens, only became public in the mid-19th century. The Sunken Garden (a replica opened in 1909) is the only reminder of the formal layout of the old gardens.

Statues of the two monarchs most closely associated with the Palace, William III and Victoria stand at the south front and the east side respectively. The statue, representing Queen Victoria at the time of her accession, was sculpted by her daughter Princess Louise and is a rare example of a monument which depicts the Queen in her young life.

O **Mon–Sat (inc BH) 09.00–17.00; Sun 13.00–17.00; £ ☎ (01) 937 9561**

Albert Memorial [2]

The Memorial to Queen Victoria's beloved Consort (excluding statue) was completed in 1872 and earned its designer, George Gilbert Scott, a knighthood. It stands 175 ft (53 m) high, the second tallest monument to an individual person in London (see Nelson's Column), and cost in total £120 000. The 14 ft (4 m) tall statue of the Prince was added in 1876 and depicts him holding the catalogue of the Great Exhibition of 1851 for which he was largely responsible. The frieze around the base of the memorial is the most populous of any London memorial, representing 169 life-sized figures of artistic heroes of the Victorian age. An arbitrary 'top ten' might read Shakespeare, Beethoven, Leonardo da Vinci, Michelangelo, Wren, Turner, Rembrandt, Mozart, Homer and Pythagoras!

> *Prince Albert died of typhoid at the insanitary Windsor Castle in 1861. Ironically, he had been a campaigner during his philanthropic career for better domestic conditions for the working classes.*

Royal Albert Hall   [3]
Kensington Gore Road

After the death of Prince Albert in 1861, public funds were raised to finance the Albert Memorial and a memorial concert hall. Unfortunately, these only covered the cost of the Albert Memorial and it was left to the ingenuity of Henry Cole, the original pro-

poser of the hall, to finance the building by selling over 1300 seats on a 999-year leasehold at £100 each. On 20 May 1867 Queen Victoria laid the foundation stone.

The Hall appears to be circular but is in fact slightly oval with outside measurements of 272×238 ft (83×72 m) and is 135 ft (41 m) high internally. The organ consists of some 9000 pipes and weighs 150 tons. It was the largest ever when built in 1924 and is still the largest in London. Its most famous regular function since 1941 has been the staging of Sir Henry Wood's Promenade Concerts which are usually held for eight weeks from July to September and culminate in what has become a major British institution, 'The Last Night of the Proms'. The Hall capacity is around 7500 people but the BBC World Service estimates that each year there is an audience of around 150 million for the 'Proms', making them the world's most popular concerts.

O Oct–Apr Guided Tours only, every ½ hour;   09.30–17.30 lasts 1¼ hrs;   £ 15.30–17.30 lasts ½ hr;   £
☎ (01) 589 3203

The 'other' Prince Albert memorial on the steps of the Royal Albert Hall. It commemorates the Great Exhibition which the Prince presided over.

Statue of Peter Pan   [4]
Kensington Gardens

Sir George Frampton's 1912 statue of Peter
Pan stands on the spot where Peter's boat is
supposed to have landed in the 'Never Never
Land of the child's mind' in Kensington
Gardens! The statue, commissioned by
Peter's creator, Sir James Barrie, was erected
unofficially overnight in the park as a
'magical' surprise for the children in keeping
with the fairy-tale qualities of its subject.
Barrie lived at 100 Bayswater Road from
1902-9, next to the Gardens from where he
wrote *Peter Pan*. The model for the statue
was Nina Boucicault, the lady who first
played Peter Pan at the Duke of York's
Theatre in St Martin's Lane on 27 December
1904. This tradition of a female Peter lasted
78 years until in 1982 Miles Anderson played
the first male Peter.

Peter Pan *has become a 'hardy Christmas annual' and the names of those who
have acted in it read like a roll call for the
British theatre. In 1913 Noël Coward
played Slightly, 1933 saw Sir Ralph
Richardson in the role of Captain Hook,
while in 1936 Charles Laughton played
the part and in the 1970s Ron Moody
appeared as Hook opposite Susannah York
and Dorothy Tutin. In 1920 a scenario was
prepared for Paramount Studios where
Charlie Chaplin was to play Peter but the
film was never made.*

London Toy and Model Museum   [5]
21-3 Craven Hill Road

This is one of the finest museums of its kind
in the world, housing a collection of over
3000 toys and models dating back to the 18th
century.

The largest and most impressive of the
eight main galleries is the Train Room which
has the best collection of toy and model trains
on public display in Europe. The trains also
run outside, where every Sunday from 11.00
to 17.00 they provide the only regular steam
service in London, carrying passengers
around the garden.

Other displays include a wooden Noah's
Ark with 90 pairs of animals, a gallery of
tin toys which includes the first ever 'jet'
propelled toy boat dating from 1898, and in
the Nursery is the well-loved collection of
teddy bears. The most famous London bear,
Paddington—named after the station a short
walk away from the Museum—has his own
show case.

O **Tue–Sat (inc BH Mon) 10.00-17.30;**
Sun 11.00-17.00;   C;   £;   ⅟ (1 step)
70%
☎ **(01) 262 7905**

Tyburn Gallows (site)   [6]
**Junction Bayswater Road and Edgware
Road**

The spot now marked with a small brass
plaque was for nearly 400 years the deadliest
site in England. The first recorded execution
took place here in 1196 but it became the
principal place for public executions in 1388
and in 1571 the 'Tyburn Tree'—London's
first permanent gallows—was erected. This
was a triangular structure some 12 ft (4 m)
high with 9 ft (3 m) cross beams on which 24
people could be hanged at one time. Public
executions were intended to act as a deterrent
to crime but almost inevitably degenerated
into riotous carnivals. The name 'Tyburn
Fair' was coined and in the 18th century
'Mother Proctor's Pews' were installed. This
was a bank of seating designed to give a

*The final journey heading westward by
horse and cart from Newgate Prison to
Tyburn thought to have introduced an
expression which lingers on—'In the cart'
meaning to be in trouble.*

grandstand view and at one single execution earned its owner, Mother Proctor, some £500. The largest ever crowd was estimated to be an amazing 200 000, assembled in 1714 to witness the hanging of the legendary Jack Sheppard (see Central Criminal Court). Almost equally (in)famous was the archcriminal Jonathan Wild, who was reputed to have picked the executioner's pockets as he adjusted the noose in 1725. One of the strangest Tyburn 'executions' was the ceremonial beheading of the dead body of Oliver Cromwell (see Statue of Oliver Cromwell). By the time of the last Tyburn execution in 1783 (after which hangings were transferred to Newgate prison) it is estimated that around 50 000 perished at Tyburn (see London Dungeon).

Marble Arch [7]

Marble Arch was designed by John Nash to symbolize the victories of Trafalgar and Waterloo and was erected at a cost of £10 000 in front of Buckingham Palace in 1827. It was moved to its present site as an entrance to Hyde Park in 1851 as a result of the redevelopment of Buckingham Palace but has since become somewhat isolated.

The unpopularity of John Nash is reflected in the long-held false myth that the Marble Arch had to be removed from the Palace because it was too narrow to accommodate the Sovereign's Royal Coach!

Hyde Park [8]

This is the largest of Central London's parks, covering some 340 acres (138 ha). Henry VIII confiscated the grounds in 1536 for hunting and Elizabeth I also hunted here. In the 17th century it became plagued by highwaymen; in 1689 as a deterrent measure William III

ordered 300 lamps to be hung from the branches of the trees between Rotten Row and St James's—the earliest example of English street lighting. (Rotten Row is thought to be a corruption of 'route du roi', as it was once the King's way from Westminster to Kensington.)

The greatest occasion the Park has ever witnessed was the Great Exhibition in 1851—the world's first major international fair. This display of the world's greatest (and most unusual) manufactured treasures included, the Koh-i-noor diamond, an eau-de-Cologne fountain, a rubber table, cuffs made from wool spun from the dogwool of a French poodle, a watch the size of a pea, a garden seat made of coal, a vase made of mutton fat and the world's most 'bladed' pen knife, the Year Knife by Joseph Rodgers and Sons Ltd of Sheffield, with 1851 blades!

The exhibition was housed in Joseph Paxton's remarkable Crystal Palace—at that time the largest glass structure the world had ever seen. Its 4000 tons of iron structure held

The Park continues to witness record-breaking occasions. The world's largest children's party, to mark the 'International Year of the Child', was attended there by the Royal Family and 160 000 children on 30–31 May 1979.

The world's largest participative sports gathering was the run in Hyde Park for Sport Aid on 25 May 1986 with c. 120 000 runners.

On the first Sunday in November each year, around 300 veteran cars (made between 1895 and 1905) leave Hyde Park Corner for the London to Brighton Veteran Car Run. This first began in 1896 to celebrate the abolition of the law which compelled a motorist to have a man waving a red warning flag walking in front of him! The speed limit was consequently raised from 4 to 12 mph (6 to 19 km/h).

some 3 million panes of glass (measuring 900 000 sq ft, 83 610 sq m) and it covered 19 acres (8 ha). (Its foundations are still under the grass of the Park.)

The exhibition lasted for 141 days during which time 6 039 195 visitors (an incredible 1/6th of the nation's population) paid some £356 000 in admission receipts.

After the exhibition the Crystal Palace was moved to Sydenham, south east of the Thames and burned down in 1936. The flames were visible as far as Portsmouth (70 miles, 113 km).

Speakers' Corner   [9]
Hyde Park

The origin of England's most famous free speech 'soap-box' dates back to 1872 when, following, frequent mass demonstrations in this corner of Hyde Park, the right of free assembly was finally granted. It is, therefore, not the speakers but their audience who have been granted full jurisdiction. Speakers' Corner is at its most lively on Sunday mornings and the only restrictions placed on the speakers are that they must not be obscene, blasphemous, treasonable or racialist, nor must they say anything to incite a breach of the peace. They may ask people to 'lend them their ears' but money is out of the question and so is amplification!

**Sunday am and pm;   starts around 11.00;
& t (subway)**

The Serpentine   [10]

This 41-acre (17-ha) lake was created by the damming of the river Westbourne in 1730. Its name derives from its winding serpent-like shape. In 1826 the frozen Serpentine provided the scene for what was then called 'the most daring feat of all time'. In order to win a wager of 100 guineas (£105) a van and four horses were driven across the ice over the broadest part of the lake. (The depth of the lake varies from 4 ft 6 in to 14 ft (1.37–4.27 m).)

Natural History Museum   [11]
Cromwell Road

The nucleus of the original Natural History Museum comprised Sir Hans Sloane's private collection of around 50 000 books, 80 000 specimens and his extensive herbarium. Originally part of the British Museum collection, these were moved in 1880 to the present building, newly designed by Alfred Waterhouse in awesome Romanesque style. The towers, spires and nave-like central hall resemble a great medieval cathedral and its 675 ft (206 m) variegated terracotta frontage makes it one of London's most attractive landmarks (particularly when floodlit). The interior is no less impressive, richly decorated with floral tiles and terracotta mouldings (those in the western half of the museum represent living creatures and organisms and those to the east depict extinct specimens). There are today some 50 million items in total, although only a small fraction of these are on public display in the 4 acres (2 ha) of gallery space. The Museum is one of the world's greatest collection of plants, animals, birds, reptiles, marine life and insects (fossil and living). Man's place in evolution, minerals, rock and meteorites, ecology and British natural history are also extensively covered.

The principal exhibition galleries and subjects are as follows:

Dinosaurs and their living relatives
The collection of dinosaurs' remains (which form only a tiny fraction of the palaeontology department's seven million fossils) is the best

The enclosed swimming area of the Serpentine, the Lido, is used by the 'All Year Round Club'—the oldest swimming club in Britain—who claim to have swum here every day since 1864!

London Bus 7.3 tons, Diplodocus 10.7 tons, African Elephant 12 tons, Blue Whale 190 tons.

known in the Museum. Its largest and most popular exhibits are:

Diplodocus—a plaster cast of one of the world's largest ever dinosaurs, measuring 87 ft 6 in (26.6 m) from head to tail. It would have weighed around 10 tons and lived 150 million years ago.

Tyrannosaurus rex—a plaster cast of the skull of the largest flesh-eating land animal ever known. It towered some 16 ft (5 m) high, was around 39 ft (12 m) long and would have weighed up to 7 tons. It roamed the earth around 70 million years ago.

The newest and most important dinosaur find in Europe this century is 'Claws' (*Baronyx walkeri*). It was discovered during excavations in Surrey in 1983. 'Claws' is a previously unknown dinosaur that lived about 124 million years ago and is the only reasonably complete skeleton of a carnivore from this age found anywhere in the world. It takes its name from its huge clawbones, 12.2 in (30.9 cm) long. It would have measured between 9–13 ft (3–4 m) tall, 29–33 ft (9–10 m) long and weighed around 2 tons.

Also displayed in this area is the Museum's rarest fish—a coelacanth, the oldest living fish whose relatives can be traced back over 350 million years.

Mammals The biggest and best known item in the Museum is a model of the world's largest and heaviest living creature, the blue whale. The model is 92 ft 10 in (28.3 m) long and a skeleton suspended above it measures 82 ft (25 m). The largest specimen ever recorded measured 110 ft 2.5 in (33.58 m) long. The heaviest weighed 190 tons, or over 15 times the weight of the world's heaviest existing land mammal, the African bush elephant (estimated 12.05 tons).

Another popular exhibit is Chi-Chi, the giant panda, who between 1958 and 1972 became London Zoo's favourite personality (Chi-Chi can be found at the top of the main staircase).

Man's Place in Evolution This includes the skull of the earliest known Briton, found at Swanscombe, Kent some 200 000–250 000 years ago. There is also a fascinating model of a Neanderthal woman, based on a skeleton found in Israel, thought to be around 41 000 years old.

Minerals, Rocks and Meteorites The mineral collection of some 130 000 rocks and gemstones includes a tiny fragment of Moon rock brought back by the Apollo 17 mission in December 1972. The adjacent Meteorite

Room is the largest such collection in the world and displays somewhat larger extra-terrestrial specimens from over 1270 falls, including the Cranbourne meteor found near Melbourne, Australia, weighing 3.5 tons.

Birds The earliest known bird is *Archaeopteryx* which is estimated to be 150 million years old. The Museum holds one of only three relatively complete skeletons ever appeared in 1681, is one of this section's most popular exhibits and is also its most tragic as a symbol of conservation failure ('As dead as a dodo').

Insects and their Relatives This section covers the largest and most diverse group of living animals. There are over 800 000 species presently catalogued and thousands of new ones are discovered each year. The largest/heaviest insect in the world is the goliath beetle which can weigh up to 3.5 oz (100 g) and has a body some 4 in (11 cm) long. Only fractionally less alarming is the world's tallest insect, the female giant stick insect which can measure up to 13 in (33 cm).

The oldest plant specimens in the Museum are the petrified trees which stand in its front gardens. These are around 350 million years old.

O Mon–Sat 10.000–18.00; Sun 13.00–18.00; C; £ (Free Mon–Fri 16.30–18.00; Sat, Sun, BH 17.00–18.00); & t 95% ☎ (01) 938 9123 or (01) 725 7866 (24 hr)

Geological Museum [12]
Exhibition Road

The Geological Museum covers the origins of the Earth, its mineral deposits and its treasures. It is divided into the following major displays:

Gemstones The Museum boasts one of the world's most magnificent collections of gemstones of which some 3000 are displayed, cut and carved stone alongside the natural crystals and rough materials from which it

originated. Models of some of the world's most precious diamonds include the Koh-i-noor and the Cullinan diamond (see Tower of London).

Story of the Earth This deals with the ingredients of the Universe and the origins of the solar system. The most valuable exhibit is a 4.5 oz (128 g) piece of Moon rock, the largest piece outside the USA. At 4000 million years old it predates any known rock on Earth by around 200 million years and was brought back by the Apollo 16, April 1972 mission.

Nearby are exhibits of the oldest rocks on earth, from West Greenland, around 3800 million years old. Various meteorites are displayed, with the comforting statistic for those of a nervous disposition, that on average, one falls only about every ten years in Britain!

An even less likely experience whilst in London is that of an earthquake, but this is exactly what is reconstructed on a vibrating platform which simulates the largest earthquake of modern times, centred on Anchorage, Alaska on 27 March 1964.

Another natural disaster is recalled by objects—glassware, teaspoons, nails etc—fused and distorted in the heat of one of the world's most deadly volcano eruptions at St Pierre,

The only earthquake fatality ever to occur in Great Britain was on 6 April 1580 when falling masonry from Christ's Hospital Church, Newgate killed two people. However, in April 1750 London experienced a major earthquake panic following two mild tremors. Doom-mongers quickly spread prophecies of impending destruction and credulous Londoners took flight from the city. The ensuing traffic jams prevented most people from getting any further than Hyde Park and amongst the crowds a quack doctor sold 'anti-earthquake' pills and women bought 'earthquake gowns' to don for the great occasion that never came!

Martinique in 1902. The town and its 30 000 inhabitants were obliterated by clouds of gas up to 1472°F (800°C) travelling at 155 miles (250 km) per hour.

Mineral Deposits of the World The most popular piece of this vast display is the model of the 'Welcome' gold nugget found on 11 June 1858 at Ballarat, Victoria, Australia.

Amongst the many mineral specimens is a mini 1/60th scale model of Stonehenge (Salisbury Plain, Wiltshire) which has been constructed from original materials. The original Stonehenge is one of the most remarkable works of prehistoric architecture in the world and it is estimated that it required a staggering 30 million man-years to erect. The earliest stage of its construction goes back to 2800 BC but whether it was a lunar calendar, a temple or an eclipse-predictor is uncertain.

O Mon–Sat 10.00–18.00; Sun 14.30–18.00; £; (Free Mon–Sat 16.30–18.00); ㄥ t 80%
☎ (01) 589 3444

Science Museum [13]
Exhibition Road

This vast collection of science, industry, technology and medicine, founded in 1857, spans antiquity to the nuclear age and comprises over 100 subject collections displayed in 60 galleries on six floors.

Ground floor

Engines and Motive Power A collection of late 18th-century giant beam and steam engines illustrates the earliest development of power on a large scale including James Watt's Old Bess pumping engine (1777), a vanguard of the Industrial Revolution.

Space Exploration The world's first large liquid-fuel rocket was Hitler's V2 (Vengeance weapon 2) (see Blitz). This pales into insignificance, however, next to the 9 ft (3 m) tall rocket motor, (just one of six) which

launched Saturn V on its Apollo and Skylab missions. The whole assembly stood over 363 ft (110 m) tall and is the most powerful rocket ever launched by the USA. Pride of place here goes to the Apollo 10 command module, 'Charlie Brown', of Apollo 10— which carried three men around the Moon in 1969. Cramped into a space about three times that of a telephone box the astronauts would have re-entered the Earth's atmosphere at 24 235 mph (39 000 km/hr). Adjacent is a full-size model of the Apollo 11 lunar lander out from which Neil Armstrong stepped, to become the first man to set foot on the Moon on 20 June 1969.

Land Transport The oldest surviving locomotive in the world, Puffing Billy (1813) and a replica of George Stephenson's famous original Rocket (1829) are dwarfed by the adjacent 79-ton Caerphilly Castle. This perfect example of 'the romantic age of steam' was the most powerful passenger locomotive in the country in 1923. Steam was replaced by diesel and in 1955 the 106-ton Deltic locomotive on display assumed the mantle as the world's most powerful single unit locomotive.

The automobile collection's oldest internal combustion motor car is a Benz three wheeler from 1888. Karl Benz patented the first motor car as we know it in 1886, but the pick of the vintage selection must be the oldest existing original Rolls Royce car dating from 1904.

Two-wheeled transport features the world's oldest bicycle built in 1839 by Kirkpatrick Macmillan of Dumfries, Scotland and the earliest factory-made motorcycle produced in 1894 by Hildebrand and Wolfmüller at Munich, West Germany.

First floor

Time and Astronomy The astronomy gallery contains some of the most beautiful objects in the museum. The orreries in particular draw a thin line between science and art. These are elaborately decorated working models of the solar system. The original orrery (so called because the first one was made for the Earl of Orrery in 1716), and the world's most elaborate 'Grand Orrery', made in 1733, are two of the Museum's greatest treasures.

The earliest time-piece is a cast of an Egyptian water clock *c.* 1415–1390 BC.

Second floor

Marine The main galleries hold one of the world's greatest collection of model ships. Of particular interest are the many attractive Chinese junks.

Third floor

Aeronautics Amongst the many pioneering and record-breaking original aircraft on display are the huge Vickers Vimy in which John Alcock and Arthur Brown were the first to fly non-stop across the Atlantic, on 14–15 June 1919, and the DeHavilland Gipsy Moth used by Amy Johnson for her 10 000 mile (16 090 km) solo flight to Australia between 5 and 24 May 1930.

Patriotic pride of place is taken by the Supermarine S6B which won outright the magnificent Schneider Trophy ('Blue Riband' for sea-planes) for Britain in 1931 and was predecessor to the Supermarine Spitfire which, together with the Hawker Hurricane (both displayed), helped to win the crucial Battle of Britain in 1940.

The collection of over 100 aero-engines in the gallery is the most comprehensive in the world.

Fourth floor

Wellcome Museum of the History of Medicine This is the largest collection of its kind in the world with a total of over 125 000 objects. The fourth floor gallery contains 43 windows featuring reconstructions of significant medical developments.

The earliest scene (window 1) is of Neolithic man practising trepanning *c.* 5000–1500 BC. This involved scraping a hole in the skull with sharpened flints probably to allow the escape of 'evil spirits' (often epilepsy). (Trepanned skulls from this period are exhibited on the fifth floor.)

The largest and most attractive exhibit is the full scale reconstruction of Mr Gibson's Northumberland Chemist Shop from 1834. By contrast, the 1930s Nigerian Ibibo medicine man (window 32) is the introduction to the Museum's outstanding collection of tribal medicine.

In the corridor between the fourth and fifth floors is the most bizarre case in the museum. Memorabilia of famous people includes Florence Nightingale's moccasins (1854-6), Napoleon's field toilet case (*c.* 1813), Captain Scott's medicine chest (1910), Nelson's razor (*c.* 1790) and an invitation to the funeral of the Duke of Wellington (1852) containing a lock of his hair. Next to these items are a dried human head carefully dissected to show vessels and nerves (probably early 19th century—English), a 4-in tall (10 cm) skeleton of a human foetus in a glass case (late 18th century) and a fake miniature 'Merman' (a small papier-mâché model of a 'fish-man') catering for the 18th- and 19th-century trade in freaks of this kind.

Fifth floor
The following galleries are of particular interest.

Galleries A–B These are devoted to tribal healing and magical beliefs. Not all of the exhibits are benevolent. An effigy from the Congo with nails driven into it is an example where black magic is thought to be able to inflict disease.

Care of the dead is illustrated by the mummy of a Colombian Inca AD 800–1400. Spectacular masks and figures from Sri Lanka (Ceylon) and the South Indian Ocean, and a tom-tom drum made of two human skulls are all used in exorcism rituals to treat the sick.

Gallery D This Egyptian display includes a mummified infant, cat and crocodile.

Gallery G A set of 16th-century wooden clappers used by lepers to give warning of their approach is a reminder of some of the dreadful conditions in medieval England. This disease was not just confined to the poor classes. One of the earliest recorded sufferers of leprosy in England was the Bishop of London in 1087.

Gallery I George Washington's ivory dentures (c. 1795) are displayed close to a 1788 report on the mental health of King George III. The mental-health theme is continued by two remarkable lifesize wood and plaster figures from the Royal Bethlehem Hospital at Moorfields. This was established as London's first asylum for 'distracted' patients in 1377 and moved to Moorfields in 1676.

Gallery V Some of the earliest space foods developed for the American programme are displayed, including mini-cheese sandwiches that would not look out of place in a doll's house!

O Mon–Sat 10.00–18.00; Sun 14.30–18.00; C; £; ⮾ t 70%
☎ **(01) 589 3456**

Victoria & Albert Museum [14]
Cromwell Road

The V & A is the national museum of art and design and is one of the world's greatest treasure-houses of fine and applied arts. It was founded by Sir Henry Cole (1808–82) in 1852 as the Museum of Manufactures with the objective (which it still retains) of stimulating students of design. It is the most complex museum in London to the casual visitor, due to its all embracing approach and sheer size, and it is impossible to see the 12 acres (4.86 ha) of treasures displayed within its 8-mile (13 km) long labyrinth in one visit. The following 'general tour' includes the especially outstanding and popular collections.

British Painting (Henry Cole Wing) This collection from 1700–1900 features Turner,

Gainsborough, Reynolds and the largest collection of the works of John Constable (1776–1837), including a full-size sketch of his most celebrated painting *The Haywain* (in the National Gallery). The National Collection of British watercolours and the best collection of English portrait miniatures in the world are also here.

Rodin Collection (Exhibition Road entrance foyer) This collection of 17 works by the great French sculptor Auguste Rodin (1840–1917) is the largest in Britain.

Continental European Art 1600–1900 (Rooms 1–9) This includes some of Europe's most outstanding furniture from the period as well as sculpture, silver, porcelain and paintings. The Jones Collection of 17th and 18th century French Fine and Decorative Art—many pieces forced out of aristocratic hands by the Revolution—is particularly important.
Note: The Jones Collection is often closed to the public.

Italian Renaissance (Rooms 11–21a) One of the most striking sculptures here is *Samson slaying a Philistine* by Giambologna, c. 1562—a piece formerly owned by Charles I.

The Morris, Gamble and Poynter Rooms (off Rooms 13 and 15) These three splendidly decorated rooms were the first museum refreshment facilities to be opened in London, in use from 1868.

Northern Renaissance and Spanish Art (Rooms 25–29a) The highlight of this collection is the huge 22 ft (7 m) high golden altarpiece depicting the gruesome martyrdom of St George (see London Dungeon). It is Valencian and dates c. 1410-20. Close by is the comparatively tiny 13 in (33 cm) high silver and gilt Burghley Nef (c. 1528). This is an aristocratic tablepiece which held the salt and indicated the position of the host at the dining table. (A nef was a medieval French sailing ship.)

Front entrance to the V & A, opened by Queen Victoria in 1857.

The Dress Collection (Room 40) Over 200 examples of dress, dating from c. 1600 to the present day, range in variety from clothes reputedly worn by James I to those designed by Pierre Cardin.

Musical Instruments (Room 40a) This beautiful collection of instruments, dating from the 16th to the 19th century, is one of the most important assembled in this country. It includes the earliest dated harpsichord in existence, made in 1521, and a Dutch 'giraffe' piano (c. 1815-20). This oddity has pedals to ring bells and to add drums, buzz and echo effects, thus making it one of the earliest types of keyboard synthesizer! Among the most elaborate instruments is a German guitar, 1693, decorated with mother of pearl, tortoiseshell, ivory, pewter and ebony.

European Art up to 1600 (Rooms 11-29a, 38, 43) (All treasures referred to below are in room 43) The earliest important English treasure displayed is the Gloucester Candlestick, an elaborately decorated gilt bronze 'wild ballet of men and monsters' dating from c. 1105. Another valuable church treasure is the Eltenberg Reliquary c. 1180, a copper and bronze gilt receptacle for holy relics, in the form of a miniature Byzantine church from Eltenberg on the German/Dutch frontier. One of the most precious sculptures is the Byzantine Veroli casket—an elaborately carved ivory panelled chest made late 10th/early 11th century.

The early 14th-century Syon Cope (a ceremonial cloak) is one of the best examples of the internationally renowned English needlework of this period.

The Medieval Tapestry Gallery (Room 38) This holds the magnificent Devonshire Hunting Tapestries (probably made in Tournai, France c. 1425-50).

Arts of Asia (Rooms 38a, 41-47E, excl 43, 46) The collection of Chinese ceramics is one of the world's greatest. One of the most valuable pieces is an 8th-century earthenware 'blood-sweating' horse which was originally part of a group of tomb figures. The collection of furnishings features a carved Ming dynasty lacquered table, c. 1426-35, which is one of the earliest and most elaborate pieces of Chinese lacquer furniture surviving in the world. The Indian section holds the most comprehensive collection of Indian art outside the subcontinent and contains one of the museum's favourite exhibits, 'Tippoo's Tiger'. This wooden effigy of a tiger mauling an English soldier was made c. 1790 and contains a hand-organ mechanism which emits roars and groans. It was a favourite piece of the fiercely anti-British Tippoo Sultan and was captured upon his defeat at Seringapatam on 4 May 1799. Another impressive relic of British campaigns in India is The Golden Throne of (Maharaja) Ranjit Singh made c. 1830.

Other highlights from the East include a 15th century pulpit from a Cairo mosque and the Ardabil carpet from Persia, woven in 1540.

The Cast Courts (Rooms 46a-b) This is one of the world's largest and most important collections of over 500 plaster casts taken from statues, tombs, architectural ornaments, etc. dating from ancient Rome to the 17th century. Room 46a is particularly striking in the enormity of its casts and is one of the most atmospheric rooms in the V & A. The largest of these is Trajan's Column which is split into two parts in order to fit it in the room. It is 125 ft (38 m) high and is adorned with a spiral relief depicting some 2500 figures. The original was built in Imperial Rome AD 113. Possibly the most awesome cast is that of the huge entrance arch from the 12th-century Spanish cathedral of Santiago de Compostela. Room 46b includes a giant cast of David by Michelangelo (original 1501-4).

Raphael Cartoons (Room 48) These 'Cartoons' (i.e. the full-scale designs on paper from which weavers worked) were painted by Raphael in 1515-16 for tapestries to be hung in the Sistine Chapel in the Vatican. They represent the single most important example of large-scale Renaissance art in England and have inspired generations of English artists and craftsmen since they were brought to England in 1623 by Charles I.

British Sculpture (Room 50 west) The most famous statue here is of George Frederick Handel by Louis-François Roubiliac. Commissioned in 1738 it was the first statue in Europe of a living artist and is acknowledged as one of the best portraits ever done of Handel.

British Art 1500 onwards (Rooms 52–8, 74a–c, 118–26) The most famous piece of furniture in the V & A is The Great Bed of Ware. It was made c. 1580 and used in several public houses in Ware, Hertfordshire. Its size made it a great tourist attraction and it was mentioned in Shakespeare's *Twelfth Night*. It is the largest bed in Great Britain, measuring 10 ft 8.5 in wide, 11 ft 1 in long and 8 ft 9 in tall (3.26×3.37×2.66 m). On the night of 13 February 1689 it was said to have been occupied by 26 butchers and their wives!

Among the many other outstanding furnishings is the splendid Kimbolton cabinet by Robert Adam (1771) and the first ever English perpetual motion clock, c. 1760, taking as its power the variation in atmospheric pressure between two jars of mercury. Two notable Royal Elizabethan relics are Queen Elizabeth I's virginals (spinet), a small wooden keyboard instrument similar to a harpsichord (late 16th century) and The Oxburgh Hangings—tapestries made by Mary Queen of Scots when imprisoned by her cousin Elizabeth during 1569–84.

Jewellery (Rooms 91–3) The V & A claims the most comprehensive jewellery collection in the world, dating from 2000 BC to the present day and covering all continents.

O Mon–Sat 10.00–17.50; Sun 14.30–17.50; £ (voluntary); **T** Mon–Sat 11.00, 12.00, 14.00, 15.00; ♿ **t** 30%; **H** ☎ (01) 938 8500

Brompton Oratory [15]
(London Oratory of St Philip Neri)
Brompton Road

This is one of London's largest Baroque churches, built in 1878–84 for the Oratory—an Italian religious group founded by St Philip Neri in 1575—which came to London in 1849. Until Westminster Cathedral was completed in 1903, the Oratory was the largest and most important Catholic church in London. It has one of the widest naves in London at 51 ft (15.54 m) and its total length is 240 ft (73.15 m). Its impressive interior decoration consists of a vast expanse of various marbles, and the chief glory of the Oratory is the altar of the Lady Chapel.

Harrods [16]
Brompton Road

The world's most famous department store began trading on its present site in Knightsbridge in 1849 as a small grocer's shop, run by Henry Charles Harrod. By 1867 turnover had reached £1000 per week and by 1880 Harrods had begun to take shape as a department store.

Between 1890 and 1910 Harrods' annual profits increased from £12 500 to £210 000 and it had become the world's largest department store. Its 1894 slogan claimed 'Harrods Serves the World' and its telegraphic address still is 'Everything London'.

The first escalator in Great Britain was installed in the store in November 1898 with an attendant at the top to administer brandy or smelling salts to anyone overcome by this new experience! Building continued apace during this period until the present 4.5 acre (1.8 ha) site was completed and the famous

---

One of the strangest orders that Harrods has ever fulfilled was in 1975 when it sold a baby elephant as a present to Governor Ronald Reagan (later President) of California.

terracotta façade was added 1901–5. Today its exterior is lit by around 11 000 light bulbs.

With a selling space of 20 acres (8 ha) administered by 250 departments on four floors, Harrods is still the largest department store in Great Britain. Its size and the number of staff accommodated, between 4000 and 6000 depending on the season, make it comparable to a small town and it is every bit as self-sufficient. It has its own power station and it draws its own water from three wells, the deepest of which is 489 ft (149 m) below the store. It is unique in having an 'in-store pub', The Green Man—named after the green uniforms of Harrods' famous commissionaires. The store claims, within reason, to be able to supply any merchandise and provides for the customer's complete life-cycle all the way to the funeral department. Harrods copes with some 30 000 customers per day; the record for a single day's business is £5.5 million. The best selling item in volume terms is Harrods' own-brand cigarettes, with sales per annum of 1.63 million packets. The best known (and possibly most ubiquitous) item is the Harrods' carrier bag, of which over 163 000 are sold each year.

The highlight of Harrods for the casual visitor is the Food Halls. The most photographed area is either the Meat Hall, beautifully decorated with 1902 tiles depicting hunting scenes, or the fresh fish display, an extravagant sea-food montage changed daily to illustrate what is on sale. The busiest time for the Food Halls is the last two weeks of Christmas, during which time the following will be sold:
¼ ton (254 kg) caviar, 3 tons (3048 kg) smoked salmon, 17 tons (17 272 kg) fresh turkey, 50 tons (50 800 kg) fresh beef, 550 tons (558 800 kg) Christmas Puddings and, to complete this gargantuan feast, 11 tons (11 176 kg) of Stilton cheese.

O; ⅋ t 80% (go early to avoid crowds)
☎ (01) 730 1234

Linley Sambourne House   [17]
18 Stafford Terrace

This is the only perfectly preserved late Victorian, early Edwardian period house open to the public in London. It was built between 1868–1874 and was the home of Edward Linley Sambourne, political cartoonist of the satirical magazine *Punch*. The original wall decorations, objets d'art and sumptuous fixtures and furniture have all been preserved to give a vivid impression of the atmosphere of an upper middle class artistic household of that time.

O Mar–Oct, Wed 10.00–16.00 and Sun 14.00–17.00
☎ (01) 994 1019

Commonwealth Institute   [18]
Kensington High Street

The centre-piece of the Commonwealth Institute is a multi-level exhibition hall in which each of the 48 member countries has its own display covering its history, people, resources, culture, agriculture, industry and technology.

Some of the more interesting of the many diverse exhibits are a towering Nigerian stilt walker, Maori wood-carvings and an ingenious mechanical transparent cow from New Zealand, demonstrating how milk is produced. The displays of Papua New Guinea, India, Sri Lanka and the history of Africa are particularly imaginative.

O Mon–Sat 10.00–17.30;   Sun 14.00–17.00;   C;   ⅋ t 90%
☎ (01) 603 4535

Leighton House   [19]
12 Holland Park Road

This was the home and studio of Frederic Lord Leighton (1830–96), one of the most distinguished Victorian artists of his day, from 1866 until his death. The rich detail of this 'House Beautiful', built 1864–66, achieved Leighton's objective of creating the first and most important surviving example of a house decorated in the style of the romantic Aesthetic Movement. The centrepiece of the house is the magnificent Arab Hall which incorporates Leighton's collection of Islamic tiles. The brightly coloured tiles are one of the finest collections in Europe and come from Rhodes, Damascus, and Cairo, dating from the 15th and 16th centuries. The Hall is based on Moorish designs, its dome was bought in Damascus, the wooden alcove is Moorish and the window screens come from Cairo.

O **Mon–Sat 11.00–17.00**
☎ **(01) 602 3316**

The Grenadier [P1]
Old Barrack Yard, Wilton Row

This 18th-century pub was originally known as the Guardsman and a sentry box stands in front of it. The Duke of Wellington's officers drank here and it is claimed that both the Duke and King George IV frequented the pub. The stone in the adjacent alleyway is by tradition the Duke's mounting block. During September the Grenadier is said to be haunted by the ghost of a guardsman who was caught cheating at cards and died from his flogging.

☎ **(01) 235 3074**

The exotic East in W14—fish-eye view of Lord Leighton's Arab Hall.

MAYFAIR AND HYDE PARK CORNER

Mayfair takes its name from a fair which was held in early May each year between 1686 and 1764 on the site of what is now Curzon Street and Shepherd Market. As modern Mayfair began to take shape in the mid-18th century, rich local residents had the riotous fair suppressed. The area has since retained its aristocratic ambience, although most of the wealthy 'upstairs-downstairs' households of the 19th and early 20th centuries have now given way to commerce and hotels.

Mayfair is well known for its early Georgian squares—Berkeley, Grosvenor and Hanover. Unfortunately, little remains of their original properties or charm.

Grosvenor Square, at 6 acres (2 ha), is the largest of these and has been dubbed 'Little America'. The United States of America Embassy is the largest embassy in Great Britain, taking up an entire side of the Square and has nearly as much usable floor space as the entire area of the Square, 5.85 acres (2.37 ha). Its building is probably also the dullest embassy in Great Britain, although its front

The estimated wealth of the Duke of Westminster, the single largest private landowner in London, who owns much of Mayfair, is £1400 million (1988). However, even his family house made way for the advance of business premises in 1928, in the shape of the Grosvenor House Hotel. In keeping with its aristocratic background it was the first hotel in London to boast a swimming pool!

Hyde Park Corner is the busiest non-motorway traffic junction in Great Britain, with up to 56 000 vehicles per day flowing to and from it, from Park Lane alone.

does feature a huge 8-9 ft (2-3 m) tall American eagle with a 35 ft (11 m) wingspan.

Hyde Park Corner was the 18th-century entrance to London from the west and the Hyde Park Screen (next to Apsley House) was designed as a grand entrance from Buckingham Palace to the Park. Modern traffic redevelopment has made this redundant and the Corner today is synonymous with London's busiest traffic roundabout. Hyde Park Corner was the Duke of Wellington's home and this area is full of 'Wellington-ia'.

Apsley House (Wellington Museum) [1]
Hyde Park Corner

Apsley House was built 1771-8 by Robert Adam (for Baron Apsley) and became the London home of Arthur Wellesley, first Duke of Wellington from 1829 until his death in 1852. During this time it became known by the famous address of 'No. 1 London' because it was the first house inside the toll-gate entrance to London from the west. It opened as the Wellington Museum in 1952 and contains a collection dedicated to the most heroic epoch of Britain's history, of

Horse-drawn buses at leafy Hyde Park Corner c. *1900. (Apsley House stands to the right.)*
This same spot today is infamous as London's busiest traffic junction.

which Wellington was the central figure, when the Empire was built by force of arms.

The Plate and China Room The magnificent silver gilt Wellington shield (*c.* 1822), depicting him victorious, was presented by the Merchants and Bankers of the City as a token of thanks to the national hero. The collection of swords includes Napoleon's court sword, the sword taken from the body of Tippoo Sahib at the fall of Seringapatam in 1799 (see Tippoo's Tiger, Victoria & Albert Museum) and the sword carried by Wellington at Waterloo (the hilt of this was ironically made by Napoleon's goldsmith). The huge Egyptian table centrepiece and dinner service were made for the Empress Joséphine, 1810–12. The Duke's many medals and decorations are also on display.

Inner Hall At the foot of the staircase is the Museum's largest and most startling piece—a colossal 11 ft 4 in (3.45 m) tall statue of 'The Little Emperor' Napoleon by Canova (1810). Napoleon is said to have disliked the

statue because it portrayed him as a god and (perhaps more importantly) because the winged figure of Victory in his hand looks away from him. In 1816, just one year after Victory did indeed desert him at Waterloo, the statue was sold to the British government and presented to Wellington.

The Duke had great respect for his arch-rival Napoleon Bonaparte (1769–1821), hence the many exhibits relating to him.

Piccadilly Drawing Room This is hung with many fine Dutch 17th-century paintings and two popular London scenes—*Chelsea Pensioners reading the Waterloo Despatch* (1822) and *The Greenwich Pensioners commemorating Trafalgar* (*c.* 1835).

Portico Room One of Europe's most famous romances is recollected by Robert Lefèvre's portraits of Napoleon and Joséphine. (It ended after 14 years in 1810, due to Joséphine's failure to bear children.)

Waterloo Gallery This grand 90 ft (27 m)

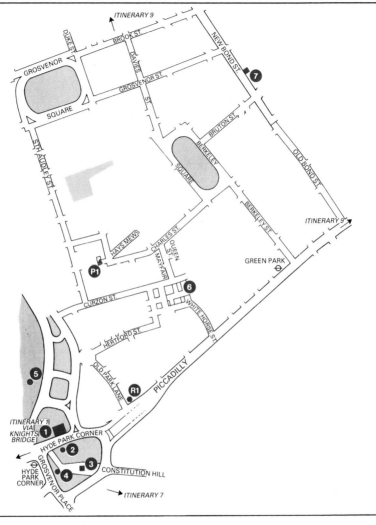

2. MAYFAIR AND HYDE PARK CORNER

1 Apsley House (Wellington Museum)
2 Statue of the Duke of Wellington
3 Constitution Arch
4 Royal Artillery Memorial
5 Statue of Achilles
6 Shepherd Market
7 Sotheby's

Pubs/Restaurants
P1 Red Lion
R1 Hard Rock Café

long room is the centrepiece of the House. Its huge Siberian candelabra were presented to the Duke by Nicholas I of Russia. The Duke's least favourite painting still hangs in its plain frame, in its original place, hidden from his gaze behind the door. (If he had known the story behind it, it would have pleased him even less!) Goya's *Wellington on Horseback* originally depicted Joseph Bonaparte (Napoleon's brother) on horseback, painted in August 1812 when Joseph was king of Spain. He was defeated that month by Wellington and so (as X-rays have recently revealed) Goya hastily painted the Duke's head over Bonaparte's. The Gallery includes some of the finest works from the Spanish royal collection, captured from the French in 1813 and then presented to the Duke. As well as the Goya, there are works by Velasquez, Murillo and Rubens. Other Old Masters include Van Dyck and Sir Joshua Reynolds. The Duke's favourite painting was *The Agony in the Garden* by Caravaggio (1520s). He was said to contemplate it in moments of stress and only he was allowed to dust it!

Yellow Drawing Room Amongst the many fine pictures is the award-winning *Passage of the Danube by Napoleon*, by Fontaine (1810) and a portrait of Joséphine in a revealing Roman style dress by Lefèvre.

Striped Drawing Room The best known portrait of the Duke by Sir Thomas Lawrence (1814) has pride of place here for its accuracy. A version of this features on the reverse of the current £5 note.

Dining Room The most impressive exhibit here is the 26 ft (8 m) long Portuguese centre-piece on the dining table which represents the four Continents paying tribute to Wellington and his allied forces.

Basement This contains caricatures of Wellington and memorabilia of his funeral.

O Tues, Wed, Thurs, Sat 10.00–18.00; Sun 14.30–18.00; £
☎ (01) 499 5676

Arthur Wellesley—1st Duke of Wellington (1769–1852)

Arthur Wellesley started his army career at 18 and his Parliamentary career at 20 and rose to the top of both. His reputation for courage and generalship was established in India in 1799 and over the next 16 years he fought in and directed 34 major battles, becoming the foremost soldier in Europe. His last and most famous battle was fought at Waterloo on 18 June 1815 when he met his arch-rival Napoleon for the first time and finally ended his ambitions of conquering Europe. He became Prime Minister in 1828 but maintained his staunch military views and resigned in 1830 over liberal reform proposals. He came back to be the head of the army and served again in the Cabinet. The greatest hero of the Victorian age was given a state funeral in St Paul's Cathedral in 1852.

The famous nickname the 'Iron Duke' was originally applied to Wellington after an iron steam boat was named Iron Duke after him and captured his indomitable character so appropriately.

The riposte 'publish and be damned' is also attributed to the Duke, in response to the threat of publication of potentially damaging letters.

The term Wellington was also passed into the English language when in 1865 the first rubber 'Wellington' boots were manufactured—named after the dress boot that the Duke had specially commissioned (see John Lobb).

The Duke is the only Prime Minister to have fought a duel whilst in office. Accused by Lord Winchilsea of double-dealing in 1829 he challenged him to meet in London's Battersea Park. Wellington is said to have fired first, deliberately wide of Winchilsea (wishing to avoid bloodshed). Winchilsea, with the heroic 60-year-old at his mercy, sensibly fired into the air and then apologized!

Statue of the Duke of Wellington [2]
Hyde Park Corner

This is one of the three statues of the Duke in London, designed by J E Boehm (1888). It shows him riding Copenhagen, his favourite charger, who carried him for over 16 hours at the Battle of Waterloo and whom the Duke buried with full military honours.

Constitution Arch [3]
Hyde Park Corner

Designed by Decimus Burton, this triumphal arch was erected in 1828 at the main entrance to Hyde Park (in line with the existing screen). It was then known as the Wellington Arch, surmounted by a huge 40-ton statue of the Duke. The Arch was moved to its present location with the massive quadriga, Peace at the reins of a four-horse chariot, dedicated to Edward VII—replacing the statue of Wellington (now at Aldershot, Hampshire). A dinner for eight was held inside the quadriga to celebrate its completion after four years' work.

Inside the Arch is London's smallest 'police station'.

Royal Artillery Memorial [4]
Hyde Park Corner

This is one of the biggest and most awesome memorials in central London. It features a huge howitzer facing towards the battlefield of the Somme in France where many of the 49 076 soldiers of the Royal Artillery 'who gave their lives for King and country in the Great War 1914–1918' died. It carries the unusual and macabre inscription 'here was a royal fellowship of death'.

Statue of Achilles [5]
Hyde Park

This huge 20 ft (6.10 m) high bronze was cast from captured French guns (including those taken at Waterloo) in 1822 by Sir Richard Westmacott. It cost £10 000 and was paid for by the women of England as a tribute to 'Arthur, Duke of Wellington and his brave companions in arms'. It is said that they were rather shocked, however, on learning they had commissioned the first public nude statue in England and a fig-leaf was added to save Victorian blushes!

Shepherd Market [6]
off Curzon Street

Formerly the site of the disorderly May Fair, Shepherd Market was laid out in the early 18th century, beginning with Edward Shepherd's food market. It is now the attractive 'village centre' of Mayfair boasting a number of foodshops, antique shops, cafés, restaurants and pubs.

Just outside Shepherd Market, at No. 9 Curzon Street, is George F Trumper, gentlemen's perfumier and hairdresser, established since 1875. They occupy one of London's most attractive 18th-century shops with original darkwood, glass and light fittings.

Sotheby's [7]
34–5 New Bond Street

Sotheby's are the oldest firm of art auctioneers in the world. They were established in London in 1744 as literary specialists and became the world's largest book auctioneers, handling great libraries, including that of Napoleon. They have been at their present address since 1917. In 1964 they acquired auctioneers, Parke Bernet of New York, and are now also the world's largest art auctioneers. World record-breaking auction prices occur frequently at Sotheby's in London and include the following categories:

Book: £8.14 million—12th century *The Gospel Book* of Henry the Lion, Duke of Saxony (6 December 1983)

Stuffed Bird: £9000—Great Auk (became extinct 1844) (4 March 1971)

Suit of Armour: £1 925 000—belonged to Henry II (1154–89) (5 May 1983)

Unusual items auctioned in London recently include:
Charles Dickens' ivory pencil £110 and John Lennon's handwritten lyrics of 'Imagine' £7150

Sotheby's oldest item is the statue of the Egyptian Goddess Sekhmet. This ancient statue dating *c.* 1320 BC sold for £1 at auction in 1835 but was never collected. Sotheby's paid the £1 and it has been kept ever since as a mascot. It surmounts the main entrance and is the oldest privately-owned outdoor work of art and the oldest statue outdoors in London.

O Previews, auctions Mon–Fri 09.00–16.30
☎ **(01) 493 8080 for details**

Red Lion [P1]

The Red Lion was built in 1723 as a 'local' for workmen engaged in the construction of the nearby Berkeley Square. It retains its intimate atmosphere and boasts one of the best preserved pub interiors in Mayfair.

☎ **(01) 499 1307**

Hard Rock Café [R1]
150 Old Park Lane

Established in London since 1971, this was the first major American 'burger-bar' in London and has spawned innumerable imitators across the country. By the end of 1987 it had served 7.5 million customers and is the most queued for restaurant in London. The Hard Rock Café has been called 'The Smithsonian of Rock'n'Roll' and holds on its walls what it claims to be the world's greatest collection of pop-music memorabilia. (This rotates between the London, Dallas, Tokyo, New York and Stockholm restaurants.)

The London collection holds 175 exhibits of gold discs, personal items, instruments, signed photographs etc. of artists such as The Beatles, The Who, Jimi Hendrix, The Rolling Stones, Elton John and Elvis Presley (including his last will and testament dated 3 March 1977).

The Hard Rock's other record-breaking claim is for their ubiquitous T-shirts and sweat shirts of which over 750 000 are sold per year.

Note: Bookings not accepted; &
☎ **(01) 629 0382**

'No drugs no nuclear weapons', but plenty of burgers, T-shirts and pop memorabilia including the last will and testament of the 'King of Rock 'n' Roll'.

CHELSEA

It is thought that Chelsea derives its name from chalk deposits in the Thames which caused it to be known as Chelchythe (meaning Chalk Wharf) as far back as AD 787. Another theory attributes the name to an old wharf at Chelsea which was a landing place for chalk and limestone building materials.

Until the development of the adjacent Belgravia area by Thomas Cubitt in the 1820s, Chelsea remained a countrified suburb separate from Central London and was well known for its healthy and attractive riverside setting. Today only the older parts retain a 'village' atmosphere although Chelsea remains an exclusive residential quarter.

Duke of York's Headquarters [1]
Cheltenham Terrace

The most imposing of this group of buildings was designed in 1801 as a school for soldiers' orphans and was founded by Frederick, Duke of York, son of George III (see Duke of York's Column). It is now used by the council of the Territorial Army (Britain's voluntary reserve).

Royal Hospital (Chelsea Hospital) [2]
Royal Hospital Road

The inspiration for the Royal Hospital came from the Hôtel des Invalides in Paris and in 1682 Charles II commissioned Sir Christopher Wren to the project. The name Hospital is misleading as it was designed as a home for 'men broken by war and old age' (and still is). It was first opened to 476 British Army pensioners in 1689. Today it houses around 420 of the world's most famous group of pensioners who are uniformed, fed, cared for and accommodated in wooden-panelled dormitory-style berths. The Pensioners may often be seen attending London ceremonies and events as guests of honour in their famous scarlet frock coats, which in design date from the 18th century. Their everyday attire consists of a navy blue uniform.

On the first Thursday after 29 May every year the Pensioners parade in the Hospital grounds next to the statue of Charles II (by Grinling Gibbons, 1692) to celebrate 'Founders Day'. The statue is decorated with oak

The area's most famous confection, the Chelsea Bun, a sugared square soft currant cake first recorded by Jonathan Swift (of Gulliver's Travels fame) in 1712, was made popular by The Chelsea Bun House which stood on Jew's Row (now Pimlico Road) until its demolition in 1839. It was the best selling cake shop of its time with crowds of up to 50 000 people reported on Good Fridays during the 1790s! On Good Friday 1839 sales of 240 000 hot cross buns are claimed. The huge crowds would have been due to the proximity of Ranelagh Gardens (see Royal Hospital), then one of London's principal pleasure gardens.

3. CHELSEA

1 Duke of York's Headquarters
2 Royal Hospital (Chelsea Hospital)
3 National Army Museum
4 Tite Street (south)
5 Peace Pagoda
6 Chelsea Physic Garden
7 Cheyne Walk
8 Albert Bridge
9 Carlyle's House
10 Chelsea 'Old Church' (All Saints)
11 Crosby Hall
12 King's Road

Pubs/Restaurants
P1 Henry J Bean's Bar and Grill
R1 The Pheasantery

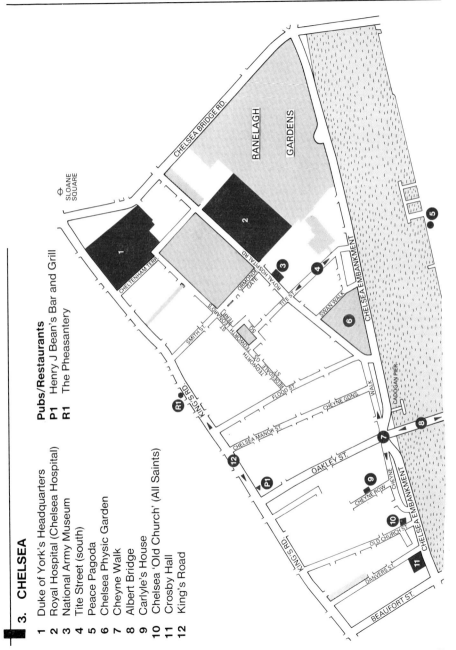

leaves and three cheers are given for the King. This commemorates Charles' escape from Cromwell's army after the Battle of Worcester (1651) when he took refuge in an oak tree. The date of 29 May marks both Charles II's birthday and the day of his restoration to the throne in 1660.

The Central Saloon block at the front of the Hospital is divided into the Hall and Chapel. The Hall is decorated with pictures of the British monarchy, pride of place (naturally) going to a huge painting of Charles II by Antonio Verrio (1687). The Hospital Museum on the east wing contains two large paintings of the Duke of Wellington and the Battle of Waterloo. The Duke lay in state in the Hall in November 1852 and in the ensuing mêlée of crowds wishing to pay their last respects, two people were unfortunately crushed to death.

It is jokingly said by the Hospital staff that the pensioners are so well kept that they are not allowed to die before they are 100 and the burial records give support to this! There have been many centenarians, the oldest being the 111-year-old William Hiseland (d 1732) who 'When 100 years old he took unto him a wife'. (This age is, however, only based on the evidence of the tombstone.)

O **Grounds Mon–Sat 10.00–dusk; Sun 14.00–dusk; Inside Mon–Sat 10.00–12.00 and 14.00–16.00; Sun 14.00–16.00;** ѣ **Grounds only** ☎ **(01) 730 0161**

▌ *The Chelsea Flower Show, the largest international gardening exhibition in the world, has been held annually in Ranelagh Gardens (east side of the Hospital) in late May since 1913. The centrepiece is the Great Marquee, Britain's largest tent at 310 ft wide by 480 ft long (94×146 m) covering an area of 3.5 acres (1.4 ha).*

Admission details: ☎ *Royal Horticultural Society (01) 834 4333.*

National Army Museum [3]
Royal Hospital Road

This collection traces the history of the British Army from 1485, when the oldest armed body in the United Kingdom, the Yeomen of the Guard, were raised by Henry VII, to the surrender of the Falkland Islands by Argentina on 14 June 1982. Outside the Museum stands one of the most formidable vehicles on display in London—a 51-ton Centurion Mark 5 tank.

The Museum boasts the most comprehensive collection of hand-held weapons in Britain. Its earliest exhibit is a long-bow stave *c.* 1545, salvaged from Henry VIII's flagship, the *Mary Rose*. One of the most unusual relics in the Museum is the complete skeleton of Napoleon's favourite horse, Marengo. Close by are the French Eagle and Standard taken at Waterloo.

The collection of military costumes, including some 20 000 items, is one of the largest of its kind in the world. Amongst these are uniforms worn by Sir Winston Churchill and Edward VIII. The latter's collection of jewels and medals, displayed here, is regarded as one of the world's greatest. The medal claiming current pride of place is the Victoria Cross awarded to Colonel H H Jones during the Falklands Campaign. The Art Gallery's collection of 17th- to 19th-century paintings includes George II at the Battle of Dettingen, 1743—the last time a reigning British monarch led his troops into battle. Among World War I exhibits are Lord Kitchener's famous recruitment posters 'Your Country Needs You' and a chilling reconstruction of trench warfare, with a section made from original materials from the battlefield of Ypres.

Notable exhibits from the Crimean War include a Turkish paper candle lantern traditionally used by Florence Nightingale and the original hand-written order (from Supreme Commander Lord Raglan) that sent the Light Brigade to the worst ever massacre in English Cavalry history.

Lord Alfred Tennyson's epic poem 'The Charge of the Light Brigade' is the most famous and enduring tribute to the tragic events at Balaclava on 25 October 1854:

'Cannon to right of them'
Cannon to left of them
Cannon behind them
Volley'd and thunder'd'

"Forward the Light Brigade!"

Was there a man dismay'd?
Not tho' the soldier knew
Some one had blunder'd:
Their's not to make reply
Their's not to reason why
Their's but to do and die:
Into the Valley of Death
Rode the six hundred'

Of the 607 men who rode into the Valley of Death 278 never rode out.

O Mon–Sat 10.00–17.30;   **Sun 14.00–17.30;**   & t 100%
☎ (01) 730 0717

Tite Street (south)   [4]

The most famous resident of this artistic street was Oscar Wilde, playwright, dramatist and leader of the aesthetic ('Art for Art's

The razor-sharp wit and repartee of Wilde has probably never been equalled in London society. He was a master of the shrewd observation and the memorable overstatement, often delivered by his literary characters:

*'Work is the curse of the drinking classes'
'There is only one thing worse than being talked about and that is not being talked about'*

His famous quote when going through customs to the USA 'I have nothing to declare but my genius!' was indicative of his huge immodesty!

sake') movement, who lived at No. 34 from 1884 to 1895. During this period his popularity was at its height, with *Lady Windermere's Fan* and *The Importance of Being Earnest* playing to packed London theatres. The 1895 courtroom revelations of his affair with Lord Alfred Douglas, however, ruined him. Wilde was sentenced to two years' hard labour in Reading gaol. His house, part decorated by his friend Whistler, was sold off to meet court costs and his wife and children deserted him. There are still several Victorian artists' studios in Tite Street. Over the years these have attracted such names as John Singer Sargent who lived at No. 31 and Augustus John who lived at No. 33.

Peace Pagoda   [5]
Battersea Park

Central London's only pagoda, built in 1985 by a Buddhist sect, may be viewed clearly across the Thames in Battersea Park from Chelsea Embankment. It is dedicated to the cause of world peace.

The Chelsea Physic Garden   [8]
Swan Walk

The Physic Garden was established by the Society of Apothecaries in 1673. It is the second oldest physic garden in England (after Oxford, 1623) but the first institute in London devoted to the study of plants, predating the Royal Botanic Gardens at Kew by 86 years. (The old meaning of the word Physic is 'of things natural'.) By 1722 the Garden was in dire financial straits and the Society of Apothecaries appealed to their landlord Dr (later Sir) Hans Sloane. Sloane had studied in the Garden during his training as a physician, and saved it by granting a lease to the Society at £5 a year in perpetuity. A statue to Sloane by J M Rysbrack stands in the centre of the Garden.

The Buddhist Peace Pagoda in Battersea Park.

In 1683 the first cedar trees in England were planted in the Garden and in 1771 England's first rock garden was arranged.

The Garden has also contributed to transforming the agricultural patterns of other countries, especially in 1722 when seeds (probably originating from the South Sea Islands) were sent to Georgia to start the United States cotton plantations.

There are today some 5000 species of plants within its 3.25 acre (1.32 ha) grounds. The most popular of these is the 'Chinese Willow Pattern Tree' claimed to be the best specimen of its type in Britain. Another specimen, remarkable for the British climate, is a 30 ft (9 m) tall Olive tree—the biggest in Britain. Other unusual trees of note include Cork Oak, Pomegranate and Cucumber Trees.

O **Mid-Apr–3rd week in Oct; Wed and Sun 14.00–17.00 and during Chelsea Flower Show (late May) Tues–Fri 12.00–17.00; £**
☎ **(01) 352 5646**

Cheyne Walk [7]

This fashionable riverside walk (pronounced Chainee) takes its name from Charles Cheyne, Lord of the Manor of Chelsea from 1660 to 1712. The late 17th century, early 18th century east side can count many famous residents:

No. 4 'George Eliot' (pen-name of author Mary Anne Evans, 1819–80) died here only three weeks after moving in. She therefore almost certainly holds the record for the shortest period of residence spent by a person to whom a blue plaque is dedicated in London!

No. 16 Dante Gabriel Rossetti, poet and painter (1828–82); Algernon Charles Swinburne, poet and critic (1837–1909); and George Meredith, author and poet (1828–1909) took this house jointly in 1862. Rossetti kept what amounted to a small zoo here including armadillos, kangaroos, a racoon, a wombat and peacocks. The latter were so noisy that neighbours forced a clause (which still exists) into all subsequent Cheyne Walk leases, forbidding the keeping of peacocks.

Nos. 19-26 This site was occupied by the Manor House of Henry VIII from 1537 to 1753. A plaque inside the alleyway next to No. 24 commemorates part of the wall of the old Manor House and claims that the mulberry trees over the wall were planted by Princess Elizabeth, who grew up here.

Albert Bridge   [8]

The pastel shades and the delicate lines of the Albert Bridge make it without doubt the 'prettiest' of the 16 road bridges that span the Thames between Kew and Tower Bridge, particularly when illuminated at night.

It was built 1871-3 as a hybrid type of cantilever-suspension bridge and named in honour of Prince Albert. It was feared that the vibrations caused by marching troops

crossing the Bridge might cause it to collapse and so signs were erected instructing troops to break step when on the Bridge.

Although a sign to this effect still exists on one of the toll booths, (which were effective until 1879) central piers were added in 1973 to cope with modern traffic loads.

The small canopied Cadogan pier close by is the finish of the world's earliest established sculling race, Doggett's Coat and Badge. It was first rowed on 1 August 1716 from London Bridge 4.5 miles (7.2 km) away and is still contested annually. Thomas Doggett was a popular Irish comedian who founded the annual race for six first-year watermen (fully trained Thames ferry men) after one such had impressed him by rowing him up river to Chelsea on a particularly stormy night. The Coat and Badge is the special uniform prize for the winner.

Pretty in Pink—the Albert Bridge at Chelsea.

Carlyle's House [9]
24 Cheyne Row

Thomas Carlyle (1795–1881), the Scottish writer and historian known as 'The Sage of Chelsea', lived in this house from 1834 until his death in 1881 and wrote his most famous works *The French Revolution* and *Frederick the Great* here in the attic. It was a meeting place for many of Carlyle's intellectual peers and friends, including Dickens, Tennyson, Browning and Thackeray. The house is preserved much as Carlyle left it and his hat still hangs on its peg.

Carlyle is also commemorated by a Lincoln-esque statue by Boehm (1882) on Cheyne Walk West.

O Apr–Oct, Wed–Sun and BH Mons 11.00–17.00; £
☎ **(01) 352 7087**

Chelsea 'Old Church' (All Saints) [10]
Old Church Street

There has probably been a church on this site since Roman times but the oldest part of the existing building (the chancel and arch of Sir Thomas More's chapel) dates back to the 13th century.

The Church contains many excellent 16th- and 17th-century monuments, particularly on the north side of the nave. The oldest monument in the Church is the tomb of Lord Bray, 1539, situated in the chancel. The grandest monument is that to Lord and Lady Dacre (1595) and contains Lord Dacre's original armour helmet.

Sir Thomas More intended All Saints to be his final resting place and in 1528 he restored the north chapel and had his tomb (including his self-penned epitaph) made. The tomb is occupied by Alice, his second wife. The church was badly damaged by bombing in 1941 but fortunately More's chapel survived and its restored roof includes original timbers. The carved capital inserted into the 13th-century arch of the chapel is a unique

surviving English work by Hans Holbein—court painter and engraver to Henry VIII. The tomb of Jane Guildford (d 1555) mother-in-law of Lady Jane Grey, is in the south east corner of the chapel.

Another great resident of Chelsea, Sir Hans Sloane, is buried at All Saints and his monument stands at the Cheyne Walk side of the church yard. He was a church benefactor and donated precious 17th- and 18th-century books, secured by chains in the Church. The 'Old Church' is a fashionable place for weddings and it is said that Henry VIII married Jane Seymour here in private before their state wedding in 1536.

A statue to Sir Thomas More, Chelsea's most illustrious resident was finally erected in front of the Chelsea Old Church in 1969. It depicts More relinquishing his position of Lord Chancellor in 1532 'weary of worldly business'. It is London's only statue to bear a facsimile of the subject's signature.

Sir Thomas More

Thomas More was born in London in February 1478. His family home was Milk Street, Cheapside and he attended school in Threadneedle Street. At the age of 12 he was placed at Lambeth Palace for two years in the service of Cardinal Morton, the Archbishop of Canterbury. This early experience at the centre of political and religious affairs of state had a significant influence on his later life. In 1496 he moved on to Lincoln's Inn where he became the most brilliant legal mind of his day. Religion was still of prime importance to him, however, and he donned the hair-shirt of a monk and entered the London Charterhouse. He eventually chose family life in preference to chastity and resumed his legal practice.

In 1518 he entered the court of King Henry VIII and soon became a personal favourite and adviser to the King. More moved to Chelsea in 1523 but any hopes of a quieter life were dashed by Henry's clash with Rome, with regard to his wish to divorce Catherine of Aragon. In 1529 More was appointed Lord

Chancellor, but only accepted the post on the understanding that he would not have to be involved in the divorce. Three years later the King assumed the title 'Supreme Head' of the Church of England and More immediately resigned from his position. In 1534 the Oath of Supremacy, making Henry (not the Pope) head of the English Church, was declared. More was summoned to Lambeth to swear to the Oath and knew as he left his Chelsea home, he would never return. On 1 July 1535 he was condemned to death as a traitor in Westminster Hall, taken to the Tower and five days later beheaded. He declared on the scaffold 'I die the King's good servant, but God's first'.

Crosby Hall   [11]
Chelsea Embankment

This is the oldest building in Chelsea, dating from 1466 and is claimed to be the oldest surviving part of a domestic household in London. It was originally the Hall of Sir John Crosby's Bishopsgate mansion, most of which burned down in the Great Fire of 1666. It was threatened again in 1908 with the development of Bishopsgate but saved by its present owners, the British Federation of University Women, who moved it, piece by piece, to its present site in 1910. It now stands on the site of the gardens of Sir Thomas More's Chelsea Home. (A plaque some hundred yards up Beaufort Street at the rear of the Hall marks the site of More's house.) This was thought a fitting site for the Hall to be relocated as More had leased it (in 1523 for the sum of £150) for entertaining, in his role as Henry VIII's Lord Chancellor.

Its other famous resident was Richard of Gloucester who reputedly learned that he was to become King Richard III whilst living here in 1483. Most of the Hall is original, including its rare intricate oak and chestnut scissor beam roof, the oriel window and the fireplace.

O Daily 14.00–17.00
☏ (01) 352 9663

King's Road   [12]

The most famous road in Chelsea takes its name from King Charles II who annexed it (as far as Old Church Street) as part of his private processional route to Hampton Court Palace. King's Road has become synonymous with fashion ever since Mary Quant opened her first boutique, 'Bazaar', on the site of No. 138 in 1955 (nothing now remains of it).

Henry J Bean's Bar and Grill   [P1]
195-7 King's Road

'Henry J Bean's But All His Friends All Call Him Hank Bar and Grill' is the longest pub name in the country consisting of 52 letters. (There is another 'Henry J Bean's' in Abingdon St, Kensington.)

It is a thoroughly Americanized bar decorated with photographs of famous Hollywood film stars autographed 'To Hank'. Its huge garden claims a mulberry tree dating back to the reign of Queen Elizabeth I (i.e. some 400 years old).

☏ (01) 352 9255

The Pheasantery   [R1]
152 King's Road

The Pheasantery is one of the oldest and most spectacular buildings on King's Road. Now a restaurant, its name derives from the 1870s when pheasants were kept there for breeding. The portico is all that remains of the original 1769 building. It was redesigned in the late 19th century to resemble a 17th-century French mansion and from 1916–34 housed a dancing school where Alicia Markova and Dame Margot Fonteyn were taught.

☏ (01) 351 3084

TATE GALLERY, LAMBETH AND SOUTH BANK

The name Lambeth is thought to derive from Lamb hythe, a dock where lambs were landed in Saxon or Norman times.

Until Westminster Bridge was opened in 1750, the horse-ferry at Lambeth was the only means of getting a vehicle across the river above London Bridge. The tariff was 2d (approximately 1p) for a man and horse, rising to 2s (10p) for a laden cart. Horseferry Road commemorates its site and Lambeth Bridge (originally opened in 1862) now connects the two banks.

The area between Waterloo Bridge and the Hungerford Railway Bridge, known as the South Bank, began development in 1951 and is synonymous with the performing arts and modern art. The latter theme is continued by the Tate Gallery on the north bank.

Tate Gallery   [1]
Millbank

The Tate Gallery is best known as Britain's most important modern art collection. In addition, it houses the most important collection of British paintings from the 16th century onwards. The Gallery was founded in 1897 by Sir Henry Tate, the sugar millionaire. Its latest extension, the Clore Gallery, opened in 1987, is dedicated to the works of J M W Turner.

British Collection This is housed in galleries 2–17, all situated on the left-hand side of the main floor. It is subject to some change but the major works mentioned

Lambeth is well known for its association with 'the Lambeth Walk', a cockney dance first made popular in 1937 in 'Me and My Girl', one of the longest running musical shows in London.

below are on permanent display (numbers refer to rooms—the following viewing order is recommended).

2/3 British School, 18th century This includes five paintings by the most notable British artist of the mid-18th century, William Hogarth.

4/5 Late 18th-century painting This includes works by George Stubbs, the greatest British sporting artist and the two outstanding portrait painters of the era, Thomas Gainsborough and Sir Joshua Reynolds, two founder members of the Royal Academy.

7 William Blake and followers The London-born Blake has been described as one of the great originals of British art. His style of work is instantly identifiable (the best known featuring muscle-bound religious and mythological figures) and shows exceptional richness of texture and vitality.

10 John Constable Constable's best known work here is *Flatford Mill*, painted in 1817, four years before *The Haywain* (in the National Gallery). Set near the same Suffolk village as *The Haywain*, it too is an evocation of the perfect English countryside.

15 Pre-Raphaelites William Holman

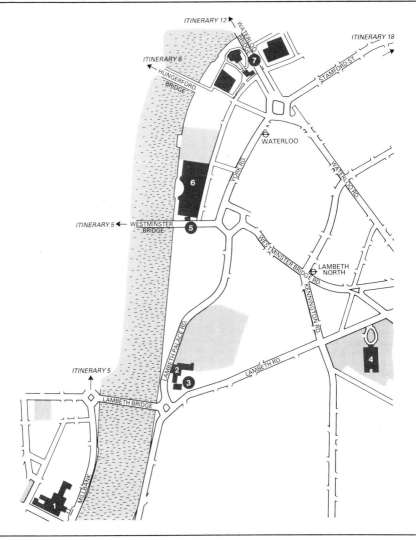

4. TATE GALLERY, LAMBETH AND SOUTH BANK

1 Tate Gallery *
2 Lambeth Palace
3 Museum of Garden History,
  St Mary-at-Lambeth

4 Imperial War Museum
5 South Bank Lion
6 County Hall
7 South Bank Arts Centre

* Specially recommended by author

Hunt's *The Awakening Conscience* (1853–7), a morality picture of a 'fallen' woman, Ford Madox Brown's *The Last of England* (1864–6), depicting a couple forced into emigration and Sir John Everett Millais' *Ophelia* (1852) are three highlights of this movement. Ophelia (taken from 'Hamlet') has been called one of the most striking and haunting images of British painting.

16 High Victorian Another romantic masterpiece by Millais, *The Boyhood of Raleigh* (1870) is contrasted by the tragic social comment of Sir Luke Fildes' *The Doctor* (c. 1891), featuring a dying child in a humble household.

17 James Whistler and his contemporaries The most controversial painting of the late 19th century was Whistler's *Nocturne in Black and Gold: The Fire Wheel* (1875). The foremost art critic, John Ruskin, enraged by what he perceived as the lack of realism in the work, accused Whistler of 'flinging a pot of paint in the public's face', to which the artist responded with a libel suit. Whistler won his case but was awarded damages of just one farthing (¼d). He was ordered to pay his costs for the case and was financially ruined.

Modern Collection This is housed in galleries 18–23 and 62 on the lower floor and 27–61 on the right hand side of the main floor. Only a part of the large collection is shown and exhibits are subject to frequent change.

18–23 and 31 British Art The Tate holds the most comprehensive collection of British modern art. It ranges in time scale from Walter Sickert (1860–1942), one of the first

> ▌ *One of the most controversial exhibits to have been displayed in the modern art section is* Equivalent VIII *by Carl Andre. It consists of 120 fire-bricks arranged in two layers and outraged the general public when it was first shown.*

English Impressionists, to the modern day David Hockney (b 1937), and in style from L S Lowry's matchstick figures to Francis Bacon's tortured images.

29 Sculpture The sculpture *Four Piece Composition: Reclining Figure* (1934) by Henry Moore, Britain's foremost 20th-century sculptor, caused controversy as one of the most abstract works of its time. It is now viewed as a typical Moore portrayal of the human body which has become familiar to the British public.

The Kiss (1901–4) by Rodin is a replica of one of the world's most romantic sculptures.

30 Cubism This features works by Pablo Picasso and Georges Braque, the prime movers of Cubism. It has been estimated that Picasso, the most prolific of all painters, produced some 13 500 paintings or designs alone during his life-time. His total works are valued at over £500 million. (Other examples of Picasso's work are in galleries 32 and 38.)

33 Impressionism and Post Impressionism A wide range of artists is featured here although none of their best known works is exhibited (see National Gallery or Courtauld Institute).

36 Surrealism Important works by members of this movement include (*The Elephant*) *Celebes* by Max Ernst, 1921, regarded as the first major surrealist painting. Salvador Dali and René Magritte are also represented.

47–48 Pop Art Andy Warhol's series of Marilyn Monroe prints in mauve, yellow, green and orange, *Marilyn Diptych*, 1962, is the most popular exhibit in this section.

The Clore Gallery This extension was purpose-built to hold the 282 oil paintings (182 unfinished) and over 20 000 drawings, sketches and watercolours of the Turner Bequest. Some of the most notable amongst the oil paintings are: the many excellent views of Venice; *Snow-Storm, Steam Boat off a Harbour's Mouth* (1842); *Peace—Burial at*

Sea (1842); *Crossing the Brook* (1815); *Richmond Hill* (1819)—one of London's most popular views.

O Mon–Sat 10.00–17.50;   Sun 14.00–17.50;   T Mon–Fri 11.00, 12.00, 14.00, 15.00;   & t 100%;   H
☎ (01) 821 1313

Joseph Mallord William Turner (1775–1851)

Turner was born in 1775 on the site of No. 21 Maiden Lane, Covent Garden. The son of a barber, he was a child prodigy and by the age of 14 was already making his living by the sale of his drawings. His work is divided into three major categories: early landscape, later mythological subjects and finally his atmospheric masterpieces of the elemental forces and the wonders of light and water. The quality of his works has earned him the accolade of the greatest British painter and the sheer quantity (see above) makes him one of Britain's most prolific major artists. He lived out his final years overlooking the Thames at 119 Cheyne Walk, Chelsea. The final words of the artist who made such a magnificent study of natural light were said to be 'The Sun is God'.

Turner is the only British artist to figure in the list of progressive records of the world's highest priced paintings. In 1980 Juliet and Her Nurse *fetched £2 729 000 and in 1984* Seascape: Folkstone, *was auctioned for £7 470 500.*

Lambeth Palace   [2]
Lambeth Palace Road

Lambeth Palace has been the official London residence of the Archbishop of Canterbury since *c.* 1200, conveniently sited for the attendance of the Palace of Westminster by the early Archbishops.

The only original part of the Palace left is the 13th-century crypt beneath the chapel. The oldest part of the Palace visible from the exterior (facing south—on far left) is the whitestone Lollard's Tower, built in 1432–5. The Archbishop's personal flag is flown from here when he is in residence. The central red-brick building is the Great Hall built in 1663. The most outstanding Palace structure, and one of the best examples of a Tudor brick building in London is the gatehouse or Morton's Tower named after the Archbishop responsible for its construction in 1486–1501. Here Sir Thomas More was interrogated in 1534 by Thomas Cromwell for refusing to sign the Oath of Supremacy.

O By appointment (groups only), write to Palace Secretary at the above address; & 80% (single steps)

Museum of Garden History, St Mary-at-Lambeth   [3]
Lambeth Palace Road

A church of St Mary has existed on this site since 1062 and has been rebuilt several times, most recently in 1851–2 by Philip Hardwick. Its oldest external feature is its fine 14th-century tower. Captain Bligh, of mutiny on the *Bounty* fame (1789), is buried in the churchyard in a fine Coade stone (see South Bank Lion) tomb which cost 45 gns (£47.25) in 1854. Alongside him are the John Tradescants, father and son. Both royal gardeners to Charles I, they were great collectors and introduced many varieties of common flowers, plants, shrubs and trees to England from abroad (e.g. Michaelmas daisies, stock, jasmine, tradescantia shrubs and the American plane, now the London plane, the capital's most common tree). Their finely carved tomb depicting crocodiles, shells and a gnarled leafy tree shows their interest in 'all things strange and rare'. The Tradescant trust was set up in 1977 to save St Mary's Church from demolition and to found the world's first Museum of Garden History.

This includes a replica 17th-century garden in the churchyard, stocked only with plants known by the Tradescants.

O Mon–Fri 11.00–15.00; Sun 10.30–17.00; Closed 2nd Sun in Dec to 1st Sun in Mar; ♿

☎ **(01) 261 1891**

> *John Tradescant the Elder (1570–1638) was the world's first organized collector of plants and his Lambeth garden established c. 1629 was probably the first genuine botanic garden in the country. Their great collection of plants and other curiosities was acquired by Elias Ashmole (d 1692, also buried in the churchyard) who passed it on to the University of Oxford. This formed the basis of the Ashmolean Museum built in 1679–83, the world's oldest surviving museum.*

Imperial War Museum   [4]
Lambeth Road

This is the country's principal museum of 20th-century war, founded in 1917 whilst World War I was still in progress. In addition to its huge and varied collection of both military and civil exhibits, it houses one of the foremost collections of British 20th-century art, including works by the Nash brothers and Stanley Spencer. The present building was completed in 1815 and until 1930 it was home to London's mental hospital, Bethlem Royal Hospital.

Note: The Museum is currently undergoing major redevelopment which is not due to be finished until the end of June 1989. Its displays will be severely curtailed until then and only a few of the exhibits described below will be on view.

The exhibits least likely to move are the last two surviving 15-in British naval guns on the front lawn, which provide a forbidding welcome to the Museum. Made in 1915–16, they

were the largest and most powerful guns of their day, each weighing over 100 tons and were capable of firing a 17.25-cwt (876-kg) shell 18.25 miles (29 km).

World War I War was declared on 4 August 1914 and the guns which fired the first British shells of the war at sea and on land are both here. The former was on 5 August by HMS *Lance* and the latter was on 22 August by the Royal Horse Artillery, close to Mons. The conditions of trench warfare are reconstructed together with its weaponry, ranging from bayonet and knuckle-dusters to the horrors of gas.

An important landmark in the war was the development of the tank which first appeared in action on the Somme in September 1916. A later version, a 29-ton Mark V tank, built in 1918, is on display. A London bus, one of the 1300 which carried troops to the front, is a rather lighter curiosity. Two notable aerial warfare exhibits are the Sopwith Camel which shot down the last Zeppelin of the war in August 1918, and the engine of Baron Manfred von Richthofen's plane. The Red Baron was the most famous World War I air ace with a total of 80 'kills' attributed to him. Other relics of famous personalities include the Lee Enfield rifle of T E Lawrence 'of Arabia'.

World War II The German onslaught of the early months is recalled by displays of the Blitz and the Battle of Britain. The Roll of the 'Few' contains signatures of 2200 of the 3080 who served with the RAF in the Battle of Britain in the summer of 1940, one of the

> *Nearly 100 million rounds of 18 pounder ammunition were fired in the British-held sector of the Western Front alone between 1914 and 1918, an average of 43 rounds for every minute of the war. (The Western Front was the opposing battle line drawn across north-west Europe stretching from Belgium through France as far as Switzerland.)*

decisive encounters of the War. A rare surviving Spitfire from the battle, credited with nine 'scores', is on display. Below it is the smallest surviving boat from the 'Fleet' of 1200 which took part in the greatest evacuation in military history, from the beachhead at Dunkirk between 27 May and 4 June 1940. A total of 338 226 British and French troops were rescued. A huge V2 rocket 46 ft (14 m) high will stand at the centre of the redeveloped galleries. This was Hitler's final 'terror-weapon' of which 517 fell in the London region between September 1944 and March 1945. An example of its predecessor, the VI flying bomb of which 2420 fell in and around London, is close by. Other exhibits in the central area include the massive 47-ton Jagdpanther Tank and a forward section of the principal British bomber, the Lancaster.

Famous documents from either end of the war include, the Anglo-German Agreement of September 1938, which prompted Prime Minister Neville Chamberlain's famous 'peace for our time' speech, the Instrument of Surrender signed on Lüneburg Heath on 3 May 1945, and Adolf Hitler's 'Political Testament', written after his wedding to Eva Braun on 29 April 1945. They both committed suicide the following day.

O **Mon–Sat 10.00–17.50, Sun 14.00–17.50;** ᚠ **t 100%;   Note: Admission charge to be introduced in June 1989** ☎ **(01) 735 8922**

South Bank Lion   [5]
Westminster Bridge

This huge Coade stone 'beast', 12 ft high by 13 ft long (3.6×4 m) and weighing 13 tons, was originally made for the defunct Lion Brewery next to Hungerford Bridge. It has now come to rest appropriately next to where London's greatest manufacturing mystery began. In the 1720s a stone-yard on the site where County Hall now stands (see below) took out a patent for a very special kind of terracotta. The yard was later taken over by Mrs

Eleanor Coade who improved the terracotta formula and supplied it under the name of Coade stone as a sculptor's material. This artificial stone was used on many distinguished buildings, e.g. The Royal Opera House, Somerset House, The Bank of England. It turned out to be the most weatherproof stone ever devised, but the factory closed in 1840 and the secret of its formula was lost. All subsequent attempts to analyse or recreate the composition have failed. The South Bank Lion is the largest surviving example of Coade stone architecture.

County Hall   [6]
South Bank

Construction of this huge complex was begun in 1912 and its main building fronting on to the river was first occupied by London's local government, the London County Council in 1922. The London County Council was superseded by the Greater London Council who occupied the building until it

The South Bank Lion—proudly defying the discovery of its secret formula.

County Hall—former seat of London government.

was disbanded in 1986.

County Hall is one of London's largest building complexes. It occupies 5 acres (2 ha) with a 700-yd (640 m) river frontage and has 2.2 million sq ft (204.4 sq m) of usable space. This includes 2415 rooms linked by 10 miles (16 km) of corridors.

South Bank Arts Centre   [7]

This compact site was developed as a national arts centre following the Festival of Britain, an exhibition of Britain's achievements in art and science, held here in 1951. The South Bank is now recognized to be the modern cultural centre of London, with three concert halls (the Royal Festival Hall, the Queen Elizabeth Hall and the Purcell Room), the Hayward Gallery, the National Theatre, the National Film Theatre and the Museum of the Moving Image (MOMI).

The National Theatre which opened in 1976 is renowned for its excellent productions of classic and experimental plays. The Hayward Gallery mounts around eight exhibitions per year with the emphasis on 19th- and 20th-century European art. MOMI is Britain's first museum of cinema and television. It is an exhibition of technological developments, ranging from 5000-year-old Chinese shadow plays to present-day satellite images, intertwined with all manner of cinema and TV *memorabilia* from Eisenstein

to Max Headroom, Mickey Mouse to Marilyn Monroe. Exhibition areas include early optical experiments, silent cinema, animation, British cinema etc. MOMI is London's most interactive museum where visitors are entertained by the eight museum actor/guides (including a Hollywood director and a Russian agit-prop cinema soldier) who help explain the historical, social and technical aspects of their own era's exhibits.

O ☎ for details of guided tours of the **Royal Festival Hall (01) 928 3191 and the National Theatre (01) 928 2252; Hayward Gallery during exhibitions Mon–Wed 10.00–20.00, Thurs–Sat 10.00–18.00; Sun 12.00–18.00; £; ⅃ t 90% (3 steps to Purcell Room); V; H ☎ (01) 928 3144 MOMI Tues–Sat 10.00–20.00; Sun 10.00–18.00; £; ⅃ 100% ☎ (01) 928 3535**

Pubs and Restaurants

There are no pubs of outstanding interest on this itinerary. Try the bars and restaurants within the South Bank Arts Centre. Nearby at Concert Hall Approach is the Archduke, a modern wine bar built into one of the arches of the 19th-century Hungerford Bridge. The Tate Gallery was the first London museum or gallery to receive high critical acclaim for its restaurant.

WESTMINSTER

Westminster is built on the prehistoric site of Thorney Island, a desolate swamp overgrown with thorn bushes, first inhabited in the Iron Age. The early Saxon development of the area and the origins of Westminster Abbey are shrouded in legend, although it is known that a Church of St Peter has been in existence for 1000 years.

Westminster Abbey and the adjacent Palace of Westminster have been the two most important buildings in the political history of Britain since the 11th century and have established the royal, governmental and ecclesiastical character of Westminster to the present day.

Westminster Bridge [1]

The construction of London's second bridge (after London Bridge) was strongly opposed and even sabotaged by the Thames Watermen in order to protect their ferry business. The bridge opened, however, in 1750 and was the first in England to use caissons (watertight cases) for its underwater foundations. Dogs were prohibited on the bridge and the maximum penalty for defacing the walls was death!

On 3 September 1803 William Wordsworth immortalized the view from the bridge with his sonnet 'Composed Upon Westminster Bridge'

'Earth has not anything to show more fair:
Dull would he be of soul who could pass by
A sight so touching in its majesty.'

Wordsworth's bridge was replaced in 1854–62 by the present bridge.

The first traffic lights in England were erected on the Bridge Street side on 10 December 1868. They were illuminated by gas and turned by hand so that motorists would see either red or green (there was no amber). The lights blew up in January 1869 injuring the constable manning them and they were withdrawn in 1872.

Looking eastwards down the Thames the 'thoroughly unsubtle' 13-storey high white Shell Mex office block is a clear landmark. It is surmounted by the largest clock face in London, which at 22 ft 8 in (6.91 m) in diameter is just 2 in (5 cm) wider than Big Ben's clock face. Predictably it has been nicknamed Big Benzene!

Statue of Queen Boadicea (Boudicca) [2]

Boadicea was Queen of the Iceni (a tribe from East Anglia who opposed the Roman occupation) and in AD 61 massacred the inhabitants of temporarily undefended London and razed the city to the ground (see Museum of London). Boadicea and her daughters are

If the Roman estimates of casualties are true, then Boadicea was involved in the two bloodiest battles ever fought on British soil. The Romans lost up to 70 000 in St Albans, Colchester and London in AD 61 but exacted a revenge of 80 000 British dead the same year (after which Boadicea committed suicide).

Time for revenge—Queen Boadicea in her war-chariot descends on London.

immortalized by Thomas Thorneycroft's 1902 bronze in their war chariot, complete with vicious knife-hubs. These and the absence of reins make this statue a favourite standing joke about 'lady drivers'!

Big Ben [3]

Big Ben, to be precise, is the name of the great bell of St Stephen's clock tower. It weighs a massive 13 tons 10.75 cwt, is 7 ft 6 in (2.28 m) tall and measures 9 ft (2.74 m) in diameter.

The clock mechanism and face took ten years to complete and cost £4080. The diameter of the face is 22 ft 6 in (6.86 m) and its hollow copper minute hands measure 14 ft (4.27 m)—the height of a double-decker bus.

The 13 cwt (660 kg) clapper first fitted to Big Ben far exceeded the bell maker's specification and it cracked the bell beyond repair. The old bell was melted down and recast in 1858 at the Whitechapel Bell Foundry—also the home of America's original Liberty Bell. Big Ben became operational in 1859 but once again the bell maker's specification was ignored and its 7 cwt (356 kg) clapper caused the bell to crack. Fortunately, the crack did not prove to be fatal and eventually a 4 cwt (204 kg) hammer was fitted! The present chime—arranged from an aria in Handel's Messiah—was first heard in 1862 when Big Ben resumed service. Since then the transmission of its chimes to all corners of the globe have made it the world's most broadcast bell.

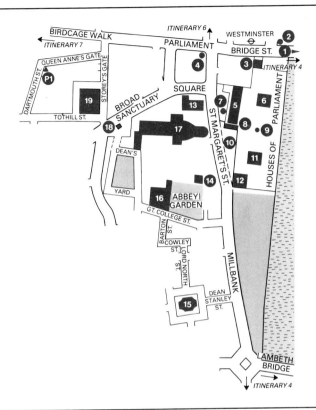

5. WESTMINSTER

1 Westminster Bridge
2 Statue of Queen Boadicea (Boudicca)
3 Big Ben
4 Statue of Sir Winston Churchill

Houses of Parliament (Palace of Westminster) *

5 Westminster Hall
6 House of Commons
7 Statue of Oliver Cromwell
8 St Stephen's Hall
9 Central Spire
10 Old Palace Yard
11 House of Lords
12 Victoria Tower

13 St Margaret's, Westminster
14 Jewel Tower
15 St John's, Smith Square
16 Westminster School
17 Westminster Abbey (see separate plan) **
18 Broad Sanctuary
19 Central Hall/Wesleyan Hall

Pubs
P1 Two Chairmen

* Specially recommended by author

** Highly recommended by author

Until the installation of automatic winding gear in 1913, two men were employed for 32 hours per week to wind Big Ben by manual labour. Its 13-ft (4 m) pendulum, weighing 685 lb (311 kg) may still be regulated by adding or subtracting old pennies. Each penny causes the clock to vary by 0.4 seconds in 24 hours!

As it is a national institution, the stoppage of Big Ben is a rare event. The longest ever 'interruption' was 13 days from 4 April to 17 April 1977 in order to effect repairs. The most unusual stoppage was in 1949 when the hands were stopped by swarming starlings!

A light above the clock face indicates that the House is sitting in the evening.

Statue of Sir Winston Churchill [4]
Parliament Square

Ivor Roberts Jones' 1973 statue immortalizes Churchill in a classic pugnacious pose, stumping the streets of Blitz-ravaged London in his army greatcoat. It is fitting that he should be so close to Parliament as it became a second home for 63 years and 360 days between 1 October 1900 and 25 September 1964—the record for the longest span of service as a Member of Parliament.

Sir Winston Churchill (1874–1965)
Churchill was born at Blenheim Palace in 1874. His early army career saw distin-

Sir Winston Churchill—'The people of London with one voice would say to Hitler, "You do your worst, and we will do our best" ' (Speech 1941).

guished action in Sudan, India and Egypt and he became a hero during the Boer War. He entered Parliament in 1900 and by 1911 had become First Lord of the Admiralty. During the inter-war years he was increasingly at variance with colleagues on international affairs, particularly his unheeded warnings against Nazi Germany. He was recalled to the Admiralty and in the darkest hours of May 1940 was asked by King George VI to form a coalition government. His epic speeches and charismatic leadership unified the nation: 'We would rather see London in ruins and ashes than that it should be tamely and abjectly enslaved'.

His leadership was not just rhetoric either, he was involved in the practical direction of the war effort down to fine detail. Churchill remarked at the end of the War, 'It was the British people who had the lion's heart but I had the luck to give the roar'. Ironically, he was not chosen again to be Prime Minister until 1951, a post he held until he was 80 in 1955.

In his 'retirement' his memoirs won him a Nobel Prize for literature. The 'greatest Englishman of the century' died on 24 January 1965 and was given a state funeral in St Paul's Cathedral. He is buried at Bladon churchyard near his family home at Blenheim.

Houses of Parliament (Palace of Westminster)

Edward the Confessor began construction of the Palace of Westminster c. 1050. The site served the dual purpose of enabling him to escape from the volatile politics of the City and to oversee the building of Westminster Abbey. His palace was completed c. 1065 and for the next 400 years became the pre-eminent royal residence. During the mid-13th century the first regular form of King's Council, known as 'Parliament', evolved. In 1512 the Palace was severely damaged by a fire and Henry VIII removed his court to Whitehall. A second, far more disastrous, fire

in 1834 burnt everything above ground with the exception of Westminster Hall, the cloisters, and the Jewel Tower. This misfortune did, however, present the opportunity to rebuild to the specification of the modern Parliament which had evolved considerably over the preceding 500 years.

A national design competition was held and the winning plan selected from the 97 submitted was that of Charles Barry who enlisted the decorative skills of Augustus Pugin to assist him.

Barry initially estimated that it would take six years to complete the Houses at a cost of £80 000. By 1860 the project, nearly complete, had cost some £2.2 million and had exhausted both Barry, who died that year aged 65, and Pugin who had died some eight years earlier in a madhouse, aged 40.

The majority of the buildings escaped major damage during World War II (with the exception of the House of Commons) and today's Houses, recently cleaned, are almost exactly as Barry and Pugin designed them.

The Houses of Parliament cover 8 acres and includes over 1000 rooms linked by over 2 miles (3 km) of corridor and 100 staircases.

They have been variously described as: 'this great and beautiful monument to Vic-

One of the reasons given for siting the Houses on the Thames was to prevent a mob ever being able completely to surround the building. The Members of Parliament may have had cause to regret this, however, in 1858, in the hot dry summer of 'The Great Stink'. This was a dreadful stench caused by raw sewage pumped directly into the Thames which by then had dried to a trickle. Conditions were so bad that the windows of the Houses had to be draped with sheets soaked in chloride of lime to hide the smell.

This incident finally brought home London's dreadful sanitary conditions and that year the first major Bill for the purification of the Thames was passed.

The river frontage of the Palace of Westminster—view from St Thomas's Hospital.

torian artifice' by architectural historian John Pope-Hennessy;
'Barry's masterpiece' by Adolf Hitler;
'A dream in stone' by Tsar Nicholas I;
'Westminster Gasworks' (a colloquial nickname!).

Westminster Hall [5]

This is the only surviving part of the original Palace of Westminster. It was constructed by William the Conqueror's son, William Rufus, in 1099 and became the central meeting place for Parliament until 1307. In 1394 Richard II set to work his master mason, Henry Yevele, to restore and transform the building into a setting worthy of Royal and Parliamentary occasions. Its crowning glory is its magnificent hammer-beam roof by Hugh Herland, completed in 1402. At 67 ft (20 m) it is the largest unsupported span in England and is acknowledged as the finest medieval timber roof in Northern Europe. King Richard further adorned the Great Hall by statues of Kings along the walls, of which eleven still remain.

From the 13th century until the late 19th century the Hall housed the Law Courts and its long history is chequered with the interchange of power.

Amongst the many famous people who have been tried and condemned in the Hall are:

Sir Thomas More—charged with treason for refusing to acknowledge the Oath of Supremacy in 1535.

Guy Fawkes—found guilty of 'the greatest treasons that ever were plotted against England' in 1605.

Charles I—'For which all treasons and crimes this Court doth adjudge the said Charles Stuart as a tyrant, traytor, murtherer and publique enimy.' A brass plate on the steps at the south end of the Hall marks where Charles sat during his trial in 1649. Four years later Oliver Cromwell was installed as England's first Protector in the Hall.

The most recent ceremonial use of the Hall was the lying in state of Sir Winston Churchill in 1965. The queue of mourners paying their last respects stretched back right across Westminster Bridge and from joining the line to passing Churchill's body took up to 5 hours.

Westminster Hall has also witnessed happy occasions, notably the coronation festivities which were held up to George IV's coronation in 1821. A colourful feature of this event was the ancient tradition of the Royal Champion, riding to the centre of the 240-ft (73.15 m) long Hall where he would throw down his gauntlet to challenge any man denying the sovereign's right to the throne to single mortal combat.

Not open to the public but may be viewed from St Stephen's Hall when passing to the House of Commons (see House of Commons).

House of Commons   [6]

The representatives from England's provincial areas or 'communes' as they were known (from which 'commons' may derive) first gathered at Westminster in 1265. They had no fixed chamber and during the mid-13th century they moved into the Abbey's Chapter House. They were eventually moved from there reputedly due to the noise of their debates disturbing the peace of the monks! By 1550 St Stephen's Chapel had become their home and they continued to meet there until the fire of 1834. Their chamber was destroyed again by an air raid in 1941 and the present chamber by Sir Giles Gilbert Scott was opened in 1950.

There are a total of 650 members who constitute the Commons but the seating accommodation of the chamber is only for 437. This is deliberate as the House is seldom full and therefore a smaller intimate chamber is more convenient for its routine conversational debates and also imparts more of a sense of urgency.

The House has two primary functions. The first is legislation—which involves reading and debating drafts of proposed Acts of Parliament ('bills') before they can become law by Royal Assent, and the second is scrutiny of government activities.

The government always sit to the side of the House nearest to the street and the opposition sit to the riverside facing them. The two parties are divided by a strip of carpet which is marked with two parallel lines measuring a distance equivalent to that of two sword-lengths. This 'no-man's land' was originally laid down to prevent bloodshed should swords be smuggled into the House and is strictly observed even today.

The Commons' most dramatic moment occurred on 10 January 1642 when Charles I stormed into the chamber to arrest five of its members who had opposed him. The House closed ranks, and the Speaker taking a particularly courageous stance, refused to inform the King as to their whereabouts. Charles stormed out with the words 'I see all the birds are flown'. This incident was the culmination of the struggle between Parliament and the King and by August the Civil War had begun. As a result of Charles' action that day the monarch has ever since been forbidden, by tradition, to enter the House of Commons.

O Members of the public queue outside to apply for 'Strangers (public) gallery' while the House sits (Summer recess generally Aug and Sept);   Mon–Thur 14.30 onwards;   Fri 09.30 onwards; &c t 90% House of Commons Information ☎ (01) 219 4272 Note: long queues are common during afternoons. To avoid these, UK residents may apply to their local MP for tickets and Foreign and Commonwealth visitors may apply to their Embassy or High Commission.

Statue of Oliver Cromwell   [7]

Parliament refused to fund William Thorneycroft's controversial 1899 statue of Cromwell due to strong opposition from the

Irish Party (Cromwell had been the hammer of the Irish some 250 years previously) and the Prime Minister, Lord Rosebery, eventually paid for it personally. Cromwell is depicted marching away from Westminster, sword in hand, as if in recollection of the incident of April 1653 when he forcibly expelled the House, who he believed were turning against him. The following day a local wit pinned a notice to the door 'This House to lett now Unfurnished'.

Charles II restored the monarchy in 1660 and took revenge for his father's execution by disinterring Cromwell's body from his Westminster Abbey grave, gibbeting it at Tyburn and placing the head on a spike above Westminster Hall. It stayed there for 25 years until blown down one night in a storm. It is now kept at Sidney Sussex, Cromwell's original Cambridge college.

St Stephen's Hall [8]

Formerly the site of St Stephen's Chapel, this was the meeting place of the Commons from 1550 until 1834 and brass studs in the floor mark the position occupied by the Speaker's chair.

O See House of Commons (no &)

Central Spire [9]

This ornate tower 300 ft (91 m) tall, acts as a ventilating shaft for Parliament's 'hot air'!

Old Palace Yard [10]

This area was formerly the courtyard of the original Palace and stretched across the present road as far as the Henry VII chapel of Westminster Abbey.

Guy Fawkes and seven of his Gunpowder Plot confederates were hanged, drawn and quartered here on 30 January 1606. He had been tortured in the Tower and was so weak that he could hardly mount the scaffold. Sir Walter Raleigh was also executed here in 1618 and his headless body is said to be buried in St Margaret's Church across the road.

An equestrian statue of Richard I, Coeur de Lion, by Baron Marrochetti (1860) stands in the centre of the Yard outside the Houses. He was the central figure among the Christian monarchs of the Crusades and it was said that even his enemies admired him, to the point where his fiercest adversary, Saladin, Sultan of Egypt, sent him choice foods when he was sick. Richard's method of financing the Holy Wars were less romantic. He raised money by robbing the Jews and selling royal lands, and is reputed to have said 'I would sell London could I find a purchaser'.

House of Lords [11]

The House of Lords has its origins in the barons who were summoned by medieval kings to council on affairs of state. There are around 1200 members, although less than 300 attend the House regularly. The membership consists of hereditary peers, life peers, Law Lords and bishops. Life peers are selected by the Prime Minister and other party leaders for their personal qualities and experience. The 'Chairman' of the House is the Lord Chancellor who sits on the Woolsack (a reminder of when wool was England's greatest export and dominated European markets).

The House has three main functions. It initiates legislation, and examines proposed legislation from the Commons. It debates

Contrary to popular belief, the searching of the cellars of the Houses of Parliament, which is conducted by the Yeomen of the Guard prior to each session of Parliament, does not date back to 1605. It was initiated during the reign of Charles II (1660–85) when a similar plot was feared.

national issues free from the constraints of party affiliation. It sits in judgement as the highest Appeal Court in the land.

One of the most famous episodes in English history occurred below the House on 5 November 1605 when Guy Fawkes was caught 'red handed' in the cellars, amongst 36 barrels of gunpowder with which he intended to blow up King James I and his Ministers at the Opening of Parliament.

The present Lords' chamber was first occupied in 1847. The centrepiece is the magnificent gold throne and canopy, designed by Augustus Pugin and used by the Sovereign at the Opening of Parliament. From here the Sovereign will read 'the Gracious Speech' at the Opening of Parliament. Around the chamber stand bronze statues of the 18 barons who forced King John to agree to the Magna Carta in 1215 at Runnymede.

O **See House of Commons; Mon–Wed 14.30 onwards, Thur 15.00 onwards Fri 11.00 onwards;** &—**Strangers Gallery inaccessible for debates—ask for alternative**
House of Lords Information
☎ **(01) 219 3107**

Victoria Tower [12]

This is the tallest part of the Palace of Westminster, measuring 336 ft (102 m) high and 75 ft (23 m) square. When built it was the tallest square masonry tower in the world. The royal standard is flown from here when the Sovereign is present and the Union Jack when Parliament is sitting. The 50 ft (15 m) high archway of the Norman porch is the royal entrance to Parliament.

The Tower contains the vast archive of the House of Commons Record Office. This dates back to 1497 and occupies 5.5 miles (8.8 km) of shelving.

St Margaret's, Westminster [13]

The original church of St Margaret was founded c. 1050–1150. It was demolished and the present church rebuilt 1486–1523 by the same masons who worked on Westminster Abbey. The interior was restored in 1877 by Sir George Gilbert Scott.

St Margaret's was adopted as the parish church of the House of Commons in 1614 and celebrated the wedding of its most famous member Sir Winston Churchill in 1908. Samuel Pepys (in 1655) and John Milton (in 1656) also married here.

The church is famous for its stained glass windows. The oldest of these is the east window commissioned in 1501 to commemorate the forthcoming marriage of Catherine of Aragon to Henry VIII's older brother, Prince Arthur. (Arthur died before the wedding and Catherine subsequently married Henry.)

Other windows commemorate John Milton and Sir Walter Raleigh who is said to be buried beneath the altar.

William Caxton (c. 1422–91) whose premises adjoined Westminster Abbey was buried in the churchyard in 1491, although somewhat ironically for England's first printer, his grave is unmarked.

Above the east entrance door a bust of Charles I stares across the road to the place of his trial, Westminster Hall, and at the statue of his deadly enemy, Oliver Cromwell.

Jewel Tower [14]

This was originally part of the south west corner of the old Palace, built by Henry Yevele in 1366 to contain the personal valuables ('Royal Wardrobe') of King Edward III. Since then it has accommodated records of the House of Lords and standard Board of Trade Weights and Measures. Eleventh-century stone carvings from Westminster Hall and some of the 97 different drawings submitted for the Houses of Parliament competition in 1854 are exhibited.

O **15 Mar–15 Oct, Mon to Sat 09.30–13.00, 14.00–18.30; 16 Oct–14 Mar closes 16.00**
Note: Often closed due to staff shortages.

St John's, Smith Square [15]

This is one of London's finest examples of baroque architecture, designed by Thomas Archer in 1713. It took 15 years to complete and at £40 875 was the most expensive church of its day. The four corner turrets were designed to equalize the weight of the building so that in case of subsidence it should at least settle uniformly into the marshy ground of Westminster. As may be seen from the angle of slope this has only been partly achieved. The interior was gutted during World War II and it now functions as a concert hall.

Charles Dickens described St John's in *Our Mutual Friend* (1864–5) as 'a very hideous church with four towers at the corners, generally resembling some petrified monster, frightful and gigantic, on its back with legs in the air'.

▌ *Between St John's and Westminster School lie three of London's most attractive Georgian streets, Lord North Street, Cowley Street and Barton Street, all built in the 1720s. Some rare surviving public air raid shelter signs from World War II are still visible on Nos. 7–10 and 13–17 Lord North Street.*

Westminster School [16]

This is one of the oldest surviving schools in London founded *c.* 1200 for clerks of the Abbey. The oldest parts of its buildings, adjoining the Abbey, date *c.* 1100 and were part of the monastic dormitory. The school's two finest buildings are the 14th-century College Hall and the 17th-century Ashburnham House. The latter dating from 1665 boasts one of the best interiors of a mid-17th-century house in London.

Ashburnham House is occasionally open during school holidays
☎ **(01) 222 3116**

Westminster Abbey [17]

According to legend the first church on this site was constructed in the 7th century by King Sebert and consecrated in person by St Peter. The earliest historical evidence records a charter from King Edgar in the late 10th century to restore the Benedictine Abbey on the site and this would have provided at least a foundation for Edward the Confessor's Abbey. Edward had vowed to the Pope that he would make a pilgrimage to the tomb of St Peter in Rome but was prevented from going for fear of being usurped. He was released from his vow on condition that he dedicate a monastery to St Peter. To this end he pledged ten per cent of his 'entire substance' and *c.* 1050 began 'The (Collegiate) Church of St Peter'—still the Abbey's official title.

The Abbey was consecrated on 28 December 1065 and just eight days later, on 5 January 1066, Edward became the first person to be buried in it as depicted in the Bayeux Tapestry (*c.* 1086).

After the defeat of Harold at Hastings, William I (the Conqueror) became the first Norman king to be crowned in the Abbey on Christmas Day 1066.

Henry III began reconstruction of the Abbey between 1245 and 1272. His chief stone mason, Henry de Reyns, was heavily influenced by the churches of Rheims, Amiens and Sainte-Chapelle in Paris. After a lull of a century Richard II directed Henry Yevele to continue work on the Abbey. Henry V and Edward IV ensured the royal patronage of the work into the 15th century and Henry VII became the Abbey's final great royal benefactor, adding his own magnificent chapel and completing the nave in 1532. The Abbey was dissolved in 1546 by his son Henry VIII but saved from destruction by its royal heritage.

The distinctive west towers of the Abbey were designed by Sir Christopher Wren who also undertook restoration work, 1698–1723. His pupil, Nicholas Hawksmoor, modified

The west towers of the Abbey—its final major addition completed in 1745.

Wren's design and completed the towers in 1745.

The north front is the Abbey's most impressive face. It was the original royal entrance and is consequently elaborately decorated. Solomon's Porch (as it is known) features Christ in Majesty with angels and apostles and is thought to date originally *c.* 1250. (It was remodelled in the late 19th century.) The rose window contains the oldest glass in its original place in the Abbey dating from 1721.

Westminster Abbey is the largest church in the United Kingdom. (There are larger cathedrals, but as Westminster Abbey does not have its own bishop it is therefore classified as a church, not a cathedral.) Its maximum overall dimensions are: length 530 ft (161 m), breadth across transept 203 ft (62 m).

Note: Memorial Dates are only given where the person is actually buried in the Abbey (see also British monarchs for dates of reigns).

The Nave This is the highest of any church in England at 101 ft 8 in (30.98 m). It measures 75 ft (23 m) across and makes a striking entrance.

Portrait of Richard II [17.1] This is the oldest contemporary portrait of an English monarch. It was executed *c.* 1390 by André Beaneve of Valenciennes, France.

Memorial to Sir Winston Churchill [17.2] This simple slab of green marble unveiled by Queen Elizabeth II reads 'Remember Winston Churchill'. His body lies at Bladon, Oxfordshire.

Tomb of the Unknown Warrior [17.3] Amongst the many tombs of royalty and great statesmen in the Abbey, this is undoubtedly the most famous and most visited. It is the only floor tomb in the Abbey that it is forbidden to tread on and even royal processions detour around it.

The Unknown Warrior was brought from Flanders and interred with earth from the battlefields on 11 November 1920 to represent the 765 399 British servicemen killed in World War I. His was the first unknown body and also the last body to be buried in the Abbey (thereafter only ashes were accepted). The artificial poppies surrounding the grave, a reminder of the poppies which grew on the battlefields, are made by disabled ex-servicemen.

The Unknown Warrior was posthumously awarded the United States' highest award—the US Congressional Medal of Honor in 1921. It is attached to the pillar to the north of the tomb.

Prime Ministers' Corner [17.4] This corner of the Abbey commemorates many statesmen and prime ministers including Clement Attlee, Ramsay MacDonald, Ernest Bevin, Sir Henry Campbell-Bannerman.

Grave of Ben Jonson (1573–1637) [17.5] This is the most peculiar burial in the Abbey. Nearing the end of his colourful life, the old court dramatist and poet, who lived on the Abbey premises, asked for a grave there, saying 'Six feet long by two feet wide is too much for me: Two feet by two feet will do'. He was consequently buried upright. Jonson is also the only person in the Abbey to suffer the indignity of a misspelled name on his epitaph, 'O Rare Ben Johnson'.

Grave of David Livingstone (1813–73) [17.6] The body of Britain's most famous African explorer lies here but his heart is buried in Ulala, Africa, where he died.

Monument to Spencer Perceval [17.7] Perceval is the only British prime minister ever to have been assassinated. He was shot at point-blank range on 11 May 1812 in the House of Commons and Sir Richard Westmacott's monument marks 'the nation's abhorrence of the act by which he fell'.

Architects and Engineers [17.8] This area contains the graves of five men who have all made indelible marks on London's landscape; Thomas Telford (1757–1834) architect of St Katharine's Dock; Robert Stephenson (1803–59) pioneer of London's railways; Sir Charles Barry (1795–1860) architect of the Houses of Parliament (his winning design is depicted on his memorial brass); Sir George Gilbert Scott (1811–78) architect of the Albert Memorial; George Edmund Street (1824–81) architect of the Royal Courts of Justice, 'The Law Courts'.

Monument to General Hargrave [17.9] This memorial to General Hargrave, governor of Gibraltar, is the most theatrical and impressive in the nave. Created by Louis François Roubiliac in 1751, it depicts an angel sounding the trumpet of doom as a pyramid behind collapses and the General freeing himself from his shroud, starts up from the tomb!

The Screen and Scientists [17.10] The magnificent gilded choir screen was designed by Edward Blore in 1834, building on to the 13th-century inner stonework. The impressive monuments to Sir Isaac Newton and to the early 18th-century English general and statesman Earl Stanhope were designed by William Kent and sculpted by John Michael Rysbrack in 1731 and 1733 respectively.

Sir Isaac Newton (1642–1727), probably the finest scientist Britain has ever produced, is buried in front of the screen.

Buried alongside Newton are: Charles Darwin (1809–82), the greatest ever English naturalist, famous for his theory of evolution and Lord Rutherford (1871–1937), 'father of nuclear physics' who in 1919 became the first man to split the atom.

Musicians [17.11] In addition to various men of science three famous English musi-

▌ *In 1816 a tooth belonging to Newton was sold in London for £730. The world's most valuable tooth was purchased by an admirer who had it set in a ring which he wore constantly.*

cians are remembered here. Henry Purcell (1659–95) was one of the greatest of all English composers and became organist of the Abbey when he was only 20. The ashes of Ralph Vaughan Williams (1872–1958) are here and a plaque commemorates Benjamin Britten, the greatest modern English composer and the first British musician to be ennobled.

Statesmen's Corner [17.12] The following record-breaking prime ministers are buried here: George Canning (1770–1827)—the shortest serving in office with only 120 days from 10 April to 8 August 1827; William Pitt the Younger (1759–1806)—the youngest to assume office in 1783 when only 24 years 205 days old. Despite the fact that he first introduced income tax in 1799 (as a temporary measure to help pay for war with France), he also became Britain's poorest Prime Minister, running up personal debts of £40 000 (now equivalent to over £1 million); Lord Palmerston (1784–1865)—the oldest first to assume office at 70 years 109 days in 1855; William Ewart Gladstone (1809–98)—holder of the record for the greatest age in office at 84 years 64 days.

The Earl of Chatham—William Pitt the Elder (1708–78) is also buried here and other Prime Ministers commemorated include Sir Robert Peel, founder of the Metropolitan Police Force (the original 'Bobby') and Benjamin Disraeli.

Chapel of St John the Baptist [17.13] The 36 ft (11 m) high monument to Lord Hunsdon (d 1596), cousin and Lord Chamberlain to Elizabeth I, is the tallest and one of the most ornate in the Abbey.

Tomb of Elizabeth I (1533–1603) and Mary I (1516–58) [17.14] Only Elizabeth's effigy rests on the tomb and the inscription reads 'Consorts both in throne and grave, here sleep we two sisters Elizabeth and Mary in the hope of one Resurrection'. Although united in death, the two were religious enemies and the catholic Mary had her protestant half-sister Elizabeth locked up in the

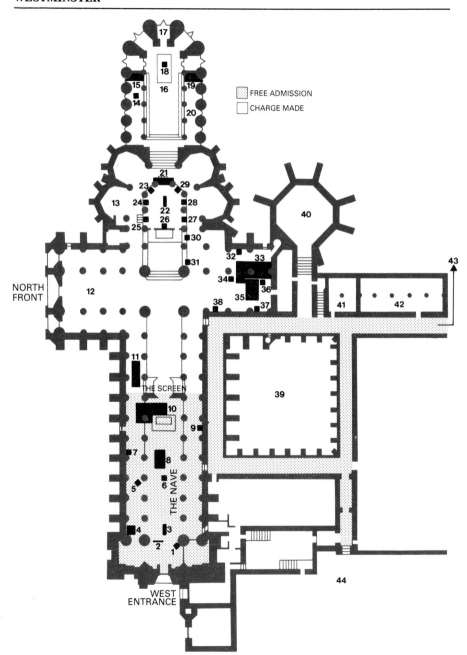

FREE ADMISSION

CHARGE MADE

17

18

15
14
16
19
20

21
23   29
13   24   28
22
26   27
25
30
31

32   33
34   36
35
37
38

40

43

41   42

NORTH
FRONT

12

39

11

THE SCREEN

10
9

7
8
5   6
THE NAVE
4   3
2   1

44

WEST
ENTRANCE

Tower in 1555. Three years later Mary died and Elizabeth succeeded her to the throne. England prospered greatly during her 45-year reign—the second longest for a British Queen—(after Queen Victoria: 63 years) and she came to be known as 'Good Queen Bess'. Elizabeth was also known as the Virgin Queen because she never married.

Innocents' Corner [17.15] This corner contains the tombs of the two youngest persons to be memorialized in the Abbey, Princess Sophia (d 1606) and Princess Mary (d 1607) aged three days and two years respectively—both children of James I. Next to them a small sarcophagus contains one of the great unsolved mysteries of English history: the bones of two young boys thought to belong to the Little Princes—Edward V and Richard, Duke of York (the sons of Edward IV) who disappeared from the Tower in 1483 (see Tower of London).

Henry VII's Chapel [17.16] This was originally commissioned by Henry VII as a memorial to the murdered King Henry VI and is thought to have been designed by Robert and William Vertue between 1503 and 1519 at an estimated cost of £14 000. The fan-vaulting of the roof is one of the architectural highlights of the Abbey, 'suspended aloft, as if by magic . . . with the wonderful minuteness and airy security of a cobweb'.

Oak doors, dating from the early 16th century, open into a chapel of magnificently carved stalls belonging to the Order of the Knights of the Bath (an ancient order of chivalry bestowed on those who have done great service to their country). Each stall is adorned with coats of arms of successive holders and the banner of the current holder hangs above his stalls. Past members include the Duke of Wellington, Field Marshal Montgomery and Earl Mountbatten. Above these stand 94 statues of popular 16th-century saints.

Battle of Britain Chapel [17.17] The stained glass window by Hugh Easton is a

The monarch most conspicuous by his absence from the Abbey is Henry VIII. He, like Britain's modern royals, is buried at Windsor.

memorial to the 1497 airmen of the Allied air forces lost in the Battle of Britain (1940). The RAF leaders Viscount Trenchard (1873-1956) and Baron Dowding (1882-1970) are buried here.

A floor tablet in the chapel marks the vault where Oliver Cromwell was buried from 1658-60 (see Statue of Oliver Cromwell).

Tomb of Henry VII (1457-1509) [17.18] This is one of the Abbey's most beautiful tombs, sculpted 'as to a king's work apperteyneth', according to Henry's own order, by Pietro Torrigiani *c.* 1518. The King's wife, Elizabeth of York and James I are also buried in this tomb.

Other royals buried in this area are: George II (1683-1760)—the last monarch to be buried in the Abbey and also the last monarch to be buried in London; Edward VI (1537-53)—Henry VIII's only son.

Tomb of the Stuart Monarchs [17.19] A monument to General Monck (1608-70), founder of the Coldstream Guards and the general whose march into London in 1660 restored the Stuart monarchy, covers the vault below which are buried: Charles II (1630-85), William III (1650-1702) and Mary II (1662-94). The last Stuart monarch, Queen Anne (1665-1714), and her husband Prince George of Denmark (1653-1708) are also buried here along with the tragic Queen's 17 children (see Statue of Queen Anne).

England's longest reigning king was George III who ruled for 59 years 96 days between 1760 and 1820. The longest reigning monarch, however, was Queen Victoria whose rule spanned 63 years and 216 days between 1837 and 1901.

Chapel of Mary Queen of Scots (1542-87) [17.20] Mary became Queen of Scotland in 1560 but was forced to flee to England when suspected of being involved in the murder of her husband, Lord Darnley (his figure is carved on the adjacent tomb of his mother, Margaret, Countess of Lennox—d 1578). Mary was held in semi-imprisonment by her cousin Queen Elizabeth I for 19 years during which time she plotted to take the English throne for herself. After her third major plot was discovered, Elizabeth ordered her execution in 1587.

Mary's became the last royal tomb chest to be erected in the Abbey in 1610 and is probably the most crowded with 27 of her family sharing the vault. At either end of Mary are the tombs of her mother-in-law, and Torrigiani's gilt bronze masterpiece of Margaret Beaufort, Countess of Richmond (1443-1509) and mother of Henry VII.

Henry V's Chapel [17.21] Henry's effigy was originally silver-plated with the head of solid silver but in 1546, when the Abbey was dissolved, the head was stolen and the silver plate stripped. The head was replaced in fibreglass in 1971, therefore making it the Abbey's newest royal tomb addition!

Henry's Queen, Katherine of Valois, now lies beneath the altar of the chantry but for 300 years her embalmed body lay in an open tomb. Samuel Pepys' diary entry for 23 February 1669 records that he was given access to the body and allowed to 'kiss her mouth, reflecting upon it that I did kiss a queen and that this was my birthday, 36 years old'.

Tomb of St Edward the Confessor (1002/5-1066) [17.22] Edward was a very religious king and soon after his death miracles were reported happening around the tomb. He was canonized in 1161 and his tomb became a shrine around which sick people would gather in the hope of miracle cures. (This tra-

▌ *During the Middle Ages, the Abbey was a major repository of objects supposed to be holy relics including hair of Mary Magdalene, a footprint of Christ in stone and St Peter's vestments.*

dition is continued to this day, on St Edward's Day, 13 October.) Sadly, during the Dissolution even this holy shrine was stripped of its covering of jewels and gold.

Tomb of Eleanor of Castile (d 1290) [17.23] Eleanor was the daughter-in-law of Henry III and the beloved wife of Edward I. Upon her death in 1290 at Harby, Nottinghamshire, Edward brought her body back in state to the Abbey and at each resting stage he erected a memorial cross (see Charing Cross Memorial).

Tomb of Henry III (1207-72) [17.24] Henry ruled for 56 years between 1216 and 1272, the longest reign of any king buried in the Abbey. The gilt bronze tomb effigies of both Henry III and Eleanor of Castile, made in 1291, were the first of their kind to be cast in England.

Tomb of Edward I (1239-1307) [17.25] Edward I claims two Abbey distinctions. He was the first to be crowned in the present Abbey (rebuilt by Henry III) and at 6 ft 2 in (1.88 m)—a veritable giant of the day nicknamed 'Longshanks'—he is the tallest monarch buried in the Abbey. His long plain tomb is inscribed *Malleus Scottorum* ('Hammer of the Scots'), another of his nicknames which commemorates his many conflicts North of the Border.

▌ *Edward I sired 18 legitimate children—a British monarchy record. The British monarchy record for the most children of any status, however, goes to Henry I who, in addition to at least one legitimate son and daughter, had at least 20 bastard children, and possibly 22 by six mistresses.*

The Coronation Chair [17.26] This was made for Edward I in 1300 from English Oak and has been used for every coronation since Edward II's in 1307. Below the seat is the Stone of Scone. This was taken from the Scots, who had used it as their throne stone since the 9th century, by Edward I in 1297. It was thought traditionally to be the original holy relic that Jacob had used as his Dream Pillow at Bethel, later taken to the sacred hill of Tara in Ireland and named 'The Stone of Destiny'. It is recorded as being used for the coronation of Macbeth's stepson at Scone in 1057. Scottish 'Nationalist' supporters stole the stone from the Abbey in 1950 but it was recovered in 1951.

Next to the Chair is Edward III's mighty State Sword, 6 ft 11 in (2.1 m) long and shield weighing 17.9 lb (8.1 kg). The Chair is turned round at coronations and placed in front of the high altar. This 'Coronation Theatre' is where every British monarch since 1066 has been crowned (excepting Edward V, Jane Grey and Edward VIII).

Tomb of Richard II (1367-1400) [17.27] Richard's tomb has suffered much at the hands of vandals. His jawbone was removed through a hole in the tomb in 1776 (since restored) and he was originally depicted holding the hand of his wife, Anne of Bohemia (1366-94); but, sadly, the arms are now broken off.

Tomb of Edward III (1312-77) [17.28] This has been built by the master stone mason of the Abbey, Henry Yevele and the master woodworker of Westminster Hall, Hugh Herland. During Edward III's 50-year reign he fathered 14 children. The niches in his tomb once held small statues of all 14 but now only six remain, including that of his most famous and eldest son Edward, The Black Prince.

Tomb of Philippa of Hainault (c. 1314-69) [17.29] Queen Philippa, wife of Edward III, is best remembered for her merciful role in begging the King to spare the lives of the six burghers of Calais who offered their lives in return for sparing their city in 1347. (A replica of Rodin's statue of the Burghers of Calais stands next to the Houses of Parliament in Victoria Tower Gardens.)

Tomb of King Sebert (d c. 616) [17.30] This is the supposed tomb of Sebert, King of the East Saxons, the legendary founder of the first Abbey. If this really is his resting place, then he is the oldest king and the most ancient person buried in the Abbey.

Tomb of Anne of Cleves (1515-57) [17.31] Anne of Cleves is the only one of Henry VIII's six wives to be buried in the Abbey. It was a political marriage and the King found her so ugly that he nicknamed her 'The Flanders Mare' and divorced her after just six months. They did, however, continue to be friends!

Poets' Corner This area is dedicated to literary, musical and theatrical personalities as well as poets.

Tomb of Geoffrey Chaucer (1343-1400) [17.32] Geoffrey Chaucer was the first poet to be buried in the Abbey, though it is probable that this honour was accorded him due to his position as Clerk of the King's works rather than as a tribute to his literary greatness. His tomb monument was not added until 1556.

Poets [17.33] There are monuments to many famous poets in this area but relatively few are actually buried here. The most popular poets' graves in this area include those of Robert Browning (1812-89)—famous for *The Pied Piper of Hamelin*, Alfred Lord

> The grave of Edmund Spenser is probably a treasure trove of unseen poetic masterpieces. He was the second poet to be buried in the Abbey and was held in such esteem by his fellow poets, including Shakespeare, that they are said to have thrown their unpublished works into his grave as a tribute.

Tennyson (1809-92)—*The Charge of the Light Brigade*, and Edmund Spenser (1552-99)—author of *The Faerie Queen*.

Grave of Thomas Parr (d 1635) [17.34] If the inscription on the grave of 1483-1635 is to be believed, then 'Old Parr' at 152 years old ('lived through the reign of ten Sovereigns') would not only be the oldest man in the Abbey but the oldest ever in the world by some 31 years! He supposedly took his first wife at 80, his second at 112, and was brought to the royal court as a curiosity.

> Even this outrageous longevity claim is surpassed in London. The burial register of St Leonard's, Shoreditch records the death in 1588 of Thomas Cam, aged 207!

Literary and Theatrical Figures [17.35] The graves of the following lie here:
Charles Dickens (1812-70): Dickens loathed public memorials and by his own insistence no public statues have ever been erected to him in London (although there are some busts). His tomb, likewise, is deliberately plain.
Rudyard Kipling (1865-1936): Kipling, an English writer born in Bombay, is best remembered for his most famous works, the (two) *Jungle Books*.
Samuel Johnson (1709-84): (see Dr Johnson's House).
David Garrick (1717-79): (see Monument to David Garrick below).
George Frederick Handel (1685-1759) (see his monument below). Handel is the only composer buried in Poets' Corner.
Sir Henry Irving (1838-1905). In 1895 he became the first actor ever to be knighted.

Monument to William Shakespeare [17.36] Shakespeare is buried in Stratford-upon-Avon but his monument by Peter Scheemakers, 1740, is one of the most impressive in Poets' Corner. It features busts of Queen Elizabeth I, Henry V and Richard III and a misquotation from *The Tempest*. It is also in current circulation, illustrated on the back of the £20 note.

Monument to George Frederick Handel [17.37] This memorial by Louis François Roubiliac shows Handel holding the score of his masterpiece *The Messiah* which was first performed on a large scale in the Abbey in 1784.

> *There is an unproven story that, although the face on Handel's statue was modelled from his death mask, the ears are not his own! It is said that Roubiliac considered the real things too large and used poetic licence to reduce them!*

Monument to David Garrick [17.38] Garrick, the greatest actor of his age, and the only actor to have a major West End theatre named after him, is shown appropriately taking his final curtain call.

O **Nave and Abbey Precinct 08.00–18.00 (Wed –20.00); 'Royal Chapels' and 'Poets' Corner' (Shaded area on diagram) Mon–Fri 09.00–16.00, Sat 09.00–14.00 and occasionally 15.45–17.00; £ (Wed 18.00–19.45 free); T, £ Apr–Oct, Mon–Fri 10.00, 10.30, 11.00, 14.00, 14.30, 15.00; Nov–Mar, Mon–Fri 10.00, 11.00, 14.00, 15.00; Sat (all year) 10.00, 10.45, 12.30; ⚇ Nave 100% (2+1 step main entry or request ramp access via cloisters) Chapels of Henry VII and Edward the Confessor not accessible but latter may be viewed from lower ambulatory level.** Note: Abbey may be closed or have restricted entry during special services ☎ (01) 222 7110 for details.**

Abbey Precinct

Great Cloister [17.39] Constructed in the 13th and 14th centuries, the North and West walks of the cloisters were used as an area for study, the South walk was a passage to the Refectory and the East walk led to the Chapter House.

Chapter House [17.40] Built *c.* 1250 this splendid octagonal building still retains its original tiled floor and many wall paintings dating from the 14th century. It was originally used as the meeting house for the monks from where the daily agenda would be set. It is one of the largest Chapter Houses in the country and could sit 80 monks around its walls. It became a parliamentary council room in 1257 under Henry III and was also used as the meeting place for the House of Commons.

O **15 Mar–15 Oct, 09.30–18.00; 16 Oct–14 Mar, 10.00–16.00; £ ☎ (01) 222 5897**

Pyx Chamber (Chapel of the Pyx) [17.41] The Pyx Chamber is a survivor of Edward the Confessor's Abbey and was originally a chapel. It contains the oldest altar in the Abbey, dating *c.* 1240, where Henry III worshipped. The name Pyx refers to its early function as a safe-room in which were kept large wooden chests (known as Pyxes) that held the standard pieces of gold and silver against which coins of the realm were annually tested. The impregnable-looking chamber was also used as a royal treasure store but in 1303 Edward I's jewels were stolen from here by a merchant named Richard de Podlicote who was caught and executed. (It is said that he was flayed alive and his skin nailed to the door of the Chamber as a grim warning.)

Exhibits include original Pyxes and a gold thread Cope (ceremonial cloak) allegedly worn by Charles II at his coronation.

O **See Chapter House (combined ticket)**

Abbey Treasures Museum [17.42] This chamber is part of the 11th-century undercroft of the original Abbey, probably used as the monks' common room. The chief exhibits are wax and wood effigies of royal persons spanning over 350 of royalty from Edward III onwards. They were used at the royal funeral, carried on top of the hearse, as a substitute for the body lying in state. These unique examples of early portraiture range in completeness from the whole body to just the head and includes a 'topless' bust of Anne of Denmark!

The effigy of Admiral Lord Nelson dressed in his own clothes was described by Lady Hamilton as a 'remarkable likeness'. This was a deliberate device by the Abbey in order to attract back some of the many visitors who had gone to St Paul's Cathedral to visit Nelson's tomb.

O See Chapter House (combined ticket)

The effigy of Frances Stuart, Duchess of Richmond (d 1702) is accompanied by her favourite pet, a West African grey parrot dating from 1702. This is the oldest known stuffed bird in England. Frances Stuart was a court favourite of Charles II and was the original model for the figure of Britannia which still appears on British banknotes.

Little Cloister and College Garden [17.43] This was originally the site of the monk's 12th-century hospital and the cloister walls date from the 14th century. The College Garden claims to be the oldest surviving in England, having been under cultivation for over 900 years.

O Apr–Sept, Thur 10.00–18.00; Oct–Mar 10.00–16.00; &
Note: Band Concerts are held Thursday lunchtimes during summer.

Dean's Yard [17.44] The east side of the courtyard dates from the 14th century and is said to be the oldest medieval domestic terrace in London. (The 16th-century Jericho Parlour and 14th-century Jerusalem Chamber in Dean's Court may only be entered on the official Abbey tour.)

Broad Sanctuary   [18]

This area takes its name from an old custom of being able to claim sanctuary (i.e. safe refuge from the law) within the precincts of the Abbey. The most famous seeker of sanctuary was Elizabeth Woodville (widow of Edward IV) who in 1483 fled here with her son Prince Richard, one of the ill-fated Little Princes.

The Gatehouse Prison stood on this site from 1370 until 1776. Its inmates included Sir Walter Raleigh, Samuel Pepys and the Cavalier poet Richard Lovelace who wrote *To Althea* from here, including the immortal lines 'Stone walls do not a prison make, nor iron bars a cage'.

Central Hall/Wesleyan Hall   [19]

This huge domed hall is London's chief Methodist Church, built in ornate French style between 1905 and 1911. It held the first regular sessions of the United Nations assembly on 10 Jan–14 Feb 1946.

Two Chairmen   [P1]
Dartmouth Street/Queen Anne's Gate

This small 18th-century pub takes its name from the sedan chair carriers who brought their customers to the Royal Cockpit, which stood on Cockpits Steps adjacent to the pub, until its demolition in 1810. (Cock fighting was finally outlawed in 1849.)

Sedan chairs were introduced to London in 1711 and were in use up until the mid-19th century.

O & (crowded)
☎ **(01) 222 8561**

Queen Anne's Gate is one of London's best preserved 18th-century streets. Originally two closes, which divided where the statue of Queen Anne stands, the eastern part (closest to the pub) is late 18th century, whilst the western part dates c. 1704.

TRAFALGAR SQUARE, WHITEHALL AND ST JAMES'S PARK

This area is the very heart of London, for government, tourists, protesters, revellers and geographers alike.

The brief thoroughfare named Whitehall (after Henry VIII's 16th-century palace) has been the country's main 'corridor of power' since the early 18th century and from here was once ruled the largest and most powerful Empire ever kown. In contrast with the grey buildings and the sobriety of government and civil service affairs is the adjacent St James's Park—the most picturesque of central London's open spaces.

Charing Cross (Eleanor Cross) Memorial [1]
Forecourt Charing Cross Railway Station

This is a replica of the original Charing Cross which stood close by on the site now occupied by the statue of Charles I. It was the last of the 12 crosses to be erected in 1290 by Edward I between Harby, Nottinghamshire, the place where his beloved wife Eleanor of Castile had died, and Westminster Abbey, her burial place. Each cross marked the resting place of her funeral cortège. It was demolished in 1647 by Oliver Cromwell's Puritan government. The present cross was erected in 1865 and features eight statues of Queen Eleanor.

St Martin-in-the-Fields [2]
Trafalgar Square

The original church on this site was built c. 1222 and stood for around 500 years before James Gibbs' present church began construction. All that remains from the old church above ground are nine of its bells which date from 1525.

The distinctive tower was rebuilt in 1824 and provides a dramatic evening sight, floodlit against Trafalgar Square.

Close to the 1740 portrait of Gibbs in the north aisle is a memorial to Far East Prisoners of War which includes portions of sleepers taken from the infamous Burma-Siam 'Railway of Death' (as featured in the film *Bridge over the River Kwai*). This was completed in October 1943, costing the lives of 16 000 allied prisoners of war and

At the Restoration in *1660*, Charing Cross was the site for the execution of eight regicides who were made to face toward Banqueting House—the site of Charles I's execution. Samuel Pepys recorded in his diary 'I went out to Charing Cross to see Major-General Harrison hanged drawn and quartered which was done there, he looking as cheerful as any man could do in that condition'!

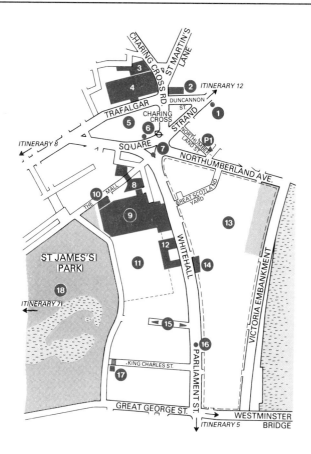

6. TRAFALGAR SQUARE, WHITEHALL AND ST JAMES'S PARK

1 Charing Cross (Eleanor Cross) Memorial
2 St Martin-in-the-Fields
3 National Portrait Gallery *
4 National Gallery **
5 Trafalgar Square
6 Nelson's Column
7 Statue of Charles I
8 Admiralty Arch
9 Old Admiralty
10 The Citadel
11 Horse Guards Parade

12 Horse Guards
13 Whitehall Palace (site – see dotted line)
14 Banqueting House
15 Downing Street
16 Cenotaph
17 Cabinet War Rooms
18 St James's Park

Pubs
P1 Sherlock Holmes

* Specially recommended by author

** Highly recommended by author

The most unusual police box in Britain, at the corner of Trafalgar Square.

probably over 100 000 native labourers who died of sickness, starvation, brutality and exhaustion.

St Martin's is famous for its crypt where many eminent people have been buried. The two most colourful were Charles II's favourite mistress, Nell Gwyn (d 1687), and Jack Sheppard, highwayman (see Tyburn) (d 1724). William Hogarth (d 1764), Sir Joshua Reynolds (d 1792), the great sculptor, Louis François Roubiliac (d 1762) and the greatest English furniture designer, Thomas Chippendale (d 1779) (whose premises were in St Martin's Lane) were also buried here. All of these graves, however, have been moved elsewhere.

The crypt has been renowned for its charity since 1918 when it was first opened to homeless soldiers returning from war. It now houses a new Visitors' Centre which includes an exhibition, tracing the history of the church, the London Brass Rubbing Centre and a restaurant.

St Martin's is also famous for its excellent lunch-time concerts which take place every Monday and Tuesday at 13.05.

O Church 07.30–21.30; Brass Rubbing Centre Mon–Sat 10.00–18.00; Sun 12.00–18.00; Restaurant Mon–Sat 10.00–20.30; Sun 12.00–18.00; ♿ church only, enter via north side
☎ (01) 930 0089, Restaurant (01) 839 4342

The most colourful occasion in the church's calendar is the Pearly Kings and Queens Harvest Festival (see Calendar of Events). These quintessential cockney characters were originally elected to safeguard the rights of market traders and adopted their pearl button-laden suits in around 1880. The 'Pearlies' add buttons to their suits throughout their lives and a fully decorated suit can hold up to as many as 30 000 buttons. They now devote their time to charitable causes.

National Portrait Gallery [3]
2 St Martin's Place

This collection was founded in 1856 as a 'Gallery of the Portraits of the most eminent persons in British History' and illustrates some of the most important themes in British History from the late 15th century onwards. There are in total some 9000 items in the primary collection, only about ten per cent of which are on display at one time. This is the world's most comprehensive portrait survey of historical personalities.

Middle Ages (Mezzanine Floor) A copy of

what is probably the earliest contemporary portrait of an English monarch, Richard II, is displayed here (the original, *c.* 1390, is in Westminster Abbey). Other notable portraits from this era include those of Chaucer (late 16th century), Henry V (*c.* 1600) and the last Yorkist king, Richard III (late 16th century).

16th century to 1837 (Top Floor) The earliest original contemporary portrait in the Gallery is that of Henry VII dating from 1505. It was painted for a prospective bride but whether or not due to the quality of the picture, she refused him!

The portrait *Descendants of Sir Thomas More* by Rowland Lockey (a copy after Hans Holbein) painted in 1593, is an important early exhibit. So, too, is a section of a large cartoon by Holbein which was made for a wall painting at Whitehall Palace *c.* 1536-7. It depicts Henry VIII with his third wife, Jane Seymour, his father Henry VII and mother Elizabeth of York. The family line is continued by two splendid portraits of Queen Elizabeth I—The 'Coronation' portrait and by contrast The 'Ditchley' portrait painted *c.* 1592 towards the end of her reign.

The raffish picture of William Shakespeare (*c.* 1610) was the first to enter the Gallery's collection. It is the only known contemporary portrait of him and is claimed to be the only true representation of 'the Bard'.

One of the finest pictures in the Gallery is said to be Sir Peter Paul Rubens' rich canvas (1629) of Thomas Howard, Earl of Arundel—the first great patron of the arts in the early 17th century. Two notable pictures of Charles II (*c.* 1680) and his mistress, Nell Gwyn, (*c.* 1675) recall late 17th-century London's most famous royal affair. Excellent portraits from the same period include Samuel Pepys—appropriately painted in 1666, during the writing of his diary—and Sir Christopher Wren, painted in 1711 by Sir Godfrey Kneller. There are few original portraits of Wren in existence and this is judged to be one of the best. Also by Kneller is a fine portrait of Sir Isaac Newton, painted in 1702.

A self-portrait by William Hogarth *c.* 1757 illustrates the most original and varied English artist of his day at work on a new canvas.

One of the most acclaimed portraits in the 'England at War' collection is that of Admiral Horatio Nelson by Sir William Beechey, 1800-1. Close to him is Emma, Lady Hamilton, painted *c.* 1785, eight years before she met Nelson.

The 'Romantic Movement' section contains the only known authentic portraits of Jane Austen, painted by her sister *c.* 1801 and of Percy Bysshe Shelley. Shelley's wife Mary wrote *Frankenstein* in 1818 and an original third edition from 1831 is exhibited in the same room.

The Regency Room is dominated by the largest picture in the Gallery—*The Reformed House of Commons* (1833) by Sir George Hayter. This contains some 375 portraits, including four prime ministers. Sittings from all 375 subjects were obtained to ensure authenticity.

Victorian and Edwardian Periods 1837 to *c.* 1910 (First Floor) Some highlights of this era include a rare group picture of the three Brontë sisters *c.* 1834, Charles Dickens 1839, Florence Nightingale at Scutari *c.* 1856, Charles Darwin 1883 and Queen Victoria 1863. One of the most celebrated of Victorian photographs shows the great engineer Isambard Kingdom Brunel, standing in front of the massive chains of the steam ship *Great Eastern* which he designed. (Launched in 1858, she had a gross tonnage of 18 914 and was then the world's largest ship.)

Sir Godfrey Kneller (1646–1723) was appointed court painter by Charles II and held this position for the reign of four monarchs up to George I. He is the only painter commemorated in Westminster Abbey but is said to have spurned the chance to be buried there with his dying words 'By God I will not be buried in Westminster . . . they do bury fools there'.

20th Century (Ground Floor) The Royal Collection includes The Royal Family (with George V and Queen Mary) at Buckingham Palace 1913 and of the present-day Royals, HM The Queen by Pietro Annigoni 1969, a pensive view of HRH The Prince of Wales by Bryan Organ 1980, and by the same artist the first portrait of the Princess of Wales 1981, painted after the news of her engagement.

Other notable portraits: T E Lawrence (of Arabia) by Augustus John 1919, Captain Robert Falcon Scott (of the Antarctic) 1911, Thomas (*Tess of the D'Urbevilles*) Hardy 1893 and James (*Ulysses*) Joyce 1935.

The 'greatest Englishman', Sir Winston Churchill is portrayed by Walter Sickert, 1927, and the most politically successful Englishwoman of the 20th century, Margaret Thatcher, is painted by Rodrigo Moynihan 1983-5.

O Mon-Fri 10.00-17.00; Sat 10.00-18.00; Sun 14.00-18.00; ⅗ (2+7 steps) 80%
☎ (01) 930 1552

National Gallery [4]
Trafalgar Square

The National Gallery houses one of the finest and most comprehensive collections of Western art in the world. This comprises just over 2000 paintings by Western European artists, dating from c. 1250 to c. 1900, whose historical stature is such to justify their representation in the Gallery.

The Gallery was founded in 1824 when the Angerstein collection of 38 works became the first paintings to be bought for the country for public display. They were exhibited in Pall Mall until William Wilkins' present classical building was opened in 1838. It is Britain's most popular gallery, attracting over three million visitors per year.

The following pictures are amongst the most famous and the most highly regarded masterpieces in the collection. (Numbers refer to rooms—generally fixed.)

(1) *The Wilton Diptych*, Richard II presented to the Christ Child by his patron saints, is thought to be of the French school (artist unknown) c. 1395 or later. It is extremely rare in its subject and its form as a portable diptych and was acquired in 1929 for £90 000.

(2) *The Battle of San Romano* by Paolo Uccello c. 1450s. This picturesque battle scene demonstrates Uccello's pioneer work in the use of perspective.

(2) *Venus and Mars* by Sandro Botticelli (late 15th century). It cost the Gallery £1050 in 1874.

(4) *The Baptism of Christ* by Piero della Francesca c. 1442. This artist, long overlooked, is now considered to be one of the greatest painters of the 15th century.

(7) *The Virgin and Child* (Cartoon) by Leonardo da Vinci, mid-1490s. In 1962, £804 361 was paid for this masterpiece—then the world's highest price recorded for a drawing.

(8) *The Ansidei Madonna* by Raphael, 1506. The National Gallery paid £70 000 for this altarpiece in 1885, making it then the world's highest priced painting.

(8) *The Entombment* by Michelangelo, c. 1506. This unfinished work is one of his very few oil paintings and cost the Gallery £2000 in 1868.

(8) *Virgin of the Rocks* by Leonardo da Vinci, 1508. A relatively small number of Leonardo's paintings still exist but the flawless and complex composition of this unfinished altarpiece panel points to his artistic genius. Another version of this hangs in the Louvre.

(9) *Bacchus and Ariadne* by Titian, 1523. This work shows why Titian has been described as one of the greatest of all colourists.

(10) *The Doge* by Giovanni Bellini c. 1501—probably the most highly regarded and lifelike of all Venetian portraits.

(19) Self-portrait by Rembrandt, 1669. This is perhaps the greatest of the 15 Rembrandts in the National Gallery and is one of the last of his many self-portraits. It depicts him tired and battered by life. He had survived his

One of the world's greatest 'picture-houses'—the upper level of the National Gallery portico.

wife, son and mistress and was in financial difficulties. That same year he was buried in a pauper's grave. The picture was bought for £430 in 1851.

(21) Equestrian portrait of Charles I by Van Dyck (late 1630s)—one of the most famous images of monarchy, it cost £17 000 in 1885.

(22) *Le Chapeau de Paille* (The Straw Hat) by Rubens *c.* 1630.

(24) *Giovanni Arnolfini and his wife* by Jan Van Eyck, 1434. This is one of the earliest, almost perfectly preserved oil paintings and gives a view into a middle-class Bruges household of the period, where a self-conducted wedding ceremony is taking place. The artist is reflected in the mirror. It cost the Gallery £630 in 1842.

(25) *The Ambassadors* by Hans Holbein the Younger, 1533—one of Holbein's largest and most important portraits. The skull (a common symbol of mortality) in trick perspective in the foreground is of unusual interest.

(28) *Young Woman standing at a Virginal* by Johannes Vermeer, *c.* 1670.

(35) *The Hay Wain* by John Constable, 1821. This is the most famous and quintessential English landscape painting. The setting is Flatford, Suffolk. It was bought for 1300 guineas (£1365) in 1866.

(35) *The Fighting Téméraire* by J M W Turner, 1838 is the most famous work of the greatest English painter. This atmospheric scene shows the old warship, which fought at Trafalgar, being towed to the breaker's yard.

(41) *The Toilet of Venus* by Diego Velasquez, *c.* 1649-51. This has been described as the most beautiful female nude ever painted. Also called *The Rokeby Venus* after Rokeby

Hall, Yorkshire, where it hung. It was bought for £45 000 in 1905.

(44) *Parapluies* (Umbrellas) by Auguste Renoir, 1880s.

(45) *Bathers Asnières* by Georges Seurat, 1883–4. This well known work is the first major example of Seurat's revolutionary new technique of divisionism, i.e. colours placed (and mixed) as a series of small dots on the canvas.

(45) *Cornfield with Cypresses* by Vincent Van Gogh, 1889—was painted during the artist's voluntary stay in a mental asylum.

(45) *Sunflowers* by Van Gogh, 1888. This is one of the series of the artist's sunflower paintings, another of which fetched a world record price of £22.5 million in 1987.

(46) *Water-lily Pond* by Claude Monet, 1899.

O Mon–Sat 10.00–18.00; Sun 14.00–18.00; T Mon–Fri 11.30, 15.00, Sat 14.00, 15.30; ⅖ t 100%
☎ (01) 839 3321
Note: July–Sept late night opening until 20.00 Wed. Tel. to confirm.

The world's highest priced painting currently is Irises *by Van Gogh, 1889 sold at auction in 1987 for £30 187 623. Like* Cornfield with Cypresses *(above) Van Gogh painted it whilst in a mental asylum.*

Trafalgar Square   (5)

Trafalgar Square was originally planned in 1812 by John Nash as part of his Charing Cross Improvement Scheme. After Nash's death, Charles Barry created the central precinct in 1840.

At the corners of the Square stand four cylindrical stone plinths, each surmounted by an octagonal bronze lamp similar to the type that would have illuminated Nelson's flagship HMS *Victory*. The door of the one at the south-east corner is a recent addition but its observation slits are a clue to its original

Admiral Lord Nelson 170 ft (51.82 m) above the city. The highest statue to an actual person in London.

purpose. It was set up in the late 19th century as a secret observation post, with just enough room for one man and a telephone in order to monitor the political marches which have traditionally congregated here.

The equestrian Roman-style statue of George IV was the first of the many statues in the Square, erected in 1843. The statue of James II (also in Roman garb), attributed to Grinling Gibbons or his studio, is regarded as one of London's finest outdoor statues. It is the oldest statue in the Square, dating from 1686 and is also the most travelled, having had three previous sites.

The famous fountains which spring into life every morning at 10.00 use 90 000 gallons (409 140 l) of water per day. They were erected in 1936, replacing the original fountains which now stand outside Parliament in Ottawa, Canada.

A huge Norwegian spruce Christmas tree has been placed in the Square every year in mid-December since 1947 as an expression of gratitude from Norway for British help during World War II. The Square is also the centre for New Year revellers.

> The Square was named after the historic naval battle which took place off Cape Trafalgar on the south-west coast of Spain on 21 October 1805. The British Fleet won a famous victory, destroying 23 of the Franco-Spanish fleet of 33 ships. The greatest casualty, however, was the architect of the victory, Admiral Lord Nelson, who was shot dead by a French musketeer (see National Maritime Museum).

Nelson's Column [6]

London's most famous monument was conceived in 1838 (33 years after the death of Nelson) when a Memorial committee was formed to raise funds. William Railton's Corinthian fluted column and pedestal surmounted by a bronze capital proved to be the winning design and was erected 1839–42. The monument (excluding the statue) is 170 ft (51.82 m) high and is London's only outdoor statue to its greatest naval hero. In order to celebrate its completion, London's most precarious ever dinner-party was held atop the column (a week before the statue was put in place) with 14 people reportedly enjoying a rump steak dinner!

A pigeon's-eye close up of London's most famous statue. Note the absence of an eye-patch!

The bronze reliefs at the base of the Column represent Nelson's four greatest battles: Cape St Vincent, the Nile, Copenhagen and Trafalgar. The statue of Nelson, weighing around 16 tons and standing 17 ft (5 m) tall was designed by Edward Hodges Bailey. On the weekend before it was hoisted aloft, it was put on public view and it is estimated that 100 000 people saw it for the last time at close quarters. Nelson is depicted with part of his right arm missing (lost in the siege of the Canary Isles 1797) but contrary to common fallacy there is no eye-patch. Nelson lost the sight in his right eye in 1775 during the siege of Corsica but his eye was saved. He faces southward to the home of the fleet, Portsmouth, and beyond to the scenes of his naval triumphs. It was not until 1867 that the four bronze lions came to 'guard' the Column. Designed by Edwin Landseer for a fee of £6000, each lion is 20 ft (6 m) long.

> The importance of Nelson's Column was noted by Adolf Hitler who planned to remove it to Berlin after the conquest of Britain as a symbol of world domination.

Statue of Charles I [7]
Trafalgar Square

This statue was cast in 1633 by the Huguenot sculptor Hubert le Sueuer and is the oldest (and one of the most impressive) of London's many equestrian statues. It stands on the site formerly occupied by the old Charing Cross and a brass tablet claims it to be the exact centre of London, from which all distances are measured.

The statue has a bizarre history which reflects this changeable period in English politics. It was originally placed in the churchyard of St Paul's, Covent Garden, and then hidden in the crypt when war broke out. Cromwell's government discovered it, however, and sold it to a brazier named John Rivett who was ordered to destroy it. Either due to royalist sympathies or with an eye to future profit, Rivett kept the bronze statue intact and to cover up the fact he sold knives and other souvenirs supposedly made from the metal. Having made a small fortune, he returned the statue to Charles II. It was erected on its present site in 1677 and on 30 January every year the Royalist Army of the Civil War Society, dressed and armed in period style, lay a wreath here to mark the anniversary of the King's execution.

Admiralty Arch [8]
Trafalgar Square/The Mall

This grand triumphal archway was built as part of the national memorial to Queen Victoria by Sir Aston Webb in 1911. It takes its name from the adjacent Admiralty building. The central gate is only opened on ceremonial occasions.

Old Admiralty [9]
Whitehall

The Old Admiralty was originally designed to accommodate the Lords of the Admiralty. The present building with its distinctive green domed roof dates from 1725 and replaced Sir Christopher Wren's original of 1695, although it retains some of its notable interior features.

It was here that Nelson took his orders and in 1806 his body lay in state in a ground floor room. The most famous First Lord of modern times (1911–15 and 1939–40) was Sir Winston Churchill. The adjacent Admiralty House was built in 1788 to enlarge the accommodation.

O By appointment only. Write to Old Admiralty, Spring Gardens, SW1

The Citadel [10]
The Mall

This grim-looking creeper-covered bunker was built in 1941 as a blastproof shelter for the communications room of the Admiralty. Its foundations go 30 ft (9 m) into the earth.

Horse Guards Parade [11]

Henry VIII indulged his love of jousting here by having a tilt-yard built on this site in 1533. Tournaments were held until the end of the 16th century to be replaced by animal baiting. The political unrest of Charles I's reign caused the Parade Ground to assume its military nature which it retains today in ceremonial form.

Horse Guards Parade is most famous for the ceremony of the Trooping of the Colour which dates from 1755. This takes place annually, usually on the second Saturday in June, to honour the official birthday of the Sovereign. The ceremony involves inspection of the Regimental Parade and a Birthday Parade. Its origin lies in the custom of parading flags and banners to the troops before battle, so that they would become acquainted with them as rallying points in the chaos of the battlefield.

London's grandest gateway—Admiralty Arch, viewed from The Mall.

Horse Guards [12]
Whitehall

The original Horse Guards was built in 1641 for Charles I as the guard house to Whitehall Palace. The existing Horse Guards was built on the same site in 1750–8 by William Kent (and John Vardy after Kent's death) as headquarters for the General Staff. It is now the office of the Commander-in-Chief of the Combined Forces and the headquarters of the Household Division who are responsible for the protection of the Sovereign.

Horse Guards Arch is still regarded as the official entrance to the royal palaces and two mounted troopers are posted daily. The Guard arrive at 11 am on weekdays, 10 am on Sundays and are inspected at 4 pm.

Whitehall Palace (site) [13]
Whitehall

Henry VIII confiscated York Place from Cardinal Wolsey in 1528 and built it up to become the largest palace in Europe, comprising over 2000 rooms by the end of the 16th century. The royal 'village' stretched almost from Charing Cross to the Houses of Parliament. Its present name is taken from the white banqueting hall which stood at the centre of the complex. Henry VIII died at Whitehall in 1547 but it continued to be the principal London residence of the Sovereign.

Charles I was executed here in 1649 and his successor, Oliver Cromwell, died in bed at the Palace in 1658. Charles II rebuilt much of the Palace and restored merry-making to the court—he even provided accommodation for four of his mistresses in grander apartments than those of the Queen who lived on the same site! Charles died here in February 1685 and the last monarch resident at Whitehall was William III who found the river-site disagreeable to his asthma and moved the court to Kensington. In 1698 the Palace was accidentally burned down, leaving Banqueting House as the only surviving building above ground.

A legacy of Whitehall Palace that has become synonymous with London's police force is the name Great Scotland Yard. These were the Palace quarters used by the kings and ambassadors of Scotland when in London. Sir Robert Peel used 4 Whitehall Place, overlooking Great Scotland Yard, as the headquarters for his newly-formed Metropolitan Police, the first uniformed statutory force in Great Britain, from 1828–90. They are now based at New Scotland Yard in Victoria Street, St James's.

Banqueting House   [14]

This was the first completed Classical style building in England, designed by Inigo Jones and finished in 1622. The Banqueting House was used for a number of royal ceremonies, including the reception of foreign ambassadors, the Maundy Thursday custom of distributing specially minted coins to the elderly, and the touching for 'King's Evil'. The latter was a custom of the Stuart kings, whereby suffers of the 'King's Evil' or scrofula (a tubercular disease of the neck glands) would be touched by the Sovereign in the hope of a 'divine cure'. (It is said that Charles II touched 90 000 sufferers in all.)

The painting of the saloon room by Sir Peter Paul Rubens was commissioned by Charles I in 1629. At 110×55 ft (33×17 m) it is the largest and most spectacular existing

work by Rubens for which he received £3000 and a knighthood. The themes in the work, the benefits of the rule of James I and his reception in heaven were to provide an ironic backdrop to the historical events of the coming years. On 30 January 1649 his son, King Charles I, walked out of the Banqueting House for the last time, stepping through a first floor window on to the scaffold that had been specially erected below the window (a bust of the King above the entrance door purports to mark the former position of the window). He made a memorable final speech declaring himself 'the Martyr of the People' going from 'a corruptible to an incorruptible crown'. His last word before the axe fell was an enigmatic 'Remember'.

The deposition of Charles I's second son James II is recalled by the weather vane (on the adjoining building) which the King fixed to warn him of a 'Protestant wind' which might aid the invasion fleet of his nephew William III. The east wind eventually brought William's fleet from Holland in November 1688 and James fled the country the following month.

O Tues–Sat 10.00–17.00;   Sun 14.00–17.00;   p
☎ (01) 930 4179

Downing Street   [15]

Downing Street was constructed in 1680 by Sir George Downing, a former diplomat, a Civil War turncoat and a property developer, whom Samuel Pepys described as 'a perfidious rogue'. In 1868 the Whitehall end of the street was replaced by the present government offices and only numbers 10, 11 and 12 of the original houses survive.

No. 10 Downing Street, the most famous address in Britain, has been the official residence of the prime minister since 1735. The house (then Crown property) was offered to the first Prime Minister, Sir Robert Walpole, by George II. He declined it as a personal gift but agreed to accept it in his capacity as First Lord of the Treasury and a brass plaque on the front door still keeps this title. The narrow front of No. 10 belies its size as it is linked to the large buildings at the rear which house private quarters, the prime minister's offices and the Cabinet Room. No. 11 is the residence of the Chancellor of the Exchequer and No. 12 is the office of the Government's Chief Whip. All three addresses are linked internally.

Note: There is no public entrance to Downing Street for security reasons. No. 10 is identifiable from Whitehall by the single protruding lamp over its porch and is generally guarded by a policeman.

Cenotaph [16]
Whitehall/Parliament Street

This is the national memorial to the 'Glorious Dead' of the two World Wars. It was designed by Edwin Lutyens and unveiled on Armistice Day in 1920. The Sovereign and leading politicians lay poppy wreaths annually at the Remembrance Service held on the Sunday nearest to the 11th of November.

The Cenotaph stands in the middle of Parliament Street, the widest street in London, measuring 130 ft (40 m) across.

Cabinet War Rooms [17]
Clive Steps, King Charles St

The Cabinet War Rooms are the most important surviving rooms of the underground emergency accommodation provided for the War Cabinet and chief military advisers during World War II. They were installed in 1938, as the threat of war increased, in the basement of the George Street Government Offices, 10 ft (3 m) below ground. Between 1939 and 1945 the Cabinet sat here over 100 times and prepared and co-ordinated operational plans. The 29 rooms and corridors cover an area of some three acres (1 ha). The most important of these are:

The Cabinet Room This was used most frequently from September to November 1940 during the Blitz and again during the German V-weapons offensives of 1944 and 1945. Winston Churchill's large wooden chair presides whilst two small red and green electric light bulbs on the wall indicated whether or not an air raid was in progress. The room has been laid out just as it was for the meeting held at 16.58 hrs on 15 October 1940 and all the clocks in the War Rooms are set at this time.

The Transatlantic Telephone Room Here was the 'hot-line' between London and the White House, from which Churchill would speak directly to President Roosevelt. The clock shows the time in London and in Washington.

The Map Room All the maps and charts displayed here were in use in the later months of the War. They include plans of fighting on the Russian front, V1 flying bomb attacks in 1944, convoy movements and the Pacific theatre.

The Prime Minister's Room This was allocated to Churchill as an office and bedroom. He slept in it on only three occasions but during 1940 and 1941 he made a number of his famous broadcasts from this office. Tapes of his stirring speeches to the nation are played and serve to heighten the atmosphere in the War Rooms.

Other interesting *memorabilia* on display include Churchill's private 'armoury' such as machine guns and pistols, a wooden rattle (to sound the alarm) and hand-bell (to sound the 'all clear') in case of gas attacks on the rooms.

O Tues–Sun 10.00–17.50 (also Easter Mon, Spring BH and Summer BH); £; ♿ t 100%
☎ (01) 930 6961

St James's Park [18]

This is the oldest and most attractive of central London's Royal Parks with an area of some 90 acres (36 ha). Henry VIII established the Park *c.* 1532 as part of his site clearance for St James's Palace. The site was occupied by St James's Hospital (from where the Park's name derives) around which used to be an area of marshy fields where its last inmates—13 young leper women—fed their hogs.

James I had gardens laid out in the early 17th century and included an aviary, from which the name Birdcage Walk derives, and a menagerie that was said to contain crocodiles, leopards, wild boars and an elephant that drank a gallon of wine per day!

The diarist John Evelyn noted a strange bird in the King's aviary: 'I saw two cranes, one of which having had one of his legs cut off above the knee had a wooden leg and thigh with a joint so accurately made that the creature could walk as well as if it had been natural'. Other animals to inhabit the park in the 17th century, and the first to provide for 'public catering', were herds of cows which were milked on the spot to provide refreshment for 1d (approximately ½p) per mug!

The Park was a great favourite of Charles II and he had it laid afresh. He was often seen walking in the park with his many mistresses and was also fond of swimming in the long thin lake known as the Canal (it was here, on 1 December 1662, that Samuel Pepys recorded the first instance of ice-skating in Great Britain).

One of the highlights of a walk in St

The Park's most famous inhabitants have been its pelicans, originally presented as a pair to Charles II by the Russian ambassador in 1665. Their 323-year long sojourn was, alas, ended recently in September 1988. The 'St James's Park Five' were convicted of upsetting London tourists by regularly supplementing their fish diet with a course of their feathered cousins—the park pigeons—and they have been sent to London Zoo! There are no plans for early parole!

James's Park is the view from the bridge in the centre of the lake, facing west to Buckingham Palace and east to the domes and towers of Whitehall: 'the most astonishing and romantic roofscape in London'.

Sherlock Holmes [P1]
10 Northumberland Street

This used to be the Northumberland Arms Hotel which was mentioned in Sir Arthur Conan Doyle's Sherlock Holmes adventure *The Hound of the Baskervilles.* In 1957 it changed its name and became a shrine to the world's most famous fictional detective. It is one of London's earliest theme pubs and the upstairs room features a 'reconstruction' of the fictional study at No. 221b Baker Street, as well as other Holmes' *memorabilia.*

The Sherlock Holmes in Northumberland Street—pub-shrine to the immortal London detective with a 'pilgrim' taking refreshment!

ST JAMES'S PALACE, BUCKINGHAM PALACE AND WESTMINSTER CATHEDRAL

This is the centre of royal London with its current royal residence, Buckingham Palace, neighbour to its predecessor, St James's Palace. Buckingham Palace is the most famous house in England, drawing hundreds of thousands of tourists each year either to see the quintessential British royal ceremony of the Changing of the Guard, or simply to view the Palace exterior hoping for a glimpse of members of the Royal Family.

Note: Neither of the royal palaces is open to the public.

Close by, Westminster Cathedral, not to be confused with the more illustrious Westminster Abbey, is one of London's most individual landmarks and also one of its most overlooked.

The Mall   [1]

The Mall was originally laid out in 1660–2 as part of the development of St James's Park by Charles II. Like Pall Mall, it takes its name from being the site of the French croquet-like

Westminster Cathedral—a masterpiece of Byzantine brickwork.

7. ST JAMES'S PALACE, BUCKINGHAM PALACE AND WESTMINSTER CATHEDRAL

1 The Mall
2 Waterloo Place
3 Pall Mall
4 St James's Palace
5 Queen Victoria Memorial
6 Green Park
7 Buckingham Palace
8 Queen's Gallery
9 Royal Mews
10 Westminster Cathedral *

Pubs
P1 Red Lion

* Specially recommended by author

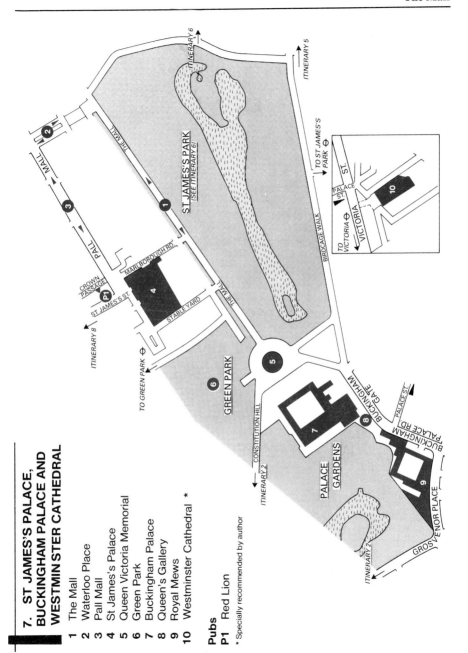

game of paille-maille, popularized by royalty during the 17th century. The Mall replaced Pall Mall as the main site for this game and over the next hundred years became London's most fashionable promenade. The present Mall runs just south of the original (now a horse path) and was designed as part of the memorial to Queen Victoria. The 115-ft (35 m) wide processional route is lined with lamp-posts topped with miniature gilded galleons. These are dedicated to Admiral Lord Nelson and, like his statue, face southwards to the scenes of his naval victories.

Waterloo Place   [2]

This small area houses the Duke of York's Column, several statues, two gentlemen's clubs and the Guards Crimean Memorial. The latter was made in 1859 from captured Russian cannons and commemorates the foot guards who fell in the Crimean War. It includes a separate statue of Florence Nightingale, depicted as the lady with the lamp (her real lamp was a paper lantern, very different from the one here—see National Army Museum, Chelsea).

The Athenaeum, founded in 1824, claims to be the most intellectually élite of all London's gentlemen's clubs and has a most impressive façade to match. The frieze is a reconstruction of that on the Parthenon in Athens and the huge gilt figure of Athene (Goddess of Wisdom, Industry and War)

> The strangest memorial of all is the small tombstone in the adjacent Carlton House Terrace: it is to Giro, a terrier belonging to the Nazi German ambassador to London. The dog was accidentally electrocuted in 1934 and buried under a tree outside where the Embassy used to stand. It therefore holds the dubious distinction of being the only surviving memorial erected by the Nazis in London.

dates from 1829. The Athenaeum has been patronised by many prime ministers, including the Duke of Wellington whose horse-mounting block is still in place in front of the

The Grand Old Duke of York, 'he marched them up to the top of the hill . . .'

club. The statue of Captain Robert Scott, the Antarctic explorer who narrowly failed in his bid to be the first man to the South Pole, was sculpted by his wife in 1915.

The Duke of York's Column, a memorial to George III's second son, Frederick, Duke of York (1763–1827) was completed in 1834. The statue is 13 ft (4 m) tall and the column is 124 ft (38 m) high. Frederick was one of the most impecunious royals and died leaving debts of some £2 million. He was Commander-in-Chief of the British Forces and so the £25 000 cost of the memorial was met by deducting one day's pay from every officer and soldier. This highly unpopular measure helped to condemn the memory of the Duke and a scathing contemporary rhyme reflected the general view of his indecisive nature:

'O, the Grand Old Duke of York, he had 10 000 men
He marched them up to the top of the hill and he marched them down again . . .'

Pall Mall [3]

Pall Mall was laid out in 1661 under the official name of Catherine Street but its colloquial name taken from the game of paille-maille (see The Mall) has outlasted it. Its most colourful resident was King Charles' mistress Nell Gwyn who was given a house freehold by the King at No. 79 and lived there from 1671 to 1687. Nell's house is long gone but this is still the only freehold non-royal property on the south side of Pall Mall. Next door is Pall Mall's oldest building, Schomberg House, parts of which date back to 1698.

On 4 June 1807 the first demonstration of gas-lighting in London was given in Pall Mall and by the end of the year 13 lampposts had been erected. A great crowd gathered to see the novel exhibition, although many were scared to touch the lamp-posts fearing that they would be hot.

St James's Palace [4]

The site of St James's Palace was formerly occupied by St James's Hospital (see St James's Park). Henry VIII acquired the land in 1532 and built it up to be the third of his royal houses in London, after Whitehall and Hampton Court Palace. Whitehall was destroyed by fire in 1698 and St James's Palace was declared the official residence of the Court in 1702. It remained so until 1837 when Queen Victoria moved to Buckingham Palace. The official status of foreign ambassadors, however, still remains accredited to 'The Court of St James's'.

The Palace was badly damaged by fire in 1809 and little remains of its Tudor buildings. The outstanding exception is the main Gatehouse in Pall Mall. Adjacent to this is the Chapel Royal which also boasts an original exterior. The building was restored *c.* 1836 and in 1840 Queen Victria and Prince Albert were married here. Friary Court retains part of its original Tudor balcony and this is one of the points from where every new British Sovereign is officially proclaimed.

Clarence House was added to the Palace in 1828 by John Nash as a temporary residence for William, Duke of Clarence (later William IV). It is a favoured residence of the present Royal Family and has been the home of Queen Elizabeth, the Queen Mother since 1953. Princess Elizabeth, later Queen Elizabeth II, lived here from 1947 to 1950 and Princess Anne was born here.

Queen Victoria Memorial [5]
The Mall

This is the grandest of the many London memorials to Queen Victoria and earned its sculptor, Thomas Brock, a knighthood on the spot at its unveiling in 1911. Designed by Sir Aston Webb, it is made from one solid block of white marble weighing around 2300 tons and stands 82 ft (25 m) high. The 13-ft (4 m) tall figure of Victoria shows her wearing her wedding ring on the right hand in the

Queen Victoria—the first monarch resident at Buckingham Palace.

German tradition favoured by her husband, Prince Albert. The figures around the Queen represent the Victorian ideals of Charity, Truth, Justice, Progress and Peace, whilst War and Shipbuilding represent some of the harsher Empire-building realities.

The gardens leading away from the Memorial were created at the same time and incorporate splendid ornamental gates, given as gifts by the countries of the Commonwealth.

Green Park   [6]

This is the smallest of the royal London parks at 53 acres (21 ha) and is the only one without a lake or any flowers. The parkland was enclosed by Henry VIII as part of his site plan for St James's Palace and created a royal park

---

There is a story that Charles II was once walking on Constitution Hill with few bodyguards and was met by his brother, James, who remarked upon the potential danger of the King being so lightly attended. Charles, known for his wit, retorted to his unpopular brother (later to become James II), 'No danger . . . for I am sure no man in England will take away my life to make you King'.

However, in later years, Constitution Hill did come to be regarded as a 'black spot' for royalty. Queen Victoria was fired upon here in 1840 and further attempts on her life were made on the Hill in 1842 and 1849. (In all, six assassination attempts were made on the Queen whilst in London.)

It was also on Constitution Hill, at the entrance to Green Park, that former Prime Minister Sir Robert Peel was thrown from his horse with fatal results in 1850.

---

in 1667 by Charles II. The 'Merry Monarch' was fond of walking alongside Green Park, in order to maintain his constitution (health) and this may be how Constitution Hill got its name.

Buckingham Palace   [7]

Buckingham Palace stands on the site of Buckingham House, built as a country house in 1702-5 for John Sheffield, Duke of Buckingham. George III purchased the House in 1762 and took up residence. By 1820 it had been decided that a new Palace was necessary and George IV set John Nash to work on the project. Nash originally estimated that the cost of the new Palace would be £250 000. Parliament considered this amount to be extravagant and throughout the next eight years designs and cost estimates were so frequently revised that the Palace became the most notorious building project of the period. A contemporary cartoon which showed a bemused John Bull (i.e. the British people) reading through Nash's final bill summarised the popular view.
'Here is a charge for building wings,
Here also is a charge for pulling down wings
then there's a charge for building them up again
But the Bill is more than double the estimate'
to which Nash replies,
'We never minds no estimates'
Nash was dismissed in 1830 and Edward Blore was commissioned to finish the project. By 1831 £640 000 had been spent.

In July 1837 Queen Victoria arrived to take up residence at Buckingham Palace and the royal standard was raised for the first time. It still flies whenever the Sovereign is in residence. She was definitely not amused by the state of the Palace. Doors would not close in its 600 rooms, many of its one thousand windows would not open, the drains did not work and the toilets were not ventilated. Repairs were effected, however, and in 1843 Victoria recorded in her diary how happy she was living there. The familiar public face of the Palace, the east front, is its most recent major addition, completed in 1913 by Sir Aston Webb.

Buckingham Palace retains its original country house setting, standing in around 40 acres (16 ha) of parkland. This includes some of the most extensive lawns in the country, where the famous Royal Garden Parties are held, which can entertain up to 9000 people at a time. The garden's history may be traced back to the early 17th century when James I planted thousands of mulberry trees here in the hope of creating a silk industry (commercial type silkworms thrive on mulberry leaves) and an original Persian mulberry tree planted in 1609 still survives.

Buckingham Palace has only ever once been seriously in danger. On 13 September 1940 the chapel, where the Queen's Gallery now stands, was bombed and badly damaged by a lone raider. The King and Queen remained in residence throughout the Blitz and a bomb fell within 30 yd (27 m) of where the King was standing in the courtyard. Queen Elizabeth, now the Queen Mother, realized that the bombing would be a unifying factor and is reputed to have said 'I'm glad we've been bombed. It makes me feel that I can look the East End in the face' (see the Blitz).

The Changing of the Guard outside Buckingham Palace is the country's most popular ceremony. The responsibility for the protection of the Sovereign rotates amongst the regiments of Footguards, in combination with the Horseguards of the Household Cavalry.

At 11.15–11.20 the St James's Palace part of the Old Guard marches down The Mall to meet the Old Guard of Buckingham Palace. There they await the arrival, at 11.30, of the New Guard with a band from Wellington Barracks. The actual change involves the ceremonial handing over of the keys of the Palace and the changing of sentries at Buckingham Palace and St James's Palace. Meanwhile, the band forms up to play a selection of informal music (snatches of West End shows and even pop tunes may be heard sometimes to the visitors' consternation!).

When all the sentries have been changed at c. 12.05, the (now complete) Old Guard marches out to return to Wellington Barracks and two minutes later the St James's detachment of the New Guard marches up The Mall to return to St James's Palace.

Note: From Mon–Sat the Old Guard of the Horseguards may be seen passing Buckingham Palace at c. 11.35. The regiments involved are the Lifeguards (with a white plume in their helmets) and the Blues and Royals (with a red plume). They are, respectively, the first and second most senior regiments in the British Army.

The ceremony takes place every day from April to 31 July and every other day from August to 31 March. Wet weather may cause cancellation.
Note: Large crowds usually gather outside the Palace gates and there are occasional variations in the times and procedures.
☎ (01) 730 3488 for details.

Queen's Gallery [8]
Buckingham Palace Road

The Queen's Gallery was originally built as a conservatory. It became the Buckingham Palace chapel in 1893 and was converted to an art gallery in 1961–2. Art treasures from the Royal Collection—the world's greatest private collection of Old Masters—are exhibited in changing displays.

O during exhibitions Tue–Sat (some BH Mons) 11.00–17.00; Sun 14.00–17.00; £ ☎ (01) 930 4832 ext. 351

Royal Mews [9]
Buckingham Palace Road

The Royal Mews houses the Queen's horses, the ceremonial coaches and cars and the finest collection of harnesses, liveries and saddleries in the country. The actual Mews (the stables) dates from 1824–5 but the grand arched entrance was built in 1763–6. The most popular and impressive exhibit is the Gold State Coach which has been used for every coronation since 1762. Built that year for George III, its panels are by Cipriani and it cost £7661. The Irish State Coach, made in Dublin in 1851, is normally used by the Queen for the State Opening of Parliament. The State Landau, built in 1902, is used by the Queen for meeting visiting heads of state and the romantic Glass Coach, made in 1910, is normally used at royal weddings, as it was at the wedding of the Prince and Princess of Wales in 1981. The Queen owns around 20 cars. The Rolls Royces used for ceremonial occasions are distinguishable by their maroon colour and their lack of registration plates.

O Wed, Thurs 14.00–16.00. Closed Royal Ascot week (mid-June); p; ♿ t 100% ☎ (01) 930 4832 ext. 634

Westminster Cathedral [10]
Victoria Street

Westminster Cathedral is London's principal Roman Catholic cathedral. Unlike its more exalted neighbour, Westminster Abbey, its roots are relatively modern. In 1850 the Roman Catholic Church government, overthrown at the Reformation, was restored to Britain, and therefore required a seat ('cathedra') for its bishop in London. It was not until 1892, however, that the eventual Cathedral architect, John Francis Bentley, was appointed by Cardinal Vaughan and in 1896 work began.

Its Byzantine design is very different from that of Westminster Abbey, partly in order not to compete, and it is one of the last major brick buildings in England. It was completed in 1903 and comprises some 12½ million hand-made bricks without any steel reinforcement. Its slender campanile (bell-tower), at 273 ft (83 m) tall, is surmounted by a cross, 11 ft (3 m) high—which, it is claimed,

contains a relic of the actual Cross on which Christ died.

The interior decoration of the Cathedral has never been completed due to lack of funds and much of its upper part and many of the chapels still have bare brick-work. It does, however, boast some of the finest and most varied marble-work of any building in the country with over 100 different types and colours from all over the world. The Cathedral's most valuable work of art is Eric Gill's series of 14 sculptures, *Stations of the Cross*, made in 1913–18, which depict the suffering of Christ. These are placed on the piers of the nave.

The North Chapels The fine mosaic and marble decoration in the Chapel of All Souls is said to be Bentley's most characteristic work and gives an idea of how the completed Cathedral chapels might eventually appear. The Chapel of St Thomas contains the tomb of the founder of the Cathedral, Cardinal Vaughan, over which the Cardinal's Red Hat hangs, to remain there according to Roman tradition until it disintegrates (his body lies at St Joseph's College, Mill Hill).

The South Chapel The Lady Chapel is the most richly decorated of all the chapels, ablaze with mosaics depicting incidents from Her life. Close by, beneath the 13th Station of the Cross, is the Cathedral's oldest monument, an early 15th-century alabaster statue of Our Lady and Child.

O ♿ 80%; The campanile may be ascended by a lift from Easter to Sept, Tue–Sun, 09.30–17.00; p

Red Lion [P1]
23 Crown Passage, Pall Mall

A pub has existed on this site for over 200 years thus making it one of the oldest licensed houses in the West End. The current Red Lion was built in 1902.

O ♿ (crowded) ☎ (01) 930 8067

PICCADILLY AND ST JAMES'S

Piccadilly and St James's are synonymous with gentlemen's clubs and high-class gentlemen's shops. Most of the clubs were formed during the 18th century by gentlemen of similar interests (e.g. the Travellers' Club, the Army and Navy Club) and were devoted to political, social and frequently gambling activities. Before World War I there were around 150 small clubs, today they number less than thirty. There is no sign on any of the clubs' doors to give its name and entry is restricted to members and guests.

Piccadilly takes its name from a grand house built by Robert Baker c. 1612 on the

Burlington Arcade—where running, whistling or singing are not the things to do!

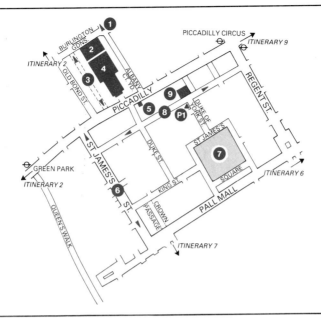

8. PICCADILLY AND ST JAMES'S

1 Savile Row
2 Museum of Mankind *
3 Burlington Arcade
4 Royal Academy of Arts *
5 Fortnum and Mason
6 St James's Street

7 St James's Square
8 Jermyn Street
9 St James's, Piccadilly

Pubs
P1 Red Lion
* Specially recommended by author

site of what is now Great Windmill Street. Baker had made his fortune selling 'picadils', a type of stiff collar made fashionable at Court, and so his house was nicknamed Piccadilly Hall.

> *No. 3 Savile Row was the headquarters of Apple Corps, the Beatles company. They played their last public performance on the roof of this building on 30 January 1969, prematurely curtailed by the police due to complaints about the noise!*

St James's, the area between Piccadilly and Pall Mall began development around St James's Square in the late 1660s and derives its name from the old St James's Hospital (see St James's Park).

Savile Row [1]

Savile Row is world famous as the street where the finest tailors in London can be found. The best known names are Hardy Amies at No. 14 and Gieves and Hawkes at No. 1. The latter building is an original survivor from 1731–3 when the street was laid out.

Museum of Mankind [2]
6 Burlington Gardens

This houses the British Museum's Ethnography Department and is the world's greatest collection of art and objects of non-western societies and cultures, particularly those of West Africa, the Americas and Oceania. There is a total of 300 000 items in the collections of which only a fraction are on display. In addition, the Museum has a series of constantly changing exhibitions which give excellent insights into various aspects of tribal and less developed life-styles throughout the world.

Its most famous exhibit (front hall) is one of the enigmatic Ancestor Figures from Easter Island, collected in 1868. It is thought that these are images of chiefs or spiritual leaders of the Polynesians who lived there and that they were carved before 1650. An excellent general introduction to the collection in Room 5 includes valuable African and Pacific wood carvings, bronze works from Benin in Nigeria, and gold Asante regalia from Ghana.

The Museum's most valuable exhibits are the nine Aztec objects decorated with turquoise mosaics in Room 1. These are some of the greatest treasures of Mexican civilization and are rare examples of the art to have survived the Spanish Conquest. The most impressive of these is a skull-mask, which may have been given to Cortés, the Spanish conquistador who won Mexico for the Crown of Spain in 1519. A sacrificial wooden knife, used to take the heart out of a living victim, is another treasure.

The Museum's biggest exhibit is an Indonesian rice barn, measuring over 16 ft (5 m) high, carved, decorated and erected by Indonesian craftsmen.

A 'Living Arctic' exhibition (running until the end of 1989) depicts the contemporary culture of the peoples of northern Canada.

O **Mon–Sat 10.00–17.00; Sun 14.30–18.00; C; ⅃ 90%**
☎ **(01) 437 2224**

Burlington Arcade [3]
Piccadilly

Burlington Arcade is London's most famous and exclusive shopping arcade. Built in 1815–19, it is still redolent of refined Victorian high society and anyone caught carrying an open umbrella or large parcel, running, singing or even whistling in the Arcade may be ejected by the uniformed beadles who maintain its regulations!

Royal Academy of Arts [4]
Burlington House, Piccadilly

The Royal Academy of Arts is the country's oldest fine arts society. It was founded in 1768 under the presidency of Sir Joshua Reynolds with the purpose of providing free art schools and an annual exhibition open to all artists of distinguished merit. The latter Summer Exhibition (held from May to August) has become a national institution. At other times of the year loan exhibitions, generally of international importance and high popularity, are staged.

Burlington House was built in the 1660s, remodelled in 1714–15 and again in 1815–18. It contains some notable 18th-century ceiling paintings and the only marble sculpture by Michelangelo in Britain, *Madonna and Child with the Infant St John*, 1504–5.

O **Exhibitions only, Daily 10.00–18.00; £; ⅃ 80%**
☎ **(01) 734 9052**

Fortnum and Mason [5]
181 Piccadilly

London's most famous 'grocery store' opened in 1707 and since the early 18th century they have been famous for supplying food parcels to British Forces and explorers abroad. During the Crimean War Florence Nightingale was sent Fortnum and Mason's concentrated beef tea by Queen Victoria. Fortnum and Mason's tradition of high quality food hampers still survives from this period. The shop-front boasts one of London's best known and most polite clocks, where figures representing the original Mr Fortnum and Mr Mason appear on the hour to a tune of 17 bells, turn and bow to each other.

O & **80%**

☎ **(01) 734 8040**

St James's Street   [6]

St James's Street holds four of London's most distinguished gentlemen's clubs. White's at Nos. 37–8 is London's grandest and longest established club. It opened in 1693 a few yards away at No. 28 where Boodle's now resides and during the next two centuries was patronized by the richest and most distinguished members of society. Around the mid-18th century White's became infamous for its betting and was notoriously depicted by William Hogarth in the *Rake's Progress*. Anything and everything was bet upon, the most trivial and extravagant example being the small fortune of £3000 wagered by Lord Arlington on which of two raindrops would reach the bottom of a window pane first! Boodle's was founded in 1765 as the country gentleman's club and moved to its present address in 1783. Opposite, at No. 60, is Brooks's, founded in 1764 for members of the Whig party (the forerunners of the Liberal party), and further down the street at No. 69 is the Carlton, the club of the Conservative party, founded in 1832.

John Lobb's at No. 9 were established in 1849 and have been bootmakers to the Crown since 1911. Inside the shop is a small museum case, featuring a miniature prototype of the Wellington boot and the last used for making shoes for Queen Victoria.

At No. 6 are the premises of James Lock and Company, known as 'the most famous hat shop in the world' in the days when headwear was *de rigueur* for men. The first James Lock came into possession of the business in 1759 and they have occupied

Boodle's Club, late 19th century—little changed today.

their current premises, built in the late 17th century, since 1764. They are the country's oldest surviving hatters. Famous clients have included Lord Nelson, who had a hat with an integral eyeshade made for him (to protect his one good eye), and the Duke of Wellington, who wore a plumed hat from Lock's at Waterloo. (Nelson's hat may be seen on his effigy in Westminster Abbey Treasures Museum.) The most famous and enduring hat that Lock's sell originated from a request in 1850, by a Mr William Coke, for a hard domed hat designed to fit closely to the head. This was originally intended for protective use when hunting in the field and in order to ensure its hardness, Mr Coke is said to have stamped on it in the shop before placing it, undamaged, on his head! The company supplying the hats were Thomas and William Bowler of Southwark and so the hat became known as the bowler. It was adopted (in a slightly modified form) by gentlemen throughout London and may still be seen today, worn by the more traditional City gents. The original bowler cost 12 shillings (60p). Lock's standard bowler today costs £75, although they still prefer to call it a 'Coke' in honour of its original wearer.

Berry Brothers and Rudd at No. 3 St James's Street, are one of London's oldest retailers. They began business c. 1699 as grocers but have established themselves as wine merchants. The existing premises are early 19th century and contain a 17th-century weighing beam which was used from 1761 until recently to weigh its famous customers, including royalty. This would then have been a great novelty as England's first public weighing machine is not recorded until 1799. Adjacent to the shop is a narrow alleyway which leads to Pickering Place, a tiny courtyard of 18th-century houses. Between 1842 and 1845 the Legation (Diplomatic Ministry) from the Republic of Texas was based here.

St James's Square [7]

The development of St James's Square, the first in the West End of London, began in the mid-1660s. The only original house left is No. 4 (remodelled in 1725), from 1912 to 1942 the home of Nancy, Viscountess Astor.

Close by is the saddest spot in St James's Square. A memorial to WPC Yvonne

> Nancy Astor became the first woman to take her seat in Parliament in December 1919, a development not greeted wholeheartedly by some of the more chauvinistic members of the House, such as Winston Churchill.
>
> It is said that on one occasion, when the redoubtable lady was feeling particularly ill-disposed towards Churchill, she remarked to him: 'Winston, if I were married to you I'd put poison in your coffee', Churchill quipped back 'Nancy, if you were my wife, I'd drink it'.

Fletcher marks the place where she fell in April 1984, after being shot by a member of the Libyan People's Bureau from the window of No. 5.

The Square has always been a fashionable address as exemplified by No. 10, the former residence of three Prime Ministers, Pitt the Elder, Lord Derby and W E Gladstone.

No. 31 is where General Eisenhower formed the First Allied Forces headquarters in 1942 and 1944. It stands on the site of the original Norfolk House, where George III was born in 1738.

The equestrian statue in the middle of the Square is of William III by John Bacon the Younger (1807). Beneath the horse's hooves is the molehill over which it stumbled and threw the King at Hampton Court in 1702. He broke his collar bone and died soon afterwards of pneumonia. Jacobite sympathizers have subsequently drunk many a toast to 'the little gentleman in the velvet jacket' (the mole!).

Jermyn Street [8]

Jermyn Street was laid out in the 1680s but none of its original buildings survives. It possesses some of London's most attractive traditional shops with gentlemen's goods predominant. No. 97, the premises of shirtmakers Harvie and Hudson, established 1890, boasts one of London's best mid-Victorian shop fronts, and similarly impressive is that of Paxton and Whitfield at No. 93. They are London's oldest and best known cheese shop, established since 1797, and have around 300 different cheeses in stock. Even older are Floris at No. 89. They are London's oldest perfumers, and were established in 1730 on this site. Turnbull and Asser at No. 71 are shirtmakers to Prince Charles, the Prince of Wales, and were established in 1885. A relief on No. 73 shows Charles II handing over the deeds of the street to Henry Jermyn, Earl of St Albans, after whom the street is named.

London's most famous cheese-board—over 300 varieties to choose from at Paxton & Whitfield.

St James's, Piccadilly [9]
Piccadilly

St James's was constructed 1676–84 and is the only one of Wren's churches to be built on a completely fresh site. It was badly damaged during World War II and has largely been rebuilt. The interior features more authenticated works by Grinling Gibbons than any other London parish church. These are the limewood carved reredos, the marble font (in which Pitt the Elder, and poet and artist William Blake were baptized) and the organ case. The organ, originally built for James II in 1678, came from Whitehall Palace as a present to the church in 1691. During repairs the miniature coffin of a bird was discovered inside it.

Red Lion [P1]
Duke of York Street

The interior of this extremely well-preserved pub dates from the 1840s and has been described as 'a perfect example of the small Victorian Gin Palace at its best'. It features rich mahogany panelling and elaborately engraved mirrors, each cut to depict a different British flower.

☎ **(01) 930 2030**

OXFORD STREET, REGENT STREET, PICCADILLY CIRCUS AND SOHO

Oxford Street is London's most visited street. It has always been a main thoroughfare to the west and was laid out in the late 18th century, taking its name from Edward Harley, Earl of Oxford, who owned land on the north side. Nearby Harley Street, famed for its medical specialists, is also named after the Earl. Initially residential, Oxford Street developed some hundred years later into London's longest and Great Britain's busiest shopping street. It now boasts over 200 shops which are visited by seven million foreign tourists each year.

Regent Street was laid out by John Nash in the early 19th century and (by contrast to Oxford Street's more vulgar appeal) its shops were to be 'appropriated by articles of fashion and taste'. It became London's most fashionable shopping street during the 19th century

There is estimated to be a total of 5 million sq ft (464 500 sq m) of selling space in Oxford Street. The department store which makes the most of its selling space is the Marks & Spencer 'Marble Arch' branch at 458 Oxford Street. It has the fastest moving stock in the world, selling a minimum of £1600 worth of goods per square foot of selling space per year. At 129 300 sq ft (12 025 sq m) its income is therefore approaching £207 million per year.

Soho is the centre of the Chinese community in London and its 'Chinatown' area around Gerrard Street is famous for its shops and restaurants. Even the street names here are subtitled in Chinese and the tops of telephone boxes are decorated pagoda-fashion. One of London's newest and most colourful celebrations takes place here on the Sunday nearest the date of the Chinese New Year (late January, early February).

but changing public taste and building redevelopment have lessened its appeal. Many of its shops, however, still retain something of its past upmarket ambience.

Soho, by contrast, has long been known as central London's most cosmopolitan area and has always enjoyed a dubious reputation. In the 16th century the area was hunting land and it is thought that its name derives from the hunting cry of 'So-ho!' or 'So-so!' (like Tally-ho!). As the village developed in the late 17th century, foreign immigrants began to settle, amongst these Greeks (hence Greek Street) and French Huguenots. Many artists came to Soho in later years and helped to establish its Bohemian reputation. In the 1920s the area became famous for its many fashionable inexpensive restaurants, attracting an even more cosmopolitan population from all parts of Europe. Unfortunately, in

No shortage of restaurants here—Gerrard Street in the heart of Chinatown.

recent years Soho has become synonymous with disreputable night-clubs and low-life. Since then improvements have been effected, however, and it remains one of London's most colourful areas.

Wallace Collection [1]
Manchester Square

The Wallace Collection, gathered in London and Paris during the 19th century, was opened to the nation in 1900. It is world-renowned for its 18th-century French treasures and its European armour.

The most famous and popular exhibits are on the first floor (Galleries 13–25).

Galleries 13–14 Both rooms feature views of 18th-century Venice made famous by Canaletto and his follower, Francesco Guardi.

Gallery 16 Amongst the outstanding Dutch and Flemish 17th-century paintings are oil sketches by Rubens and works by Rembrandt.

Gallery 18 More 17th-century Dutch works include Aelbert Cuyp's *Avenue at Meerdervoort* (early 1650s) which fetched a world record price for a landscape of 140 000 francs in 1868. This was equivalent to approximately £14 000, i.e. ten times the sum paid for *The Haywain* by John Constable (in the National Gallery) in 1866.

Gallery 19 This is one of the finest picture rooms in the world, containing 70 paintings, mostly dating between 1620 and 1670. The star attraction is Frans Hals' *Laughing Cavalier*. Originally entitled *Portrait of a Man* its more cheerful present name was first given to it by the press in London in 1872. Hals' works were greatly undervalued until recently and in 1774 the asking price for the *Laughing Cavalier* was only £15. (The world's highest priced painting at that time, by Raphael, had fetched £8500 in 1759.) The many other paintings of outstanding quality here include:

Perseus and Andromeda by Titian (1554), *Dance to the Music of Time* by Poussin (c. 1640), *Rainbow Landscape* by Rubens (c. 1636), 'Mercury' Landscape by Claude (1660), *Lady with a Fan* by Velasquez (1638–9), *Titus* (Rembrandt's son) by Rembrandt (c. 1657).

Gallery 21 This is considered to be the finest collection of French 18th-century paintings and furniture to be found in a single room. The collection of paintings by Watteau is the most extensive of his work. Some of the furniture is from the Palace of Versailles, including pieces from Marie Antoinette's apartments.

In the corridor before entering Gallery 24 is an extremely rare enamelled copper perpetual almanac (a form of wall calendar) made for Louis XV in 1741–2.

Gallery 25 The Riesner Roll-top desk (1769) is one of the Wallace Collection's greatest treasures.

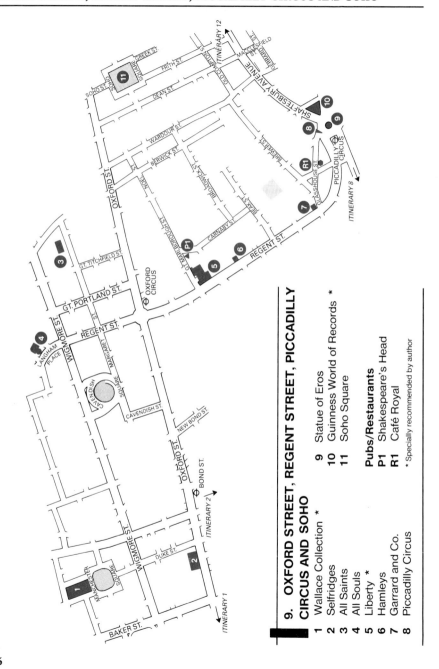

9. OXFORD STREET, REGENT STREET, PICCADILLY CIRCUS AND SOHO

1 Wallace Collection *
2 Selfridges
3 All Saints
4 All Souls
5 Liberty *
6 Hamleys
7 Garrard and Co.
8 Piccadilly Circus

9 Statue of Eros
10 Guinness World of Records *
11 Soho Square

Pubs/Restaurants
P1 Shakespeare's Head
R1 Café Royal

* Specially recommended by author

On Oxford Street it's impossible to miss the bus—some of London's 5100-strong fleet.

Ground Floor

Gallery 2 The wardrobes and cabinets designed by André Charles Boulle are some of the finest pieces of surviving 18th-century French furniture. This gallery also holds part of the French royal porcelain collection from Sèvres (mid-18th century), one of the finest of its kind in the world.

Gallery 3 Most of the objects here are ecclesiastical .works of art, including an important medieval collection dating back to the 13th century.

Galleries 5, 6, 7 The Wallace collection of European armour is the finest in Great Britain outside the Tower of London and is one of the greatest in Europe. It is particularly rich in decorated armour and 16th- and 17th-century swords.

Gallery 5 The centre-piece is a superb equestrian armour made in Nuremberg, 1532-6. The special left-handed 'comb-tooth' bladed daggers, used for catching and breaking an opponent's sword, are of unusual interest.

Gallery 6 The most important piece in the European armoury collection is considered to be the unique Gothic war-harness for horse and rider made in South Germany, 1475-85.

Gallery 7 This collection of medieval and early Renaissance arms and armour contains five excellent mid-16th-century parade helmets and a very rare English tilting helmet c. 1515.

Gallery 8 holds an exotic collection of Oriental armoury of the 18th and 19th century.

Gallery 10 The best known of this collection of early 19th-century paintings is Edward V and the Duke of York (the 'Little Princes') in the Tower, by Delaroche. Early watercolour works (1809-13) by J M W Turner are displayed in the corridor.

O Mon–Sat 10.00–17.00; Sun 14.00–17.00; ᵫ 100% (request entry ramp); T (tel for times)
☎ (01) 935 0687

Selfridges [2]
400 Oxford Street

Selfridges was opened on Oxford Street in 1909 by Gordon Selfridge of Wisconsin, USA. Its imposing frontage features 22 giant Ionic columns and over the main entrance is the 11-ft (3 m) tall figure of 'The Queen of Time'. Selfridges is London's second largest department store (next to Harrods) and its perfumery department is claimed to be the largest in Europe.

O ᵫ t 100%
☎ (01) 629 1234

The first public demonstration of television (albeit only in rough silhouette images) was given at Selfridges, Oxford Street by John Logie Baird on 25 March 1925.

All Saints [3]
Margaret Street

All Saints began construction in 1850 and its designer William Butterfield aroused much controversy by the first important use of 'constructional polychrome' i.e. different coloured brickwork, (pink and black), to decorate the church. Whatever the merits of the contemporary arguments, Sir John Betjeman (former Poet Laureate and an authority on London's churches) was moved to describe All Saints as 'one of the hidden wonders of London'. The interior is richly decorated with a multiplicity of marbles and other decorative stones. The Lady Chapel altar screen (1911) and the panels above the altar (1909) are particularly impressive as are the high Gothic arches which give the atmosphere of a 'great soaring mysterious place'.

All Souls [4]
Langham Place

All Souls was designed by John Nash to mark the end of Regent Street and was built 1822-4. It is one of central London's most unusual church designs with its sharp spire encircled by two tiers of Greek columns, and in its day was ridiculed as another example of Nash's excesses.

It was severely damaged by bombing in 1940 and its interior is completely modern.

O ♿ **t 100%**

Liberty [5]
260–78 Regent Street

Liberty were first established in Regent Street by Arthur Lasenby Liberty in 1875 and are renowned for their printed fabrics which have had a considerable influence on late 19th- and 20th-century fashion and taste. The 'Tudor building', fronting on to Great Marlborough Street, was built in 1924 and is one of the most impressive large scale Tudor reproductions in the country. The interior consists of a series of galleries four storeys high, grouped around a central well. The timbers used throughout the building came from two of the last sailing ships in the British navy, broken up in 1921, and have been fashioned by master-craftsmen to form London's most beautiful store interior, featuring carved balustrades, linenfold panelling and oak staircases. The Regent Street frontage was completed in 1925 and incorporates a frieze 115 ft (35 m) long which shows goods being transported from the East to Britain by camel, elephant and ship. Above the archway, linking the two main buildings, is a clock on which figures of St George and the Dragon 'fight' on the hour.

In 1898 the first ever table tennis sets were brought to Hamleys of Regent Street and sold exclusively by them. The original brand name of Gossima did not catch the public imagination but in 1901 it was renamed 'Ping Pong' (after the sound made by the ball) and became a world-wide craze. (Early sets of Gossima are on display in Pollock's Toy Museum, Bloomsbury.)

Liberty today is a department store but its highlight is still the Oriental department, selling the type of silks and fabrics with which Arthur Liberty established his reputation.

☎ **(01) 734 1234**

Hamleys [6]
188–196 Regent Street

Hamleys was first established at High Holborn, London in 1760 under the name of Noah's Ark and in 1881 transferred their 'infinite variety of toys, games, magical apparatus and sports goods' to 200–202 Regent Street. In 1981 they moved to their current premises and with selling space of 45 000 sq ft (4180 sq m) on six floors they are the world's biggest toy shop.

O ♿ **t 100% (Note: very crowded)**
☎ **(01) 734 3161**

Hamleys—Toying with visitors' affections for over a century.

Garrard and Co.   [7]
112 Regent Street

Garrard and Co. have been established as goldsmiths and silversmiths since 1735, although the first Mr Garrard did not assume control until 1802. They became the finest and largest goldsmiths and jewellers in the West End of London and in 1830 were appointed to King William IV. They have remained Crown Jewellers ever since and are therefore responsible for preparing the regalia for coronations and other state occasions. Their severest test in this respect was in 1862 when they were asked to recut the famous Koh-i-noor diamond (see Tower of London, Crown Jewels). Among the many other works commissioned from the firm, the most famous is the Royal Yacht Squadron's Cup made in 1848 for 100 guineas (£105). In 1851 it was won by the schooner *America* and has since been known as the America's Cup.

☎ (01) 734 7020

Piccadilly Circus   [8]

London's most famous Circus first took shape in 1819 as a crossroads between Piccadilly and Regent Street. In 1880 it acquired its present name and Shaftesbury Avenue was driven through it during the next decade. It is one of London's busiest road junctions and is also one of the most garish, due to its famous illuminated advertising hoardings. The first electric signs appeared in 1890 (thought to have been for Bovril).

Tourists taking a rest beneath the statue of the Greek god of erotic love.

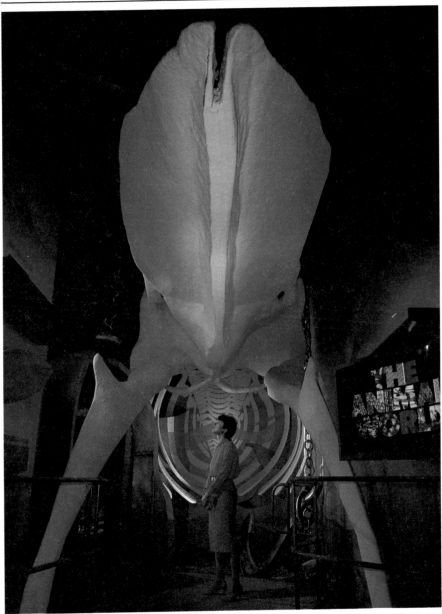

'Whale I never!'—in the belly of the world's largest living creature at the Guinness World of Records where amazing facts, feats and figures come to life.

Statue of Eros [9]
Piccadilly Circus

The full title of Sir Alfred Gilbert's monument is the Shaftesbury Memorial Fountain. It was erected in 1893 to honour the 7th Earl of Shaftesbury (1801–85), a well-known philanthropist, much of whose work had been done for the poor in the area around Shaftesbury Avenue. Its famous 8-ft (2 m) tall statue, the first in London to be cast in aluminium, was intended to represent the Angel of Christian Charity and not, as it has become known, Eros, the Greek god of sexual love! Indeed, Gilbert's creation aroused so much hostility with Victorian society that he left the country in bitter disappointment and did not return until 1932. Ironically, Eros is his greatest memorial.

> *Even in 1901 the area around Piccadilly Circus experienced severe parking problems and in May of that year the world's first multi-storey car-park was opened at Denman Street, just off the Circus. At 19 000 sq ft (1765 sq m) it then claimed to be the world's largest garage.*
>
> *London's only underground theatre, the Criterion, was built in 1874 on the south side of Piccadilly Circus. The adjacent Criterion Restaurant Long Bar (now the Criterion Brasserie) built at the same time, was one of the earliest buildings to use ornamental tile work for decoration and its gilded ceiling and gemstone tiles are valued at £1¼ million.*

Guinness World of Records [10]
Trocadero Centre, Piccadilly Circus

The Guinness World of Records is an exhibition which illustrates and recreates some of the world's most fantastic and fascinating record-breaking facts and feats. It is effectively the show of the *Guinness Book of Records*—the world's all-time best selling copyright book (excluding versions of the Bible).

Human World A life size model of Robert Pershing Wadlow—the world's tallest ever man at 8 ft 11.1 in (2.72 m) towers over the shortest ever person, Pauline Musters, who measured just 23.2 in (59 cm). A film of Wadlow shows him as a 6 ft (1.83 m) tall eight-year-old playing with his (normal size) friends. One of the most mind-boggling statistics is provided by digital displays which shows the world's population 'exploding' before your eyes at the rate of 155 per minute, i.e. before you leave the World of Records there will have been a net world population increase of around 10 000 people! Exhibits include Britain's most tattooed lady, Rusty Field, with 85 per cent body coverage and the world's highest shallow diver, Henri la Mothe is shown plunging 28 ft (8.53 m) into 12⅜ in (31.43 cm) of water.

Videos of the world's greatest guzzlers (e.g. 250 oysters downed in 2 min 52 sec) and a highly creative marathon domino-toppling are compulsive viewing.

Animal World This is entered Jonah-fashion through the jaws of the world's largest animal—the Blue Whale. A 'Noah's Ark' of extremes includes replicas of the world's largest tusks and horns and the heaviest snake (the anaconda). A 'greatest leaps' display makes interesting comparisons between man, a kangaroo, a frog and a flea.

Planet Earth This shows the physical extremes of the Earth as well as the exploration of outer space. Weather extremes include a model of the heaviest hailstone at 2.25 lb (1.02 kg), more than the weight of a standard bag of sugar.

Structures and Machines A replica of a section from the Humber Bridge—the world's longest suspension bridge at 4626 ft (1410 m) hangs above displays of engineering achievements. The world's tallest structures set against the London skyline shows the National Westminster Tower dwarfed by the world's tallest building, the Chicago Sears Tower, at 1559 ft (457 m). Another comparative visual display shows speed records ranging from man chugging along at 22.53 mph (36.25 km/h) to a jet plane clocking over 2193 mph (3528 km/h) (blink and you'll miss it!).

Sports There is a reconstruction of the exact length and trajectory of Bob Beamon's world record breaking long jump set at the Mexico Olympics, 18 Oct 1968 when he reached 29 ft 2.5 in (8.90 m). Still intact after 20 years, it is the world's longest unbroken athletic record.

Entertainment A mini cinema screens excerpts from box office record breakers (*ET*, *Gone With the Wind*, etc.), a juke box blasts out the greatest hit records ('She Loves You', 'Rock Around the Clock', etc.), while the first British TV advertisement, for Gibbs SR Toothpaste in 1955 is screened.

Shop of the world's most valuable items In addition to copies of such treasures as the *Mona Lisa* (valued at $100 million—then £35.7 million—for insurance purposes in 1962) actual items on display include the world's most expensive pair of ruby and gold embellished mink lined golf shoes which retail for £9250 or $17 000 in the USA.

O **All year excl. 25 Dec; 10.00–22.00; C; £; & t 100% (request assistance to enter Trocadero)**
☎ **(01) 439 7331**

Soho Square [11]

Soho Square was laid out in the 1680s and the original houses built around it during the next decade. Of these, Nos. 10 and 15 still exist. Soho Square was then named King Square in honour of Charles II whose weather-beaten statue stands in the square. It is one of London's oldest outdoor statues, dating from 1681, and appears to have stood in the original square. It was removed in 1870 to Grimsdyke House, Harrow, later to become the home of William Gilbert (of Gilbert and Sullivan fame) and into whose possession the statue passed. It was returned to Soho Square by Gilbert's widow in 1938.

At the Greek Street corner of the Square is the House of St Barnabas. This is a rare example of a domestic building open to the public in London. It boasts the finest preserved interior in Soho, dating from *c.* 1754, including fine woodcarving and excellent decorative plasterwork. Dr Manette and Sidney Carton met here in Charles Dickens' *Tale of Two Cities* (1859).

O **Wed 14.30–16.15; Thurs 11.00–12.30**
☎ **(01) 437 5508**

Shakespeare's Head [P1]
29 Great Marlborough Street

The Shakespeare's Head was built in 1735 and for the first nine years it was owned by two brothers, Thomas and John Shakespeare, who claimed to be distant relatives of William Shakespeare. A modern life-size bust of the Bard peers down from the first floor, looking out of the window (perhaps searching for his missing hand which was blown off during World War II!)

☎ **(01) 734 2911**

Café Royal [R1]
68 Regent Street

The Café Restaurant Nichols was first opened in Glasshouse Street in 1865 by Daniel Nicholas Thévenon, who had been forced to flee France as a bankrupt wine merchant. By 1868 it had expanded to its current address as the Café Royal and soon became one of the best known restaurants in London. During the 1890s the Café became London's most fashionable Arts Club, patronized by amongst others James Whistler (who always signed his bills with his butterfly mark) and Oscar Wilde. The Café was rebuilt in 1923–4 but still attracted regular arts patrons such as, T S Eliot, J B Priestley and Anna Pavlova. The literati no longer meet at the Café but its original cosmopolitan atmosphere still lingers on in the baroque Grill Room.

☎ **(01) 437 9090**

REGENT'S PARK AND ENVIRONS

The traffic fumes and noise from Marylebone Road, one of London's busiest east–west arteries, contrast with the clean air and tranquility of the adjacent Regent's Park. Buildings, too, change dramatically across the Marylebone Road 'divide'. On the town side, drab and featureless 20th-century styles predominate with the notable exception of Park Crescent, whilst on the Park side is the best preserved complete collection of glistening white Regency houses in London. The old village of St Mary by the bourne (later compressed to Marylebone) has given way to commercial development, and its bourne, the Tyburn stream, now only runs underground.

Madame Tussaud's   [1]
Marylebone Road

The world's most famous waxworks has its roots in one of the earliest collections of life-size wax figures of living people, opened in Paris in 1770 by a Frenchman named Dr Curtius. Madame Tussaud (then Marie Grosholtz) became his pupil and during the French Revolution was ordered by Dr Curtius, a friend of the Revolutionary leaders, to make death masks of the victims of the guillotine. She acquired the business in 1794, moved to England in 1802, and after exhibiting around the country, set up permanently in Baker Street in 1835. Her sons moved to the present site in 1884. Today it attracts over 2¼ million visitors per year.

The exhibits are arranged in the following order:

Tableaux These are reconstructions of historical and famous fictional scenes, including The Princes in the Tower (see Tower of London), Guy Fawkes in the Parliamentary cellars and the Sleeping Beauty. The latter, breathing gently due to a hidden mechanism, is a likeness of Madame du Barry, the last mistress of Louis XV. Originally made in 1765, it has since been recast from the original mould and is the exhibition's oldest figure.

Conservatory A gathering of stars from the arts, entertainment, music and sporting worlds mingle informally here. Record-breakers include the Beatles, à la mode of 1962, Agatha Christie, Pelé and Martina Navratilova.

Superstars This section features current entertainers, with audio-visual effects added to enhance such figures as Dolly Parton, the world's highest paid cabaret entertainer, Michael Jackson whose *Thriller* album is the best selling of all time, and Daley Thompson, the great all-round athlete.

Grand Hall At the entrance are figures of Madame Tussaud (self portrait, aged 81),

The most amusing waxwork is the trick figure of a 'sleeping tourist', generally to be found on a public seat in the Grand Hall.

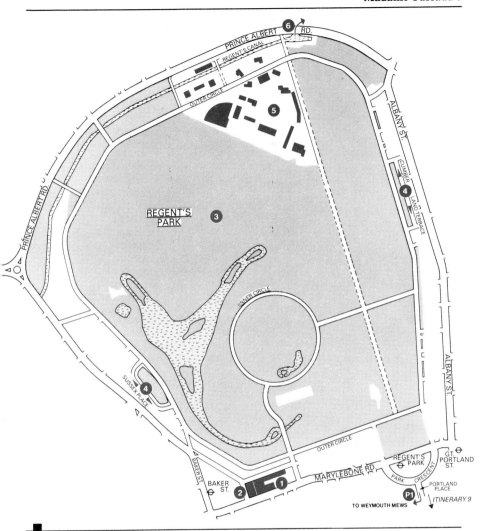

10. REGENT'S PARK AND ENVIRONS

1 Madame Tussaud's
2 London Planetarium
3 Regent's Park
4 Regent's Park Terraces and Villas
5 London Zoo
6 Camden Lock

Pubs
P1 Dover Castle

Marie Antoinette, Louis XVI and the Revolutionary writer Voltaire. The latter is taken from the mould of the oldest surviving original sculpture made personally by Madame Tussaud in 1778.

The Hall features all the senior members of the present British Royal Family and many of the British monarchs dating back to Richard I. The most popular exhibit is that of Henry VIII and his six wives. Famous statesmen and world-leaders include the Duke of Wellington, Napoleon, Abraham Lincoln, Lenin, Sir Winston Churchill and Charles de Gaulle.

Chamber of Horrors Madame Tussaud's macabre relics of the French Revolution are some of the oldest exhibits here and include the guillotine blade that sliced off the heads of Louis XVI and Marie Antoinette in 1793 and their death masks. Amongst the exhibits illustrating the history of various methods of execution is the old bell of Newgate (see Central Criminal Court). An eerie recreation of the cobbled streets of London in 1888 is the setting for the Jack the Ripper killings, London's most mysterious unsolved murders. Exhibits of other London murderers includes Dr Crippen (hanged 1910)—the first murderer to be caught by the use of radio; John Haigh (hanged 1949)—a real life Vampire who drank the blood of at least six victims; John Christie (hanged 1953) who murdered at least seven women at 10 Rillington Place and finally Donald Nilsen, the worst English murderer of all time who admitted to 15 one-at-a-time killings between December 1978 and February 1983.

Battle of Trafalgar This is an atmospheric recreation of below decks of HMS *Victory* during the decisive five-hour battle which finally ended Napoleon's invasion hopes on 21 October 1805. This tableau opened in 1966 and cost £50 000—almost as much as the cost of building HMS *Victory* in 1765.

O **All year excluding 25 December; weekdays 10.00–17.30, weekends and holidays 09.30–17.30; C; £;** & t 70% **(Tel in advance)** ☎ **(01) 935 6861** Note: **Long queues at peak times of year.**

London Planetarium [2]
Marylebone Road

This is a separate part of Madame Tussaud's, opened in 1958 as the first planetarium in the United Kingdom. Accurate images of between 8000 and 9000 stars can be projected on to the 70-ft (21 m) high copper dome. In the evening this changes to 'Laserium'—a music and light show using a laser projector to produce a kaleidoscope of images set to recorded pop and rock music.

O **All details for Planetarium as Madame Tussaud's except no** &. **Combined ticket for Madame Tussaud's and Planetarium at reduced price.** ☎ **(01) 486 2242 for details of Laserium's performances.**

Regent's Park [3]

Regent's Park, originally covered by the huge Forest of Middlesex, was appropriated by Henry VIII from Barking Abbey at the Dissolution of the monasteries and cleared for use as a hunting park. Marylebone Park, or Fields, as it was then known, changed hands again in 1649 when it was sold by Cromwell's government for £1774. As London spread northwards in the late 18th century, it was decided to develop the Park, by now farmland, as a new estate. The Prince Regent's architect, John Nash, had a vision of a grand garden city of perimeter terraces and villas within the park, including a grand villa for the Prince. The plans were ridiculed but with the support of the Prince Regent, after whom the Park is named, some of it went ahead (see below).

The Outer Circle of the Park encloses 487 acres (197 ha). At its heart in the Inner Circle is Queen Mary's Garden where in summer the display of roses is renowned. The adjacent Open Air theatre holds plays on summer evenings, dependent on the weather (☎ (01) 935 1537).

Regent's Park Lake is all that is visible of the old Tyburn stream and in 1867 was the scene of London's worst ever ice-skating disaster when 41 drowned after the ice broke. As a consequence of this, regulations (still in existence) were introduced, specifying a minimum thickness of 5 in (13 cm) of ice before skating is permissible on lakes in London's parks.

The Park's greatest claim to fame is the London Zoo (see below).

Sherlock Holmes—the character most frequently appearing on the silver screen— played here by Peter Cushing, one of 67 actors to have portrayed him in 186 films.

London's most famous fictional address, No. 221b Baker Street, where Sherlock Holmes 'lived', lies just a short distance away from Regent's Park. In reality the address does not exist, but it is generally accepted that it would have been located on the site now occupied by the Abbey National Building Society. The Abbey National still receives mail addressed to the great detective and a member of staff is assigned to reply on behalf of Sherlock Holmes in the appropriate spirit!

Regent's Park Terraces and Villas [4]

The vast sweep of white stuccoed buildings around the Park were laid out according to the designs of John Nash between 1820 and 1828. It remains the most elegant example of town planning in central London. Sussex Place is the most distinctive of the terraces, comprising 26 houses, topped with pointed cupolas. Cumberland Terrace is the most splendid, embellished with decorative reliefs and statues which were intended to provide a suitable view from the Prince Regent's villa opposite (planned but never built).

Park Crescent, now isolated by the Marylebone Road, was planned to be part of a full circus entering into the Park. At its east end is a memorial to J F Kennedy, unveiled by the President's brothers Robert and Edward in 1965.

London Zoo [5]

The collection of the Zoological Society of London founded in 1826 is the oldest existing privately owned zoo in the world. The largest part (approximately 80 per cent of specimens) is housed within 36 acres (14 ha) of Regent's Park, the remainder is at Whipsnade Park, Bedfordshire. Stocktaking on 1 January 1988 accounted for a total of 11 243 creatures, the most comprehensive collection in the country.

It is not possible to see everything in one day but the following are some of the more popular and record-breaking attractions.

Cumberland Terrace, designed by Nash, 1826–8. The figures represent Britannia and the glory of the Empire.

Apes and Monkeys Ever since Tommy the chimpanzee first arrived in 1835 and dressed in 'a cap and Guernsey shirt' the inmates here have delighted the crowds. The gorilla is the primate most closely related to man and is the tallest at up to 6 ft 4.75 in (1.95 m). The most popular London Zoo gorilla was Guy, so named because he arrived on 5 November ('Guy Fawkes Day') 1947. He has two statues dedicated to him in London, one here and one at Crystal Palace Park.

'Big Cats' The most magnificent animals in the Zoo are also some of the most lethargic. The lions, 'king of the beasts' and amongst the largest of the cat family, doze around 20 hours per day. The cheetah is the fastest land animal, with probable maximum speeds of 60–63 mph (96–101 km/h) over level ground.

Penguins and Sealions These delightful aquatic favourites provide the Zoo's most popular feeding spectacles (see the notice boards near the Zoo entrance for feeding times).

Elephants and Rhinoceroses The Zoo's first male elephant was Jumbo who arrived in 1867 with his mate Alice, and immediately gave his name to anything of large size. Some years later, poor Alice lost some 12 in (30 cm) of her trunk to a morbid souvenir hunter! The African elephant is the world's heaviest land mammal, estimated at up to 12.24 tons.

> *It is possible to 'adopt' an animal for a year by paying (in total or in part) the cost of its annual keep. This ranges from a mouse which costs £10 up to an elephant which costs £5000!*

London Zoo's two elephants, Dilberta and Layang-Layang, by the Elephant House which they share with three Black Rhinos—June, Jasper and Stumpy.

Reptiles The Zoo's only fatality caused by animal attack occurred in 1852 when a keeper was bitten on the nose by a cobra. The Indian cobra is one of the world's most dangerous creatures, killing between 10 000 and 20 000 people each year. The Zoo has also hosted the world's largest ever venomous snake, a King cobra measured in 1937 at 18 ft 9 in (5.71 m) long.

Aquarium This is the most comprehensive in the United Kingdom, stocking over 2000 specimens.

Giraffes The first giraffe to arrive at the Zoo in 1836 was an immediate fashion 'hit', giving rise to new dress patterns copying its markings. The giraffe is the tallest land animal and can measure up to 20 ft (6 m), which

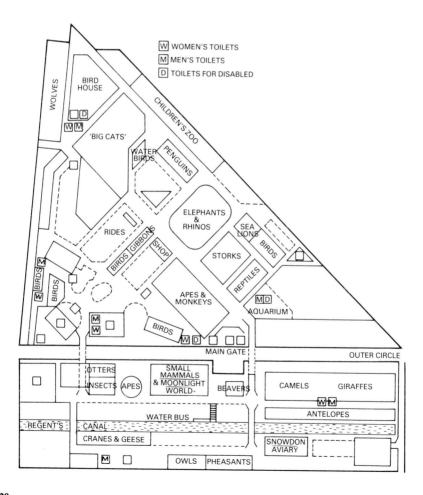

is nearly 1½ times taller than a double-decker bus.

Insect House This is the oldest insect collection in the world, opened in 1881. It features some of the Zoo's most repulsive creatures, such as the 2-in (5 cm) long Hissing cockroach or the Malaysian dung beetle, and also some of the most deadly, such as the desert scorpion and the black widow spider.

O All year excluding 25 Dec; Mar–Oct 09.00–18.00 (or dusk, whichever is earlier); Sun and BH 09.00–19.00; Nov–Feb 10.00–dusk; C; £; ⅄ t 75% ☎ (01) 722 3333

Camden Lock [6]
Camden High Street

This is one of London's busiest and most attractive street markets. Amongst the pleas-ant canalside setting of cobbled courtyards and warehouses, its warren of shops and market stalls specialize in crafts, fashion and antiques. The best way of getting there is by the frequent narrow boat service which runs along the Regent's Canal from Paddington Basin (Little Venice) via Regent's Park, London Zoo to Camden Lock.

O 10.00–18.00 Sat and Sun only

Dover Castle [P1]
43 Weymouth Mews

This mews pub dates back to the 18th century. It was originally divided into several small bars, and frequented by coachmen. The narrow strip mirrors on the ceiling enabled the coachman to see over the wall when his employer was ready to leave, whilst drinking in a separate bar.

☎ (01) 636 9248

The Regent's Canal, opened in 1820—in its heyday one of the busiest waterways in Britain.

BLOOMSBURY

The development of Bloomsbury began in the early 1660s with Southampton Square, the first designated Square in London (later renamed Bloomsbury Square). The land around it was let off in an early successful example of 'town planning' which stipulated size and character of properties to be built. It soon became one of London's most fashionable suburbs and the development of squares was to characterize the area. Around the turn of the 19th century, Bedford Square, Fitzroy Square, Tavistock Square and Brunswick Square were all laid out.

During the 19th century Bloomsbury became a favourite haunt of artists and writers, the most famous of these being Charles Dickens who lived at Tavistock Square in 1851–6 and 48 Doughty Street in 1837–9. In the early part of the 20th century the Bloomsbury Group, an association of artists and writers including E M Forster, Roger Fry, John Maynard Keynes and Virginia and Leonard Woolf re-established the area's literary reputation. Bloomsbury's erudite atmosphere lives on today both in its institutions, chief amongst these being the British Museum and the University of London, and

in its many varied specialist bookshops. In the shadow of the British Telecom Tower, Charlotte Street is famous for its numerous restaurants.

British Museum and British Library [1]
Great Russell Street

The British Museum was founded in 1753 around some 80 000 objects left in the will of the great collector Sir Hans Sloane. The first national museum in Great Britain, it was originally universal but its natural history collection has long since been removed to South Kensington, to form the nucleus of the Natural History Museum, and its ethnography department constitutes the Museum of Mankind in Burlington Gardens.

The British Museum today comprises one of the largest and finest collections of antiquities in the world, magnificent medieval treasures, one of the greatest collections of European prints and drawings and, within the British Library, many of the world's oldest and most famous documents and books.

11. BLOOMSBURY

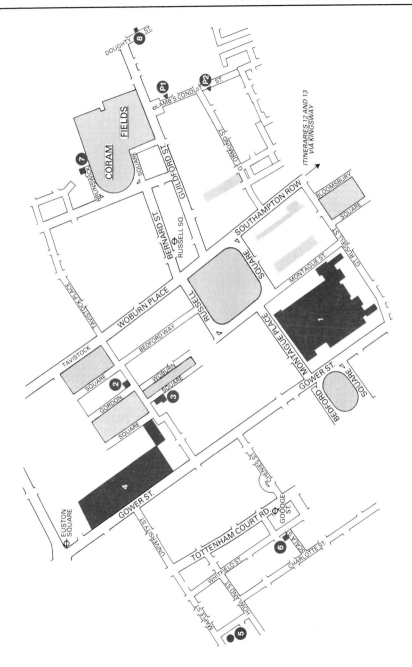

DOUGHTY ST.

8

P1

P2

LAMB'S CONDUIT ST.

ORMOND ST.

CORAM FIELDS

7

BRUNSWICK SQUARE

GUILDFORD ST.

BERNARD ST.

RUSSELL SQ.

SOUTHAMPTON ROW

BLOOMSBURY SQUARE

GT. RUSSELL ST.

ITINERARIES 12 AND 13 VIA KINGSWAY

TAVISTOCK PLACE

WOBURN PLACE

RUSSELL SQUARE

BEDFORD WAY

MONTAGUE ST.

1

MONTAGUE PLACE

TAVISTOCK SQUARE

2

GORDON SQUARE

WOBURN SQUARE

3

GOWER ST.

BEDFORD SQUARE

EUSTON SQUARE

4

GOWER ST.

UNIVERSITY ST.

CAPPER ST.

GOODGE ST.

6

TOTTENHAM COURT RD.

CHENIES ST.

RIDGMOUNT ST.

CHARLOTTE ST.

WHITFIELD ST.

HOWLAND ST.

MAPLE ST.

5

The construction of the main building was begun in 1823 and has a total floor area of 17.57 acres (7.11 ha). It is the largest and most visited museum in London. In 1986 it attracted over 4.14 million visitors, which is more than any other indoor attraction in the country.

Due to its sheer size and all-embracing nature it is impossible to do even a small number of the collections justice in one visit. The following is the recommended viewing order of a selection of the greatest and most popular treasures.

Ground floor

Assyrian Sculptures and Reliefs (Rooms 16-17) The British Museum is considered to have the greatest collection of Assyrian sculptures in the world.

Room 17 contains magnificent stone panels which depict lion-hunting scenes. These decorated the state apartments of Ashurbanipal, the last great king of Assyria (now North Iraq), in his palace at Nineveh. They date from 668-627 BC.

Room 16 is dominated by two colossal human-headed winged bulls, each weighing around 16 tons, c. 710 BC, which come from the entrance to a royal city at Khorsabad (similar lion-like figures from Nimrud stand in Room 26).

Sculptures from the Parthenon 'The Elgin Marbles' (Room 8) This is one of the most famous sets of sculptures in the world and is widely held to be the greatest. They were collected by the Earl of Elgin in 1801-3 (thus being saved from almost certain destruction) and sold to the British Government. The important sculptures come from the Parthenon, the great Temple of Athena on top of the Acropolis in Athens. Many were worked on between 447 and 432 BC by Pheidias, the great architect of the Parthenon, as internal and external decoration work. The larger part of this was a huge frieze, originally some 500 ft (152 m) long, of which half is preserved here, which ran

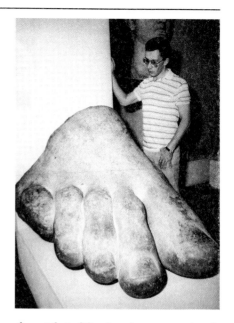

A great feat of Greek sculpture—remains of a colossus.

around the interior of the Parthenon. It depicts the Panathenaic festival—a four-yearly event involving athletic feats and a religious procession towards the Acropolis, to honour Athena. It may also be a memorial to the heroes of the Battle of Marathon (490 BC). The sculptures at either ends of the gallery show the metopes (a frieze round the outside of the temple) and the free standing sculpture in the pediment.

These sculptures are the cause of one of the art world's knottiest problems. The Greek people would like them to be returned 'home', the British Museum (and many a museum around the world) fear this would be the thin end of the wedge and the start of the break up of museum collections as we know them.

Mausoleum of Halicarnassus (Room 12) This room is unique in the world in containing works from two of the Seven Wonders of the World. It is dedicated mostly to sculptures from the Mausoleum, the giant tomb of King Mausolus built at Halicarnassus (now in Turkey) in the 4th century BC. There is also a sculpture from the Temple of Artemis built at Ephesus (also in Turkey) in the 6th century BC. In addition lions from the Mausoleum flank the main stairs from ground to upper floor in the entrance hall.

Rosetta Stone (Room 25) This tablet of black basalt, discovered in 1799, was the first key to being able to read hieroglyphics. The name derives from its find-place and its bilingual text is a priests' decree, dating from 27 March 196 BC. This is translated from hieroglyphics into Greek, thus enabling the language of ancient Egypt to be decoded.

Egyptian Sculptures (Room 25) The huge red granite head and arm comes from the colossus of a king thought to be Amenophis III *c.* 1400 BC.

Further down the gallery is a particularly striking statue of a seated nobleman and his wife, hand in hand, entering into eternity, *c.* 1350 BC.

The most dramatic of the many excellent statues here is the remaining upper part of the Colossus of Rameses II, *c.* 1250 BC. Rameses II (also known as Ozymandias) was the great builder of the temple of Abu Simbel, of whom Shelley wrote:

'My name is Ozymandias, King of kings:
Look on my works, ye Mighty and despair!'

Upper floor

Egyptian Mummies (Rooms 60-1) The British Museum is considered to have the greatest collection of Egyptology outside Cairo and its collection of mummies is one of the most visited in the whole museum. Not only are there mummified humans but also sacred mummified animals which range in size from a small bull to a tiny shrew. Also on show are many brightly painted coffins and mummy cases—the scenes on them being designed to help the dead in the afterlife.

'She who must be obeyed'—this is thought to be Hatshepsut who reigned supreme 1503–1482 BC, one of the four Egyptian Queens to rule as Pharaoh.

Ironically, one of the most popular exhibits here is an 'unmummified' body of a man which has been naturally preserved by dehydration after burial in the hot sands. He is nicknamed Ginger after the colour of his hair and died *c.* 3300 BC thus making him the oldest man in the British Museum.

Babylonian Room (Room 54) Objects here illustrate the rich culture and daily life of the world's second oldest civilisation, established by the Sumerians *ante* 3500 BC. Many of the pieces come from the Royal Cemetery at Ur (in Iraq) and date *c.* 2500 BC. This find is regarded as one of the 20th century's most important.

Prints and Drawings (Room 67) Selections from the Museum's treasures, which include works by Michelangelo, Raphael,

Welcome to 'the greatest jackdaw's nest in the world'. Above the portico 'The Progress of Civilization' by Richard Westmacott.

The oldest man in the British Museum—'Ginger', born over 5000 years ago.

Dürer, Rubens, Rembrandt and Botticelli are on temporary display here.

Celtic Britain—Lindow Man (Room 37) The body of a man murdered between 300 BC and AD 100, possibly by Druids as a fertility sacrifice, was discovered in a peat marsh at Lindow Moss, near Wilmslow, Cheshire in 1984. He has been almost perfectly preserved due to being waterlogged and the face of 'Pete Marsh' is the only one to have survived from British pre-history.

Roman Britain—Mosaic Pavement from Hinton St Mary, Dorset (Room 35) This remarkably preserved 30×20 ft (9×6 m) 4th-century mosaic is one of the major Christian antiquities of the Roman World.

Roman Britain—The Mildenhall Treasure (Room 40) This hoard of 4th-century

The Reading Room of the British Library—focal point of over 16 million volumes.

silver tableware found in Mildenhall, Suffolk contains some of the finest pieces of Roman silverware to have been found anywhere in the Roman Empire.

Early Medieval—The Sutton Hoo Treasure (Room 41) This treasure trove comes from the royal burial ship of an ancient English king, dating *c.* AD 625. It was found at Sutton Hoo, Suffolk and has been called 'the most marvellous find in the archaeological annals of England'. Highlights include the king's garnet-encrusted gold shoulder clasps and his reconstructed helmet.

Medieval Gallery (Room 42) The beautifully carved Lewis Chessmen found on the Isle of Lewis, Outer Hebrides, is the largest and most outstanding collection of early chessmen in the Western World. They are of 12th-century Scandinavian origin, carved from walrus ivory. Close by is another of the Museum's most outstanding possessions, the Royal Gold Cup of the kings of France and England, made in Paris *c.* 1380.

Clocks and Watches (Room 44) This collection of magnificent time-pieces from the 16th to the 20th century is claimed to be one of the finest in the world.

Ground floor

Manuscript Saloon (Room 30) This holds one of the world's greatest collections of historical and literary manuscripts, including handwriting of many of the world's leading names in art, science, music and literature (Michelangelo, Leonardo da Vinci, Beethoven, Dickens, etc). One of its earliest

English exhibits is the Lindisfarne Gospels *c.* 689, the greatest masterpiece of early English book illumination. Also here are two of the world's oldest and most important copies of the Bible—the 5th-century *Codex Alexandrinus* and the 4th-century *Codex Sinaiaticus.* The latter is claimed to be as old and as important as *Codex Vaticanus*, the world's oldest bible, *ante* AD 350.

The King's Library (Room 32) The most famous pieces of paper in the British Library relate to the Magna Charta. The very document (called 'the Articles of the Barons') that King John sealed at Runnymede in 1215 is displayed along with his seal and two of the four original copies of Magna Charta made from the Articles. The effect of this document is incalculable—among others, it directly influenced the US Constitution and the UN Declaration of Human Rights. Book milestones include: the world's first printed book, the *Diamond Sutra* dated May AD 868; the earliest mechanically printed book, the Gutenberg Bible *c.* 1454; the first book to be published by an Englishman: *The Recuyell of the Histories of Troye* by William Caxton 1473–4; the first publication of the collected works of William Shakespeare, *First Folio*, 1623. Next to this is one of the only four existing authentic signatures of 'the Bard'.

> The Portland Vase will not be on display until late 1989. It was shattered into about 200 pieces as a consequence of an infamous drunken attack in 1845. It was then painstakingly reassembled but the glue has since discoloured and grown brittle. The vase has therefore been recently broken down again by the Museum and it is currently in the process of restoration. Its new location is not yet known. There is a copy of the Vase in Room 47 and in the same room is Josiah Wedgwood's Pegasus Vase, described by him as 'the finest and most perfect I have ever made'.

Islam, S and SE Asia and the Far East (Room 34) The respective collections of Chinese antiquities and Indian sculptures in this gallery are unrivalled in the West and contain many outstanding pieces.

British Library Reading Room The domed Reading Room of the British Library is the principal room of the largest library in the United Kingdom which houses over 16 million volumes. A copy of each new publication produced in the United Kingdom is required to be kept here and stock increases require over 8 miles (13 km) of new shelving annually. Famous readers of the past include Marx, Lenin and George Bernard Shaw.

Portland Vase (Room – see below) The world's most precious vase is thought to date from the late first century BC. It is of unknown Roman origin and takes its name from the Dukes of Portland who once owned it. It is usually regarded as the most priceless example of the art of glass-making and the virtuosity of its workmanship has inspired many modern craftsmen, including the greatest of all modern 'potters', Josiah Wedgwood, to imitation.

O **Mon–Sat 10.00–17.00; Sun 14.30–18.00; T; £ Mon–Sat 10.30, 11.00, 13.30, 14.00, Sun 14.45, 15.15, 15.45;** & **t 95%; V**
Reading Room: brief conducted visit on hour, 11.00–16.00. Readers must apply in advance for a pass.
☎ **(01) 636 1555**

Percival David Foundation of Chinese Art [2]
53 Gordon Square

This small museum is dedicated to Chinese ceramics and holds some 1500 pieces dating from the 9th to the 19th century. A number of these have been in the possession of Chinese emperors and the collection is of priceless documentary, historical and technical importance. It is especially noted for its Ming

Dynasty (1368–1644) wares and also includes the earliest dated pieces of blue and white ware (the 'David Vases') dating from 1351.

O **Mon–Fri 10.30–17.00**
☎ **(01) 387 3909**

Courtauld Institute Galleries [3]
Woburn Square

These intimate galleries were founded in 1931 by the industrialist Samuel Courtauld, who was later to bequeath the finest collection of Impressionist paintings in the country to the Institute. Further bequests have contributed many masterpieces of European painting from the 14th to the 20th century, but due to the confines of space in the present building only a fraction of these are on display (the galleries move to Somerset House in late 1989).

The Princes Gate Collection— Italian and Netherlandish 14th–18th centuries

Gallery 1 The small altarpiece Triptych (1410–20) by the 'Master of Flémalle', one of the earliest Dutch Old Masters, is of outstanding early importance. Two of Europe's finest 16th-century painters, Pieter Bruegel the Elder and Titian, are represented here.

Gallery 2 This is devoted mostly to the 17th-century Dutch masters, Rubens and his famous pupil Van Dyck. Most of the works are of religious subjects.

Gallery 3 This holds one of the world's greatest collection of Rubens' paintings. He was a fashionable portrait painter and the most striking example here is *Family of Jan Brueghel the Elder* (*c.* 1612). *Landscape by Moonlight* (late 1630s) is considered to be Rubens' finest landscape.

Gallery 4 18th-century Italian paintings here include the work of the church and palace artist Giovanni Tiepolo.

The Courtauld Collection—French Impressionist and Post-Impressionist

Galleries 5 & 6 The most popular and best known work here is *Bar at the Folies-Bergère*, 1882, by Manet, his last important work. *Portrait of the Artist with Bandaged Ear* by Van Gogh, 1889, recalls the famous gesture of the depressed genius who cut off part of his ear and sent it as a present to a girl with whom he was in love. Other popular works are *Two Dancers on the Stage* by Dégas, *c.* 1877, *Card Players* by Cézanne, *c.* 1892, and *La Loge* (The Theatre Box) by Renoir, 1874. Also on display are works by Gauguin, Monet, Pissarro, Rousseau, Seurat, Sisley and Toulouse-Lautrec.

Galleries 8 & 9 These are used for changing exhibitions which will include some of the vast collection of over 5000 drawings (including work by Michelangelo, Rembrandt, Rubens, Picasso).

O **Mon–Sat 10.00–17.00; Sun 14.00–17.00; £; ﴾ 3 steps**
☎ **(01) 580 1015**

University College [4]
Gower Street

University College was founded in 1826 as the first English university for non-Anglicans and acquired the nickname of 'the godless college'. The main building was constructed 1827–9 by William Wilkins in the style of the same architect's National Gallery. To the far right of the building on the ground floor is London's most unusual memorial, the remarkable 'auto-icon' ('self-statue') by Jeremy Bentham (1748–1832) enclosed in an air-tight glass and mahogany case. Bentham was a philosopher and one of the founders and administrators of University College. He was determined not to be excluded from it even when dead and so he left appropriate instructions that his embalmed, fully clothed body should be put

Towering highest in London—the British Telecom Tower at 620 ft (189 m).

on display close to where the College committee held its meetings.

(Extract from the will of Jeremy Bentham) *'My body I give to my dear friend Doctor Southwood Smith. The skeleton he will cause to be put together in such manner as that the whole figure may be seated in a chair usually occupied by me . . . when engaged in thought.'*

The face is made of wax and the actual skull is kept in the University safe but everything else is original. The auto-icon even used to preside over meetings of the College committee and was then noted in the minutes as 'present but not voting'. The presence of the ghost of Bentham is also well-documented by college staff!

At the back of the College is the University Church of Christ the King. It began construction in 1835 and is a striking example of Victorian Gothic revival. It has one of the tallest naves in London at 88 ft (27 m) high, featuring a hammerbeam roof and its overall architecture is most cathedral-like.

O College—Mon–Fri 09.30–17.00;
&. ground floor
☎ (01) 387 7050

British Telecom Tower   [5]
Maple Street, off Tottenham Court Road

The Telecom Tower was begun in 1962 (then known as the Post Office Tower) and when opened in 1965 it was the tallest structure and tallest building (i.e. an occupied structure) in Great Britain. The Tower comprises 36 floors and is 580 ft (177 m) high, surmounted by a 40-ft (12 m) high radar mast. It lost its record as tallest building in 1980 to the 600 ft (183 m) tall National Westminster Tower but it is still the tallest structure in London at 620 ft (189 m). The foundations of

The fastest times recorded for racing up the 814 steps to the top observation floor was 4 min 21.4 sec on 6 February 1970 (thereafter discontinued).

this 13 000-ton colossus penetrate just 25 ft (8 m) down and in a 90-knots wind it sways up to nearly 6 in (15 cm). The Tower used to boast a revolving public restaurant on its top floors. On a clear day a diner would be able to see for 40 miles (64 km) in all directions in the 23½ minutes it took the restaurant to turn 365°. The Tower is unfortunately now closed to the public.

Pollock's Toy Museum   [6]
1 Scala Street

This is one of London's most charming museums, occupying two small adjoining houses, dating from 1760, connected by narrow winding staircases. A small alcove in Room 1 represents a toy shop of around 1910–20, selling one of the very first games of table tennis, then marketed as Ping-Pong or Gossima (see Hamleys, Regent Street). Room 3 claims a doll dating from 1822 which has crossed the Rockies in a covered wagon both ways and also a tiny Egyptian clay mouse with moving jaw and tail over 4000 years old! Teddy Bears feature in Room 4, the oldest being Eric, a battered one-eared specimen, 'born' in 1905, just three years after the origination of the world's first Teddy.

The original Mr Benjamin Pollock (d 1937) was the very last publisher of cardboard toy theatres and an 1820 theatre is displayed in Room 6. He single-handedly kept the toy theatre tradition alive at his East End shop and inspired Robert Louis Stevenson to write 'If you love art, folly, or the bright eyes of children, speed to Pollock's'.

O Mon–Sat 10.00–17.00;   all year except
BH;   C;   p
☎ (01) 636 3452

Thomas Coram Foundation   [7]
40 Brunswick Square

The Foundation began in 1739 when Captain Thomas Coram (1688–1751), ex-mariner, ex-American colonist and philanthropist was granted a royal charter to care for the abandoned young children (foundlings) he had seen on the streets of London. In 1745 the Foundling Hospital was built on the site of Coram Fields and the present building where it covered 56 acres (23 ha). Admission to the Hospital was determined by a 'lucky dip' system whereby mothers had to draw coloured balls from a bag. A white ball meant admittance, a black ball meant refusal. This heartbreaking system was later reformed to admit the first child of an unmarried mother as long as certain other conditions could be met. In 1826 the Foundation moved out of London and the Hospital was demolished. The present building was constructed in 1937, to house the Foundation's art collection and to be its London headquarters from which it still operates adoption and adolescent care projects.

Its strong connection with the arts was initially prompted by William Hogarth, one of the original governors. He devised a clever scheme to attract the paying public to the Hospital (to contribute to its upkeep) by arranging an annual exhibition of the best contemporary artists' works here (thereby inspiring the founding of the Royal Academy in 1768).

On the first landing is Hogarth's portrait of Captain Thomas Coram (1740). Hogarth said that this outstanding portrait gave him more pleasure than any other. A more typical Hogarth scene of London low-life is *The March of the Guards to Finchley* (1746) in the Court Room lobby.

The Picture Gallery holds one of the Foundation's most valuable treasures, part of the *Massacre of the Innocents* from the studio of Raphael. This is the largest surviving fragment of a series of cartoons designed for tapestries (woven 1520-4) now hanging in the Vatican.

The other great benefactor of the Hospital was George Frederick Handel and next to the cartoon is the original keyboard of the organ Handel presented to the Hospital chapel. Amongst the exhibits in the showcases, the most poignant are coins and tokens left with the children by their mothers. This was the only way of identifying them in later years as the children would have been given new names to give them a fresh start in life. The Court Room is reconstructed to its original form and Hogarth's *Moses Brought Before Pharaoh's Daughter* (1746) is meant to depict the 'original foundling'.

O Mon-Fri 10.00-16.00; Closed PH & BH; p; ☖ 6 steps, small lift
☎ (01) 278 2424
Note: Rooms subject to closure for private purposes.

Dickens House Museum [8]
48 Doughty Street

Number 48 Doughty Street dates from 1801, and is the only surviving house in which Charles Dickens lived for any significant period of time whilst in London. The success of *Pickwick Papers*, which had been running for a year in serial form, meant that in April 1837 Dickens could afford to move to this smart middle class private road. He stayed until December 1839, a relatively short time but enough for the prolific genius to secure his reputation by writing the final instalments of *Pickwick Papers*, almost all of *Oliver Twist*, *Nicholas Nickleby* and the start of *Barnaby Rudge*. In addition, he completed several other minor works here.

The House was opened as a museum in 1925 and is the finest collection of Dickens' *memorabilia* in the world. The exhibits particularly reflect the novels which were written here.

Ground Floor The glass case in the Morning Room contains several interesting curios

---

On the site of the old hospital in Coram Fields is a children's playground, administered in the spirit of the Foundation with the unusual sign (on Guildford Street) stating that: 'Adults are not admitted unless accompanied by a child'.

---

from Dickens' early life, including the types of shoe blacking pots on to which the 12-year-old had to stick labels during his traumatic factory period, and from the same year the earliest example of his handwriting. The china monkey here was a favourite desk top item without which Dickens claimed himself unable to settle down to write!

First Floor   The Study contains the elegant desk from his Gad's Hill home near Rochester and the table on which he was writing his last (unfinished) novel *The Mystery of Edwin Drood*. Nearby is a copy of *David Copperfield* taken by the ill-fated Scott expedition to the Antarctic in 1910–13.

Second Floor   Mary Hogarth's Room recalls the most heartbreaking occasion for Dickens whilst at this house. He had fallen in love with Mary, his wife's 16-year-old sister, and she had moved in to No. 48 with them. After only a month, however, she died suddenly of a heart attack. Dickens was so shocked that he immediately stopped work and withdrew himself so completely that it was even rumoured that he had died (as may be seen from his letter refuting the suggestion!). Later, Mary was the model for some of Dickens' tragic heroines, the most famous being Little Nell (see Old Curiosity Shop).

The Suzannet Room features Dickens' theatrical work and his own reading tours.

Ignoring his doctor's advice, he gave strenuous dramatic readings of his own works late into his life and he was one of the day's great theatre attractions.

O **Mon–Sat 10.00–17.00;**   £
☎ **(01) 405 2127**

Charles Dickens (1812–70)

Charles Dickens was born at Portsmouth in 1812 and came to London in 1823. His early career as a lawyer and reporter (plus a short period of factory work) shaped his conception of the harsh realities and social injustices of Victorian London. His first short story *A Dinner at Poplar Walk* appeared in an obscure magazine in 1833. More short stories

('sketches') followed under the pen-name of Boz and during 1836–7 Dickens' first novel, *Pickwick Papers*, which like many of his stories was published first in serial-form, became a major success. Dickens went on to write a further 13 major novels, becoming the greatest writer of his time and probably the greatest ever English novelist. The freshness and wit of his observation, the vitality and colour with which he invested his characters and the ability to tell a story, capturing the spirit of the age, made him indeed 'The Inimitable' (his own immodest description!).

The Lamb   [P1]
94 Lamb's Conduit Street

Both the pub and the street take their name from a wealthy merchant, William Lamb, who built the water conduit under the street in 1577. The present pub is an 18th-century building of matchboarded walls and ceilings, and retains much of its original bar woodwork and glass, including rare glass 'snob-screen' panes which swivel to shut off the view of the bar-tender if so required! It contains one of the oldest types of juke-boxes in London, a late 18th-century polyphon which plays, not so compact, large metal discs when primed with an old penny (available from behind the bar). On the walls is a unique collection of old sepia music-hall photographs.

☎ **(01) 405 0713**

The Sun   [P2]
63 Lamb's Conduit Street

This small basic bustling pub sells more different types of draught beer than any other pub in London. It boasts over twenty different brews at any one time and in the course of a week will rotate these to feature over fifty types per week. This extravagant choice is helped by its huge cellars which are occasionally open to the public.

☎ **(01) 405 8278**
Note: Meals not available in evenings.

COVENT GARDEN, STRAND AND EMBANKMENT

The site of Covent Garden was formerly owned by the Abbey or 'Convent' (the old term for a religious community, not necessarily female) of St Peter at Westminster. Produce was cultivated here for the monks of the Abbey and the present name is a corruption of 'Convent Garden'.

In 1536, after the Dissolution of the monasteries, the land was granted to the Dukes of Bedford and in 1627 they commissioned Inigo Jones to lay out the first square in London. His work was considerably influenced by the Italian style of market-place and the name 'Piazza' lives on. The market for fruit, vegetables and flowers was established in 1670 and by the mid-18th century the first

Off the beaten track in Covent Garden—fish-eye view of Neal's Yard.

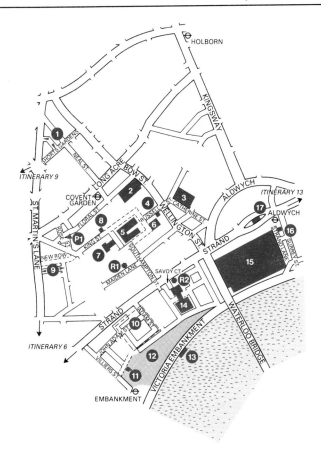

12. COVENT GARDEN, STRAND AND EMBANKMENT

1 Neal's Yard
2 Royal Opera House
3 Theatre Royal, Drury Lane
4 Theatre Museum
5 Central Market
6 London Transport Museum
7 St Paul's, Covent Garden
8 No. 43 King Street
9 Goodwin's Court
10 The Adelphi (site – see dotted line)
11 York House Watergate

12 Victoria Embankment Gardens
13 Cleopatra's Needle
14 Savoy Hotel
15 Somerset House
16 'Roman' Bath and Watch House
17 St Mary-le-Strand

Pubs/Restaurants
P1 Lamb and Flag
R1 Rules
R2 Simpson's-in-the-Strand

135

shops and coffee houses were being built. The area had by now acquired a large number of brothels and a very dubious reputation (as depicted in John Cleland's saucy novel, *Fanny Hill*, 1749). Permanent market halls were built between 1830 and 1870 and the market continued to flourish, albeit in an unruly way.

It was sold by the Bedfords in 1918 and in 1974 moved to Nine Elms in Battersea. The market area was restored by the Greater London Council and is now one of London's most popular shopping and entertainment precincts.

The Strand was originally a path running alongside the Thames, hence its name. It reached its zenith between the 16th and 18th centuries by which time a total of seven grand palaces faced on to the river. All of these have now disappeared. Today's Strand is better known for its theatres, a legacy of the 1890s when it held more theatres than any other street in London.

Victoria Embankment was completed between 1868 and 1874 and the extent of the land reclamation is graphically illustrated by the York House Watergate which now stands some 100 yd (90 m) back from the river.

Neal's Yard   [1]
Off Short's Gardens

This tiny enclosed courtyard is a peaceful oasis of 'healthy living' shops in an almost rustic setting. Around the corner, in Short's Gardens, Neal's Yard Wholefood Warehouse boasts one of London's most eccentric clocks—the only outdoor working water clock in London, constructed in 1982, (there is also a steam clock by the same designer in the Farmer's Market, Sydney Street, Chelsea).

Royal Opera House   [2]
Bow Street

The first theatre on the site of the present Royal Opera House opened in 1732 and at the time was said to be London's most luxurious ever. Its opulence, however, was torn apart by incensed theatregoers in what came to be termed 'The Half-Price Riots' of 1763 when the customary rule of admission at half-price after the third act was stopped. The building was destroyed by fire in 1808 but rebuilt, incorporating its original Coade stone frieze (see South Bank Lion) of literary figures. Prices were increased for the new theatre and once again riots ensued. These 'Old-Price Riots' continued for 61 nights. The Riot Act was even read from the theatre stage by the police—but the management eventually gave in and prices were reduced. This theatre, too, burned down and the present building was designed by Edward Barry in 1858. This now houses the Royal Opera and the Royal Ballet.

Opposite the Royal Opera House is Bow Street Magistrates Court and Police Station. The original court was established in 1740 and its second magistrate was Henry Fielding (the author of Tom Jones*). In 1750 he established the first small detective force in England of six non-uniformed 'thief-takers'. Around the turn of the century 'Mr Fielding's people', some 70 strong, acquired the better known name of the Bow Street Runners. Henry Fielding's half-brother, John Fielding, was Bow Street's most remarkable magistrate. Although totally blind, he was reputed to be able to recognize some 3000 thieves by their voices.*

Bow Street police station is most unusual in as much as a clear 'white' lamp shines outside it, instead of the traditional blue glass lamp. This was installed at the request of Queen Victoria who found the blue lamp depressing after the bright lights of a show at the Royal Opera House. It it said that this reminded her of the Blue Room at Windsor Castle in which Prince Albert died.

The Royal Opera House boasts numerous English premières. Notable plays include *She Stoops to Conquer* (1773) and *The Rivals (1775)*, operatic premières include *The Barber of Seville* (1818), *The Marriage of Figaro* (1819), *Madame Butterly* (1905) and *Der Rosenkavalier* (1913).

O **Tours by appointment only;** £
☎ **(01) 240 1911**

Theatre Royal, Drury Lane [3]
Catherine Street

The present theatre is the fourth on the site and staged its first performance in October 1812, thus making it the oldest theatre in London on its original site. It was granted its first royal charter by King Charles II in 1663. Every English monarch since then has occupied the Theatre's Royal Box and there have been a number of royal incidents at the Theatre. Assassination attempts were made on the life of (the future) George II in 1716 and that of his grandson, George III in 1800. It was also here that Charles II met Nell Gwyn. The popular story of Nell as an orange-seller at the Theatre is unproven but she did make her stage début here in Dryden's tragedy *The Indian Emperor* in 1665, and by many accounts went on to become a very accomplished actress.

The first Theatre Royal burnt down in 1672. The second building was designed by Christopher Wren in 1674 and became home to some of the English stage's greatest performers. David Garrick, the first great English naturalist actor, débuted here in 1742 and became manager in 1747. In 1889 he was accorded the honour of the first British theatre to be named after an actor—the Garrick Theatre in Charing Cross Road. Richard Brinsley Sheridan succeeded Garrick and commissioned the third building which opened in 1794. The most amazing performance of the period was by child prodigy William Betty, who played *Hamlet* at the age of 13. The Prime Minister specially adjourned

the House of Commons so that its members could all witness it for themselves! In 1800 Sheridan's theatre was the first in the world to install a safety curtain (partly to guard against fire), yet in 1809 it completely burned down for the second time. Sheridan was fetched to the scene of the disaster and sat in a neighbouring bar drinking and contemplating his ill-fortune. When his agitated friends asked him what his next action would be, he is said to have remarked philosophically 'May not a man be allowed to drink a glass of wine by his own fireside'.

During rebuilding, a man was found bricked-up in a hollow wall, reputedly with a knife through his ribs. This is said to account for 'The Man in Grey'—the Theatre's resident ghost. He has only been seen in daylight and is considered a lucky omen for the production that is playing!

The present building was completed in 1812 by Benjamin Wyatt at a cost of £400 000. Since 1945 the theatre has become famous for its musicals with the longest-run being *My Fair Lady* which between 1958 and 1963 played 2281 times.

O **Tours by appointment only;** £
☎ **(01) 836 8108**

Theatre Museum [4]
Russell Street

The Theatre Museum, opened in 1987 as an exhibition of all major performing arts, illustrated and created by stage models, costumes, prints and drawings, posters, puppets and props.

The earliest London theatre was built in 1576 by James Burbage near Finsbury Fields and called simply 'The Theater'.

His brother, Richard, was also in the theatrical trade and his epitaph (d 1619) in St Leonard's, Shoreditch is one of the shortest and most appropriate epitaphs in London. It reads simply 'Exit Burbage'.

The Museum's largest exhibit is the Angel that used to surmount the Old Gaiety Theatre, Aldwych, and now stands in the Museum foyer. The Old Gaiety, demolished in 1903, was the first London theatre to be lit by electricity on the outside in 1878 and it was the venue for Gilbert and Sullivan's first comic opera, *Thespis*, (or *The Gods Grown Old*) performed in December 1871.

Some of the most popular exhibits in the main gallery are as follows:

Pop Music The most famous costume here is the black 'Beatles suit' worn by John Lennon. Flamboyant outfits worn by Mick Jagger and Elton John contrast with costumes worn by the somewhat more staid Beverley Sisters some twenty years earlier.

Magic Prop umbrellas and flowers from the collection of Tommy Cooper (1922–84), England's most famous recent comic magician, contrast with Hindu Cups—believed to be the earliest trick for which sleight of hand was used. This ancient version of 'Find the Lady' dates back at least as far as the reign of Tutankhamun (1358–1340 BC) and may have been around for centuries before.

Ballet Costumes worn by Dame Alicia Markova (b 1910)—the first British-born prima ballerina of international status—and costume gear from The Royal Ballet's production of *The Sleeping Beauty*, which was in performance from 1946 to 1970, take pride of place.

London Theatre This traces the development of the British and London Theatre from Shakespeare to the present day. It includes the brass plaque of London's Windmill Theatre, boasting 'We never closed'. It was the only London theatre not to close during World War II (except for 12 compulsory days in 1939). Founded in 1931, it presented non-stop revue, featuring nude tableaux, which were permissible as long as the girls kept still (introducing the expression 'If it moves it's rude' into popular English language).

Opera Items relating to both classic and popular opera (particularly Gilbert and Sullivan) are displayed, including the first major successful popular opera, John Gay's *Beggars Opera*, first performed in 1728 in Lincoln's Inn Fields Theatre (demolished in 1848).

Personalities The smallest individual to command his own display case is Charles Stratton, the American midget transformed by showman extraordinaire Phineas T Barnum ('There's a sucker born every minute') into General Tom Thumb who came to London in 1844 and started an outbreak of 'midget-mania'! The youngest personality to amaze the London stage was the 13-year-old William Betty (see Theatre Royal, Drury Lane) with his performances of *Hamlet* and the strangest personality was the performing dog Carlo who was the star of London's theatreland around the same time. Joseph Grimaldi (1778–1837), 'The Father of Clowns' is also featured. He made his first appearance at the age of two at Sadler's Wells Theatre but never acted in a circus (in his day the clown only appeared in pantomimes).

The Paintings and Picture Collection The most unusual exhibit is the wheelbarrow of the legendary tightrope walker Charles Blondin (real name Jean François Gravelet, 1824–97) with which he made the earliest crossing of the Niagara Falls on 30 June 1859—a distance of 1100 ft (335 m).

O Tues–Sun 11.00–19.00; £; ⅃ t 100% ☎ (01) 836 7891

Central Market [5]
The Piazza

This elegant structure was erected in 1830 at a cost of over £70 000 in an attempt to accommodate and therefore control the tolls on the sprawling market stalls. Within only 25 years, it was too small to hold the burgeoning market and has now been developed into units for small shops and restaurants.

London Transport Museum [6]
39 Wellington Street

This comprehensive historical collection of London transport—the largest urban passenger transport undertaking in the world—opened in Covent Garden's renovated Victorian flower market in 1980. Historical pride of place is claimed by a replica of London's first omnibus which commenced service on 4 July 1829. A newspaper advertisement described it as follows:

OMNIBUS

G. Shillibeer, induced by the universal admiration of the above Vehicles called forth at Paris, has commenced running one ... from Paddington to the Bank ... the fare charged from Paddington to the Bank being one shilling and from Islington to the Bank or Paddington, only sixpence.

Shillibeer's omnibus (right)—London's original horse bus and successors.

At a time when the average weekly working class wage was around 30 shillings (£1.50) George Shillibeer's elegant horse-drawn coach was far beyond the means of most people.

Other notable London Transport firsts on display are:

—the first Trolleybus (commenced service on 16 May 1931). This type of vehicle required an overhead electric power cable but did not need tracks and therefore replaced the London tram. They ran in London until May 1962.

—an 1866 steam-powered locomotive—one of the first types to enter service on the original Metropolitan underground line in 1863.

—an original 1890 carriage from the City and South London Railway—the world's first underground electric railway which ran between King William Street (near London Bridge) and Stockwell.

One of the Museum's most popular exhibits is a simulation of an underground train travelling along the Circle Line as viewed from the driver's seat. The average speed of an underground train is 20.5 mph (32.9 km/h) but the confined space gives an illusion of far greater speed.

O All year excl 25 & 26 Dec, 10.0-18.00; C; £; ♿ t 80% ☎ (01) 379 6344

St Paul's, Covent Garden [7]

This is the only building to survive from Inigo Jones's original Covent Garden. In view of its longevity, dating back to 1633, it is ironic that Jones was instructed by the Earl of Bedford (the owner of the estate) not to go to any considerable expense in its construction. The Earl is reputed to have told Jones, 'I would not have it much better than a barn'. 'Well then, you shall have the handsomest barn in England' was the reply. The odd feature of its design is that the great Tuscanstyle portico is not the main entrance to the

> During an average working day, London Transport carries over six million passengers and its buses and underground trains run a total of around 500 000 miles (804 500 km).
>
> The first section of the London Underground—the world's first urban underground railway—was opened on 10 January 1863 between Farringdon Street and Edgware Road, forming what is now part of the Metropolitan line. The network today is one of the most extensive of the 67 in the world with 251 miles (404 km) of track of which 102 miles (164 km) actually runs underground.
>
> There are 272 stations and the record time for touring all of them is 18 hr 41 min 41 sec set by a team of five on 30 July 1986.

church. This is because the church was built facing eastward on to the square and therefore the altar would have had to be placed at the west end in order to face the main entrance. This break from tradition was not allowed by the Church and therefore the portico entrance was never used. St Paul's was gutted by fire in 1795 but restored by Thomas Hardwick and reconsecrated in 1798.

St Paul's is known as 'The Actors' Church', and memorial services for distinguished members of the profession are held here.

Its array of wooden memorial plaques reads like a *Who's Who* of stage and screen. The youngest remembered is Richard Beckinsale (1947-79). The most popular (certainly for American visitors), is Vivien Leigh (1913-67). Other famous names include Marie Lloyd (1870-1922) 'the beloved Queen of the British Music Halls', and Boris Karloff (real name William Henry Pratt) (1887-1969). On the same wall is a wreath of limewood carved by Grinling Gibbons for St Paul's Cathedral. This was presented to St Paul's Church in memory of Gibbons and his wife who are buried in the crypt (destroyed by the fire of 1795).

On the north wall are memorials to Sir Noël Coward (1899-1973), Thomas Arne, composer of 'Rule, Britannia!' who was baptized and buried in this churchyard (1710-78) and Sir Charles Chaplin KBE (1889-1977).

On the south wall is a silver funeral casket containing the ashes of Dame Ellen Terry (1847-1928) and next to it a tablet to Dame Edith Evans (1888-1976) whose ashes are buried nearby.

The most unusual memorial, depicting a mask with a dagger through the eye, is dedicated to the colourful actor Charles Macklin (d 1797). He stabbed a fellow actor in the eye, backstage at the Theatre Royal, Drury Lane in 1735. He was found guilty of manslaughter but was never imprisoned and continued to act at the Theatre until the age of 90.

The Church's most famous modern theatrical association is with the opening scene of *My Fair Lady* (see Theatre Royal, Drury Lane) when Henry Higgins meets Eliza Doolittle sheltering from the rain under the portico.

A plaque at the front of the church commemorates England's first Punch and Judy show—'near this spot, Punch's Puppet show was first performed in England and witnessed by Samuel Pepys on 9 May 1662'. To commemorate this, Covent Garden hosts two annual Punch and Judy festivals (see Calendar of Events).

No. 43 King Street   [8]

King Street was built as part of the original Covent Garden development in the 1630s and named in honour of Charles I. No. 43 was constructed in its present form in 1717 and is one of the oldest and most attractive buildings in Covent Garden. In January 1774 it opened as Low's Grand Hotel—the first

hotel in England (i.e. a public residence with the emphasis on accommodation for families rather than an inn or tavern whose primary business was refreshment). It continued as a hotel up until the 1880s.

Goodwin's Court   [9]

This narrow gas-lit alleyway, parts of which date back to 1690, is the oldest residential part of Covent Garden. The delightful bow-windowed houses numbered 1–8 date from the late 18th century.

The Fire mark over the alley entrance is a rare example of the type of badge that was used from the early 1700s until 1833 to denote that a building was protected by a particular insurance company. The insurance companies ran the only effective fire brigade until 1833 (when the first London Fire Engine Establishment was formed) and therefore the badge was a recognition sign to the firemen.

The Adelphi (site)   [10]

The Adelphi riverside development of 24 terraced houses set above arched vaults was begun by the Adam brothers, John, Robert, James and William in 1772 and occupied 3 acres (1.2 ha) of land stretching back to the Strand. (The name is taken from the Greek

One of the original seven Strand Palaces that stood on the site covered by the Adelphi was Durham House (recalled by Durham House Street). This was the home of Sir Walter Raleigh from 1583-1603 and is one of the traditional settings for the famous incident in 1586 when his servant saw him smoking for the first time and attempted to extinguish him with a tankard of ale!

Garden Centre—refreshments in the Central Market.

'Adelphoi', meaning brothers.) The most attractive of the few original buildings that remain are No. 8 John Adam Street—the home of the Royal Society of Arts since 1774 and No. 7 Adam Street, the offices of *The Lancet.*

York House Watergate [11]
Watergate Walk

This gateway built in 1626 led from the gardens of York House, on the Strand, to the Thames, before it was reclaimed by the Victoria Embankment in the 1870s. The first Duke of Buckingham, a powerful influence in the court of James I, lived at York House until his murder in 1628; the second Duke,

George Villiers moved in after the Restoration. The Watergate still bears the Villiers arms.

York House was demolished in the 1670s but the Duke, determined not to be forgotten, insisted that all the streets on its former site should commemorate every part of his name and title even down to 'Of Alley' (at the top of Villiers St).

Victoria Embankment Gardens [12]
(East side of Charing Cross)

This section of the gardens includes two excellent, contrasting statues. Robert Burns, the great Scottish poet, is immortalized by a huge bronze statue (1884) by Sir John Steel. In front of him is the comparatively tiny, but superbly crafted, memorial to the Imperial Camel Corps of World War I by Cecil Brown (1920), depicting a soldier riding a camel.

> *A few yards away from this miniature memorial towers the 68 ft 6 in (20.88 m) tall Cleopatra's Needle. It is thought-provoking to consider whether this camel really could pass through the eye (if one existed) of Cleopatra's Needle!*

Cleopatra's Needle [13]
Victoria Embankment

Cleopatra's Needle, some 3450 years old, is London's oldest outdoor monument. Its colourful history also qualifies it as one of London's most interesting artefacts. This pink granite obelisk is the largest in the United Kingdom, standing 68 ft 6 in (20.88 m) high and weighing around 186 tons. It was cut from the quarries of Aswan *c.* 1475 BC and erected in front of the temple of the sun god at Heliopolis. (It was one of a pair—the other now stands in Central Park, New York.) In 23 BC it was removed to Alexandria and stood in front of the palace in which Cleopatra had died in 30 BC—hence the popular name. It collapsed in the sand in the 16th century and lay there until 1819 when it was offered to the British Government as a memorial to Nelson and Abercrombie, who had defeated the French at the Battle of the Nile in 1798. Problems of transportation and cost, however, meant that the monument did not reach London until January 1878. Its five month long journey, towed from Alexandria in a huge cigar-shaped iron pontoon, cost some £15 000 and the lives of six seamen who were drowned in a gale. The 19th-century sphinxes at the base of the monument were originally positioned facing outwards (i.e. on guard). A contractor's mistake some years later, however, positioned them facing

Paying homage to the Gods and Pharaohs of an ancient civilization—hieroglyphics and symbols on Cleopatra's Needle.

inwards where they have remained! The hieroglyphics and symbols on the obelisk are dedicated to various Egyptian gods and rulers, including Tuthmosis III and Rameses II. Buried beneath it is a 'time-capsule' of two

> *The Egyptian theme is extended to the iron seats (c. 1860-70) on the Embankment. Those in the City of London feature camels and those in Westminster feature sphinxes. The other notable street furniture are the iron lamp standards depicting entwined dolphins. Made around the same time, these are the most elaborate lampposts in London.*

earthenware containers recording for future posterity various Victorian artefacts, including portraits of 'twelve of the prettiest English ladies', a set of British currency, a copy of *Bradshaw's Railway Guide*, the *Holy Bible* and a bronze 35-in (86 cm) scale model of itself.

Savoy Hotel   [14]
Strand

The Savoy Hotel was begun in 1884 by opera impresario Richard D'Oyly Carte who, 13 years earlier, had financed the adjacent Savoy Theatre. It opened in 1889 as the first hotel in Great Britain to provide private bathrooms, 70 in all, out of a total of around 100 rooms. This was seen at the time to be an incredible luxury and it is said that the builder asked D'Oyly Carte whether he expected his guests to be amphibious! By comparison the Savoy's nearest rival, the Hotel Victoria in Northumberland Avenue, only provided four bathrooms between 500 guests!

Its first manager was Swiss hotelier César Ritz and the first chef, the great Auguste Escoffier. This formidable team elevated the

The forecourt to the Hotel, Savoy Court, is the only road in Great Britain where traffic is required by law to drive on the right hand side. This was originally conferred as a special privilege by Parliament in order that visitors to the Savoy Theatre would be let out of their carriage straight into the theatre, without having to cross Savoy Court. In the early days the forecourt was rubberized in order that guests would not be disturbed by the clatter of horses' hooves.

The most unusual 'member of staff' at the Hotel is Kaspar 'the Savoy cat'. Kaspar is in fact a model who is seated at any dinner party for 13 at the Hotel (thus avoiding the unlucky number).

Savoy to the height of fashion and luxury. The hotel is still world renowned with its Savoy Grill Room, one of London's most famous hotel restaurants.

☎ (01) 836 1533

Somerset House   [15]
Strand

The original Somerset House was the first Renaissance Palace in England, built in 1547–50 for the Duke of Somerset (1506–52), who became Lord Protector of England on the death of Henry VIII in 1547.

Inigo Jones, who designed some of the old palace, died at his Somerset House apartment in 1652 and Oliver Cromwell lay in state here in September 1658. Catherine of Braganza (wife of Charles II) retired to the palace in 1665 and introduced the first ever Italian opera to be performed in England (*c.* 1685).

The palace was demolished in 1775 and the following year Sir William Chambers was appointed as architect for the first block of purpose-built government offices in England.

The most impressive view of Somerset House is the 267-yard (244 m) long façade fronting the Thames. The bronze statue in the courtyard of George III with Neptune at his feet is by John Bacon the Elder (1788).

Somerset House has become best known in modern times as the offices of the General Registry of all births, deaths and marriages in Great Britain. This system of compulsory registration commenced on 1 July 1837 and transferred to St Catherine's House, Kingsway in 1973.

O **Courtyard only Mon–Sat**

'Roman' Bath and Watch House   [16]
Strand Lane

This red-brick bath house was first mentioned and dubbed as 'Roman' in 1784. This is now thought to be unlikely and it may only date back to the early 17th century. Nonetheless, this would still qualify it as London's oldest surviving public bath house.

Note: It may only be viewed from outside.

The Regency style early 19th-century Watch House which overlooks the Bath and the river, was used as a Customs payment point for goods landed here, subject to a tax payable to the church of St Mary-le-Strand.

> *The first public baths in London were Turkish-style baths established by the Romans AD 77-83 in Upper Thames Street. When the Romans left London, so did the custom of public baths and it was not until 1845 that they returned to London at Glasshouse Yard in Docklands.*

St Mary-le-Strand   [17]

The original church of St Mary, *c.* 1143 was demolished to make way for Somerset House in 1548 and was not replaced. A giant maypole reported to be 134 ft (41 m) high—the tallest one ever recorded in England—was put up on the site in 1660. James Gibbs started work on the present baroque-style church in 1714, when the maypole was removed. St Mary's was completed in 1717 and in 1809 John Dickens and Elizabeth Barrow, the parents of Charles Dickens, married here.

> *The first ever rank for Hackney Carriages, the horse drawn predecessor of today's taxis which still retain the name, was established outside the church in 1634.*

Lamb and Flag   [P1]
33 Rose Street

This is the oldest surviving pub in Covent Garden, and is one of London's few original wooden-framed buildings. A building has existed here since 1639 although it has only been a public house since 1772. It used to be known as 'The Bucket of Blood' because of the bare-fist prizefighting that used to go on upstairs. The poet, John Dryden, also suffered a bloody beating here in 1679, apparently in retribution for writing satirical verses about one of Charles II's mistresses. The incident is recorded on a wooden plaque in the passageway adjacent to the pub.

Rules   [R1]
25 Maiden Lane

Established by Thomas Rule in 1798, this is certainly Covent Garden's oldest restaurant and also claims to be the oldest in London still trading on its original site. Its most famous patrons were the Prince of Wales, later to become King Edward VII, and his mistress Lillie Langtry, who dined here secretively in the 1870s. A special doorway leading into a curtained-off alcove was built so that they could enter unnoticed. Their signed portraits are still here to see. Other celebrity diners have included Charles Dickens (who presented to Rules some of his own playbills which still hang on the walls).

☎ (01) 836 5314

Simpson's-in-the-Strand   [R2]
100 Strand

Simpson's was first opened as a traditional English roast restaurant in 1848 and has since become a bastion of English food. The original 1818 building held 'The Grand Cigar Divan' where chess was played by gentlemen who sat on the divans (or sofas) and smoked cigars. The present building dates back to 1904.

The restaurant remains a traditional luncheon meeting place and has received royal patronage from George IV onwards.

☎ (01) 836 9112

THE CITY

General Introduction

The City of London, colloquially known as 'The Square Mile', is the ancient heart of the capital, with its 677 acres measuring in fact just over one square mile. It is therefore the smallest of the 33 administrative departments that make up Greater London. The City boundary is a meandering line which may be crossed unwittingly at many points. The only boundary markers of the modern City are statues of dragons (the badge of the City) which, either singly or in pairs, 'guard' nine points that were formerly the main City entrances.

It is widely accepted that the site of the earliest settlement of London was on the two hills of Cornhill and Ludgate Hill, occupied by the Romans in AD 43.

Just 18 years later London was razed to the ground by the army of Queen Boadicea. It was soon reconstructed, however, and surrounded by London Wall built in the late 2nd century. The powerful independent nature of the City has survived ever since.

The City of London is the oldest municipal corporation in the world. It held its own laws and freedoms before the Norman Conquest and succeeded in negotiating a special charter of similar rights with William the Conqueror in 1066. This was confirmed by Magna Charta and the privileges and wealth of the medieval City assured by the Merchant Guilds.

The shaping of the modern City has been influenced by two dramatic historical events. Firstly, the Great Fire of London in 1666 which razed over 80 per cent of the City and secondly World War II bombing (1940–5) which destroyed one third of the City's buildings and devastated its infrastructure.

In the intervening period between these disasters, London had reached its peak (particularly during the reign of Queen Victoria, 1837–1901) as the centre of the British Empire and the City became established as one of the commercial and financial centres of the world—a vital international role it still plays today.

In common with the business centres of other major cities, the City depopulates drastically in the evenings and at weekends from around 300 000 to its resident population of around 6000.

There are some 50 miles (80 km) of streets, lanes, alleys and various thoroughfares in the City but there is not one single 'road'! The term 'road' only came into use after the street pattern of the City had already become well defined. There is also plenty of greenery in the City with over 190 open spaces (of various sizes) and some 2500 trees tended by the Corporation.

The City of London has its own police force whose uniform is distinguished by its Roman-type helmets and gold-buttons. The minimum height stipulated for a City police-officer is 5 ft 11 in (180 cm) for men and 5 ft 6 in (168 cm) for women, i.e. more than 3 in (8 cm) and 2 in (5 cm) taller respectively than officers in the Metropolitan police!

The Heart of the City—(left to right) Bank of England, Stock Exchange, National Westminster Tower, Royal Exchange.

City Churches

Before the Great Fire the City held 97 parish churches, dating back to Saxon and Norman times. Eighty-nine of these were destroyed and it was decided to rebuild 54. Sir Christopher Wren was commissioned for 51 City churches, all of which have certain common features. The pulpit, the font and the altar are all very prominent with the latter backed by an elegantly carved and painted altarpiece (reredos). The darkwood fittings are the work of many craftsmen, the most famous being Grinling Gibbons, although his work is often attributed and seldom proven in City churches. Most City churches also have decorative wrought-iron, mid to late 17th-century sword rests. These were designed to support the Lord Mayor's ceremonial sword (turned to point upwards in the rest) when he attended City church services.

Almost all of the churches were damaged during World War II and eleven were lost forever. Today there are around 40 City churches which may be visited freely by the public. Most are open Monday to Friday, at least between 10.00 and 16.00 (and for Sunday services). They afford rare havens of peace for tourists and office-workers alike and are often fascinating historical oases in the modern City.

General Notes

To get your bearings in a church, remember the altar is nearly always built at the east end. Architectural terms (without explanation) are avoided in the text with the possible exception of:

Nave: the body of the church where the congregation sits.

Chancel: the extension of the nave where the altar is, reserved for choir and clergy.

Capital: top section of a column, usually decoratively carved.

147

CITY—WEST AND ENVIRONS

This area has been the centre of legal London since the mid-14th century, housing some of the world's oldest surviving legal training establishments, the four Inns of Court. These 'Honourable Societies' are responsible for the training and appointment of barristers, those members of the legal profession entitled to plead in the superior English and Welsh law courts.

The grounds and some buildings of the Inns (refer to text for details) are generally open to the public and provide some of the City's most elegant and peaceful oases. The better known legal face of this area is the imposing Royal Courts of Justice.

This itinerary also encroaches on to Fleet Street, famous as the traditional home of English journalism (see City Central).

Inns of Court

The Inns of Court resemble small University campuses. Much of an Inn comprises rooms which are either offices or residential quarters for practising barristers (inn meant house or mansion in old English). Each Inn has its own dining hall which students must attend 24 times during their period of training to 'eat dinners', as part of their education in not only legal but also social etiquette, and each Inn also has its own library and chapel. The students' academic training, however, is carried out elsewhere at London colleges under the auspices of the Inns of Court School.

St Clement Danes [1]
Strand

The connection of the church with the Danes is thought to come from a 9th-century Danish settlement in the area and it is recorded that King Harold Harefoot (son of Canute) was buried here in the original wooden church. This was replaced around the turn of the 11th century by a stone church. By 1679 this had fallen into disrepair and was rebuilt by Wren in 1680–2. The steeple was added by James Gibbs in 1719. The church was gutted in December 1941.

St Clement Danes is famous for England's best known church-bell chimes 'Oranges and lemons say the bells of St Clement's' according to the 18th-century children's nursery rhyme (see also St Clement Eastcheap). An orange and a lemon have been given to each child of the St Clement Danes Primary School at the annual service on 31 March every year since 1920, commemorating the restoration of the church bells.

In post-war years the church has been adopted by the Royal Air Force. The ashes of England's most famous RAF hero, Douglas Bader, who flew into combat with two artificial legs, are in the crypt. Dr Samuel Johnson was a regular church-goer here and a plaque inside, and statue outside, commemorate him.

In front of the church entrance stands the huge memorial to W E Gladstone. He held four Prime Ministerial terms but always failed to charm Queen Victoria, who once complained of his dour manner, 'He speaks to me as if I were a public meeting'!

O ♿ **1 step**

Twining's [2]
Devereux Court, 216 Strand

Thomas Twining began his business here in 1706 as Tom's Coffee Shop but in 1717

I *Tea was first sold in England in 1670 at Thomas Garraway's Coffee house in Exchange Alley, Cornhill. It cost the exorbitant price of between 16 and 50 shillings (80p–£2.50) per pound. It was, however, recommended 'for the cure of all disorders'!*

---

changed to the more fashionable beverage of tea. Twining's hold the London longevity record for the same family on the same site in the same business.

O ♿ **1 step**
☎ **(01) 353 3511**

Wig and Pen Club [3]
229–30 Strand

This is an eating and drinking club for lawyers and journalists. The club is made up of two old timber framed houses, No. 229 which dates from 1625 and No. 230 built some hundred years later. Internally, it is a quaint old building leaning at various angles and claims the only wooden suspended staircase (i.e.

Law and the Gothic order—the Royal Courts of Justice.

Fish-eye view of Twining's—providing Londoners with their 'Rosie Lee' since 1717.

without any external support) in London. This dates from 1625 and is the club's only original feature.

O The club may normally be viewed by non-members before 11.30 but overseas visitors (with passport) may be granted free temporary membership.
☎ **(01) 583 7255**

Royal Courts of Justice ('The Law Courts') [4]
Strand

These remarkable buildings were designed by George Street and built 1874–82. They resemble more a fairy-tale Bavarian castle than the home of English civil law, complete with Gothic turrets.

Modern extensions now provide a total of 60 law courts in over 1000 rooms (all upheld by 35 million bricks). These courts hear the majority of English civil law cases that have been brought to the High Court. These include the bankruptcy courts at the rear of the complex in Carey Street (from which the old saying 'to be in Carey Street', meaning financially ruined, derives).

The highlight of the annual calendar of the Law Courts is the second Saturday in November, the Lord Mayor's Show. The newly elected Lord Mayor will enter the Law Courts where he promises to perform his

13. CITY—WEST AND ENVIRONS

1 St Clement Danes
2 Twining's
3 Wig and Pen Club
4 Royal Courts of Justice ('The Law Courts')
5 Temple Bar Monument
6 Prince Henry's Room

Temple
7 Middle Temple Hall *
8 Temple Church

9 St Dunstan in the West
10 Dr Johnson's Memorial House
11 Public Record Office Museum
12 Staple Inn
13 Prudential Assurance Building

Gray's Inn

Lincoln's Inn *
14 Lincoln's Inn Old Hall
15 Lincoln's Inn Chapel
16 Lincoln's Inn New Hall and Library

17 Lincoln's Inn Fields
18 Sir John Soane's Museum *
19 Old Curiosity Shop

Pubs
P1 Ye Olde Cock Tavern
P2 Ye Olde Cheshire Cheese
P3 The Cittie of Yorke
* Specially recommended by author

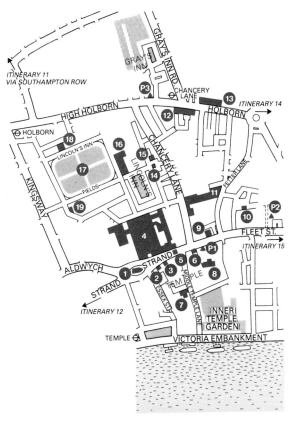

duties and signs the Declaration before the Lord Chief Justice and Judges.

O **Mon– Fri 09.30–16.30**
☎ **(01) 936 6000**
Note: Courts in session may be visited by the public (children must be 14+) 10.00–16.30 except during summer recess in August and September.

Temple Bar Monument [5]
Fleet Street/Strand

This huge monument, built in 1880 by Horace Jones, features the largest of the City's 12 dragons (see City General Introduction) guarding the City's 'royal entrance'. Since Queen Elizabeth I passed through Temple Bar in 1558 a brief ceremony is always enacted on state occasions. The Sovereign will request of the Lord Mayor permission to enter the City. The Lord Mayor will then offer the Pearl sword as a sign of loyalty. The Sovereign will touch the sword to signify that it should be kept in the safe hands of the Lord Mayor and it is then carried before the Sovereign to show that they are in the City under the Lord Mayor's protection.

The panels on the base of the monument depict Queen Victoria entering the City in 1837 and Wren's old Temple Bar gateway monument. Wren's gate was built c.1670 and from 1684 until 1746 was used to display the heads of executed traitors. It eventually became a major traffic obstruction and was removed in 1888. (It now stands in Theobald's Park, Hertfordshire.)

Prince Henry's Room [6]
17 Fleet Street

Prince Henry's room has stood over the gateway to the Inner Temple since 1610 and is the oldest surviving domestic dwelling in the City. It boasts a rare original Elizabethan timbered façade and a well preserved interior. It was named in honour of Prince Henry, the son of James I who became Prince of Wales in 1610. It is now used to exhibit Samuel Pepys memorabilia.

O **Mon–Fri 13.45–17.00, Sat 13.45–16.30; p;**
☎ **(01) 353 7323**

Temple

The Temple comprises the Inner Temple (to the east) and the Middle Temple (to the west)—two of the four Inns of Court. (Outer Temple, further to the west, no longer exists as a legal entity.) There is no physical division between the Inns although the Inner Temple property carries the badge of a winged horse whilst Middle Temple's insignia is the Lamb of God.

The Temple takes its name from the Order of the Knights Templar, an Order of monastic knights founded in France in 1118 to protect travellers on their pilgrimage to the Holy Land, a number of whom settled in the Temple area in 1162. These Crusaders in turn took their name from the place of pilgrimage—the Holy Temple of Solomon in Jerusalem. In 1312 the Order was disbanded by Pope Clement V, after false confessions of devil worship were extorted from the Templars in order to seize their wealth and lands. The Temple then briefly passed to the other monastic fighting Order of that period, the Knights Hospitaller of St John (see St John's Gate). They were already accommodated at Clerkenwell, so the land was leased to the legal profession in 1320 and granted freehold in 1608.

The Temple was the last area of London where gas lights were lit manually until 1986 when the 'last lamplighter in London' was superseded by automatic switching devices!

Grounds: O Daily 08.00–20.00

Middle Temple Hall [7]

This magnificent hall built by Edmund Plowden c.1562–70 acts as a dining hall for students and members of Middle Temple and contains much original Elizabethan woodwork. This includes a double hammerbeam roof structure, a huge intricately carved Elizabethan screen and a table reputedly made from the hatch of Sir Francis Drake's Flagship *The Golden Hind*. Suits of armour dating from the same period (late 16th century) surround the hall. The Hall's collection of royal pictures includes an equestrian painting of Charles I attributed to Van Dyck.

O Mon–Fri 10.00–12.00; 15.00–16.00 when Hall is not in use. Closed BH and PH.

☎ **(01) 353 4355**

Temple Church   [8]

The round Temple Church was constructed by the Knights Templar in 1185 as a model of either the Church of the Holy Sepulchre or the nearby Dome of the Rock in Jerusalem. It was visited and consecrated by Heraclius, Patriarch of Jerusalem, in the presence of Henry II. It is the only circular church in London and one of only four Temple Churches in Britain (Holy Sepulchre, Cambridge; Holy Sepulchre, Northampton; Ludlow Castle Chapel).

Extensive restoration work in the 19th century unfortunately swept away much of its medieval character and the round section of the church suffered major interior damage in May 1941. The 13th-century effigies of Crusader Knights on the church floor have been restored to their original appearance and around the walls are a number of stone-carved 'grotesque Gothic heads that gape and grin'. These are said to represent souls in heaven and hell.

In the north aisle stands the richly decorated 16th-century altar tomb of Edmund Plowden (d 1584), builder of Middle Temple Hall. On the south wall lies an excellently preserved 13th-century Purbeck marble effigy of a bishop, possibly Heraclius of Jerusalem. The altar-piece was carved by William

Emmett in 1682 under the direction of Christopher Wren.

O ♿ (1 step)

St Dunstan in the West   [9]
Fleet Street

St Dunstan was built 1829–33 by John Shaw on the site of a church first mentioned in 1237. It boasts two unusual London firsts: its clock, made in 1671 for the sum of £35 was the first public clock to tell the time in minutes, and the statue of Elizabeth I by Kerwin (1586) is the earliest public statue of an English monarch. (A 14th-century statue claimed to be King Alfred was removed form the site of Westminster Hall in 1822. It now stands in Trinity Church Square in Southwark.)

St Dunstan is also notable for its statues of early English mythical figures. Inside the doorway of the church stand 16th-century statues of King Lud and his two sons and above the church the giants Gog and Magog strike the church bell (see Guildhall).

In 1653 the world's most famous encyclopaedia of fishing, Izaak Walton's *Compleat Angler* was published in a workshop in St Dunstan's churchyard and there is a memorial window and plaque in honour of the author.

Note: Often closed to the public.

Dr Johnson's Memorial House   [10]
17 Gough Square

This is the only surviving house in which Dr Samuel Johnson was resident in London and is the only original house in this courtyard, dating *c*.1700.

Dr Johnson lived here from 1749 to 1759, paying a rent of £30 per year and it was in this house that he compiled his famous Dictionary. He had already started work on it in 1747 but it was here in the attic, aided by six clerks, that he completed it after a further six years. This was the first definitive and comprehensive English dictionary and became the standard language reference for around a hundred years. A first edition, published in 1755, is on display in the dining room.

The most curious of the *memorabilia* relating to Johnson and his contemporaries is a brick from the Great Wall of China, donated to the 'Johnson Club' in 1922. Johnson once stated that he would dearly like to see the world's longest wall but his wish was never realized. The donor of the brick probably considered that bringing part of the wall to him, even 138 years after his death, was the next best thing!

O May–Sept, Mon–Sat 11.00–17.30; Oct–Apr 11.00–17.00; £ ☎ (01) 353 3745

Dr Samuel Johnson (1709–84)

Dr Johnson arrived in London in 1736 and was to spend 19 long years earning a meagre living as a freelance writer until the publication of his Dictionary in 1755. This catapulted him to instant fame and he became the centre of London's literary world. Standing well over 6 ft (1.80 m) tall and of heavy build he was a giant of his day. According to his biographer, James Boswell, he was 'a man of most dreadful appearance, slovenly and with an uncouth voice. Yet his great knowledge and strength of expression command vast respect and render him very excellent company'. He formed the Literary Club, a select gathering of wits and intellectuals and it is as a wit that he is best remembered. His most famous quotation is also the most often heard tribute to London 'When a man is tired of London, he is tired of life; for there is in London all that life can afford'.

Public Record Office Museum [11]
Chancery Lane

This spectacular mock-tudor building, designed by James Pennethorne in 1860, is the national archive of central government

and legal documents. This is the most complete set of records of any nation state in the Western World, due largely to Britian's freedom from invasion since 1066. At 1 January 1988 the total collection occupied over 350 000 ft (107 km) of shelving.

The oldest and most valuable document (and the only one on permanent display) in the Museum is the Domesday Book. This was the first comprehensive survey of England ever undertaken—ordered by William the Conqueror in 1085 to evaluate the lands and resources of his recently acquired kingdom. It is a fiscal inventory, a feudal statement and a legal record. The name 'Domesday' (Day of Judgement) meant that its evidence was final and not subject to appeal.

Temporary displays of other famous documents will include such favourites as:
Shakespeare's will (1616)
Guy Fawkes' confession (1605)
Nelson's log book from HMS *Victory* (1805)

O Mon–Fri 10.00–17.00 ☎ (01) 876 3444

Staple Inn [12]
Holborn

Staple Inn was founded in 1378 and became part of Gray's Inn in 1529. Its name originates from its use as a wool warehouse and market place (wool traders used to be known as 'Staplers').

Staple Inn was originally an Inn of Chancery which functioned as a school for Chancery clerks (see Lincoln's Inn Old Hall) and as a preparatory school for the Inns of Court. There were at one time or another some 30 such Inns but by the end of the 17th century they had ceased to perform a useful function and they were disbanded and eventually demolished. Today the only Inns of Chancery buildings that survive are Barnard's Inn Hall and Staple Inn.

Natural History Museum revisited—the Prudential Assurance Building, Alfred Waterhouse's other great Gothic Revival structure in London.

The front of the Inn facing on to Holborn is the only surviving half-timbered Elizabethan terrace in London, dating from 1586.

The Hall was built in 1580 but was destroyed by a flying bomb in 1944. It was rebuilt in 1950 and retains its original windows which had been removed during the war.

Prudential Assurance
Building [13]
Holborn

Alfred Waterhouse's huge red brick and terracotta building was constructed in 1879, concurrent with his other London masterpiece, the Natural History Museum. It is the last major Gothic revival work to be built in London.

The building occupies the site of Furnival's Inn—one of the Inns of Chancery (see Staple Inn) dissolved in 1817. Just inside the yard a plaque and a bust commemorate Charles Dickens who had lodgings in Furnival's Inn from 1834 to 1837 where he wrote most of *Pickwick Papers*.

Gray's Inn

Gray's Inn stands on land formerly belonging to Sir Reginald le Gray, the Chief Justice of Chester. The hall and lands of the Gray family were passed on to the lawyers in 1370 and the name and the golden Griffin emblem have been retained ever since.

The Inn has notable Shakespeare connections through the Bard's patron, the Earl of Southampton, who was a member of Gray's Inn. In 1594 *Comedy of Errors* was premièred in the Hall. The Inn's most famous member was Sir Francis Bacon (1561–1626), philosopher, statesman and part of Shakespeare's literary circle. It has frequently been claimed, though never proven, that he may have been the true author of Shakespeare's works. Bacon's statue stands in South Square.

> *Sir Francis Bacon's advanced philosophy of science and practical experimentation resulted in the first ever frozen chicken which Bacon himself packed with snow at Highgate Hill in 1626. The chicken was well preserved but Bacon was rather less fortunate. He contracted a chill which developed into pneumonia and his eventual death. Bacon's Lane, off Highgate Hill, recalls the fateful experiment.*

The Hall dates from 1556 but only the walls are original. It was gutted by bombing in 1941 and has been rebuilt as a replica (not open to the public). Charles Dickens was apprenticed at No. 1 South Square to a solicitors' firm in 1827 for a wage of 13s 6d (67½p) per week.

Grounds O Daily 08.00–19.00

Lincoln's Inn

Lincoln's Inn is the oldest of the four Inns of Court with legal records dating back to 1422, although the Inn may have been in existence for some 75 years before then.

The name is thought to derive from the Earl of Lincoln who formerly owned the land the Inn stands partly on and whose lion emblem the Inn has incorporated into its badge.

Lincoln's Inn New Hall—the centrepiece of the oldest of the Four Inns of Court.

Lincoln's Inn claims the most distinguished membership list of the four Inns, including eleven Prime Ministers dating from the first, Sir Robert Walpole, to Mrs Margaret Thatcher. The 18-year-old Oliver Cromwell studied at the Inn in 1617 and his room is believed to have been above the Chancery Lane gatehouse.

Grounds O Mon–Fri 08.00–19.00;   ♿ **use Lincoln's Inn Fields gateway.**

> *Charles Dickens who worked as a lawyer's clerk in Lincoln's Inn New Square in 1828, used the Old Hall as the setting for scenes in* Bleak House *(published in 1853)—a damning indictment of the period's obscure and laborious legal machinery.*
>
> *Dickens's view was echoed in reality 18 years later when in 1871 the Tichborne personation case, spanning 1025 days, became the longest trial in British history.*

Lincoln's Inn Old Hall [14]

The Hall began construction in 1490 and was restored in 1924. A window on the east side (visible from outside) commemorates Sir Thomas More, who at the age of 18 in 1496, became the Inn's youngest ever bencher (one of the committee of barristers who presides over the Inn's affairs).

King Charles II and the royal party took dinner here in February 1672. Tradition has it that everyone dined and drank so well that there was some difficulty in finding a bencher able to rise to propose the Loyal Toast. Since then, the Honourable Society of Lincoln's Inn has enjoyed the unique privilege of drinking the Loyal Toast sitting down.

The hall was used as the High Court of Chancery (the division of the High Court particularly concerned with property disputes) from 1737 to 1882.

O T only Mar–Sept Mon–Fri 09.30–11.30 (depart from Lincoln's Inn Fields Gate) inc. Chapel and New Hall; £

Lincoln's Inn Chapel [15]

The foundation stone of the chapel was laid by John Donne, Chaplain of the Inn and Dean of St Paul's Cathedral, in 1620. The Chapel bell is said to have been brought back from Spain in 1596 as part of the spoils of Cadiz. For at least a century it has been the custom to ring the bell between 12.30 am and 1.00 pm when news of the death of a bencher is received. It was reputedly upon hearing the toll of the Chapel bell and observing the lawyers anxious for news of the demise of a colleague that Donne wrote the immortal lines 'No man is an island entire of itself . . . Any man's death diminishes me because I am involved in Mankind, And therefore never send to know for whom the bell tolls; it tolls for thee'.

The chapel boasts a well-preserved undercroft where in past centuries unwanted babies could be left in the knowledge that the lawyers would care for them.

O Mon–Fri 12.00–14.30; T (see Old Hall)

Lincoln's Inn New Hall and Library [16]

Philip Hardwick's original 1845 building was extended in 1871 by Sir George Gilbert Scott, the designer of the interior of the hall. The library collection which dates from 1497 is one of the oldest in London, comprising some 130 000 legal volumes.

O T only (see Old Hall)

Lincoln's Inn Fields [17]

One of the earliest mentions of Lincoln's Inn Fields records that this was a jousting ground in 1150 for the Knights Templar (see Temple). Although the Fields later became a fashionable place in which to live, they have a bloody history. In 1586 Anthony Babington and 13 co-conspirators were hanged, drawn and quartered here for plotting against Queen Elizabeth I. A plaque in the bandstand in the middle of the Fields commemorates the last execution here in 1683 of Lord William Russell who was beheaded for treason. The square of buildings around the field began construction in the 1630s and has the distinction of being the oldest surviving traditional square and the largest public square, 6.84 acres (2.76 ha) in London.

The only original surviving house is No. 59–60 credited to Inigo Jones (1640). Spencer Perceval, the only British Prime Minister ever to be assassinated, lived here between 1790 and 1807.

Sir John Soane's Museum [18]
12–14 Lincoln's Inn Fields

In terms of layout and size this extraordinary labyrinthine museum is the most unusual collection of art treasures and antiquities in London. It was formerly the home of the designer and architect, Sir John Soane (1759–1837) and has been preserved in its original condition—an eccentric 18th-century 'time capsule'.

The tiny Picture Room is remarkable in itself, so designed as to accommodate enough pictures to fill a gallery more than three times its length. In order to save space, the walls consist of a series of hinged panels which open out to reveal the pictures hung behind. The most famous of these are the two series by William Hogarth, *The Rake's Progress* (1735) which charts the rise and fall of a young rake about town and *The Election* (1755-8) which satirizes the greed and corruption of such an event. In the New Picture Room and Ante-Room hang works by Turner and Canaletto.

The largest and most valuable treasure amongst Soane's huge collection of funerary objects is the sarcophagus of Seti I (1303–1290 BC) from the Valley of the Kings.

O Tues–Sat 10.00–17.00;   T Sat 14.30
☎ **(01) 405 2107**

William Hogarth (1697–1764)

Hogarth was England's first great native painter and has been called the only true cockney painter, as he was born near Old Bailey, lived in Leicester Square and never worked out of London. He was principally a satirical artist, levelling his brush against the prevailing social evils and excesses of 18th-century society. His best known works, aside from those in Sir John Soane's Museum, are *Marriage à la Mode* (1745) (in the National Gallery), *The Harlot's Progress* (1732) (paintings destroyed, original engravings in Hogarth's House) and *Gin Lane* (1751) (engraving only, at Hogarth's House). The latter plumbs the depths of degradation of London street life where gin (then untaxed) is consumed in vast quantities by the masses—'Drunk for a penny and dead drunk for two pence' was the popular ironic maxim of the day. Hogarth's paintings may also be seen at the Tate Gallery and the Thomas Coram Foundation. Most of his original

A curious question—was it really the model for the novel?

engravings are on display at Hogarth's House, his country summer retreat in Chiswick.

Old Curiosity Shop [19]
13-14 Portsmouth Street

This is a rare example of an Elizabethan London building which is perfectly intact in its original form and is open to the public. It was built in 1567 and is thought to have first been used as a dairy, served by cows grazing on Lincoln's Inn Fields. It became one of London's many 'Curiosity' shops in 1780 and although there is much debate about whether or not this was the model for Dickens' famous novel of 1841, it is certain that the author would at least have known this shop. Around 1883 Mr Clayton Clarke (Dickens' illustrator, better known as 'Kyd') suggested to the shop proprietor that he should add the words 'Immortalised by Charles Dickens' to the shop front.

This is the only 'Curiosity' shop of the Dickens era that is still standing in London; it is also claimed to be the oldest shop in London.

Note: Also open on Sunday

The shop was the fictional home of Little Nell—the young heroine who obsessed the public and Dickens alike during his serialization of the book. Her 'killing off' reduced both author and public to tears (see Dickens's House).

Ye Olde Cock Tavern [P1]
22 Fleet Street

The 'Cock' lays claim to be the oldest of the many historic public houses in Fleet Street, dating originally from 1549, although at that time it stood on the other side of Fleet Street and the present building dates from 1887. The original cellars still run beneath Temple Church and its most prized relic is its 17th-century pub sign—a splendid wooden cock said to have been carved by Grinling Gibbons—displayed in a glass case behind the ground floor bar.

Samuel Pepys is said to have carried out some of his many flirtations in the Cock. Other regular customers included Charles Dickens and Alfred Tennyson, who commemorated the pub in verse:

'O plump head-waiter at The Cock
To which I must resort
How goes the time? 'Tis five o'clock,
Go fetch a pint of port.'

A similar order nowadays would not only cause heads to turn but wallets to empty as at 1989 prices a pint of port at The Cock would cost over £10.

☎ (01) 353 3454

Ye Olde Cheshire Cheese [P2]
Wine Office Court, 145 Fleet Street

This ramshackle building survives in its original form from 1667. It is one of London's least altered pubs and its old wooden furnishings and sawdust 'carpet' help to make it one of the most atmospheric. It claims patronage by Charles Dickens, Samuel Johnson and many other literary names.

☎ (01) 353 6170

The Cittie of Yorke [P3]
22-3 High Holborn

A pub has stood on the site of The Cittie of Yorke since 1430, although from 1695 to the 1890s it was called Gray's Inn Coffee House. The present building was reconstructed as The Cittie of Yorke in the late 19th century, using much of the old original material. The long row of vats (barrels) ranging from 500 to 1100 gallons (2273–5000 l) tucked beneath the trussed wooden beams is a particularly impressive sight.

☎ (01) 242 7670

CITY—NORTH

The area to the north of Holborn Viaduct and London Wall lay mostly outside the original Roman Wall and did not become part of the City until much later.

The Barbican, the City's newest settlement, dominates the north of the City and was built (somewhat ironically) just outside the old protective boundary wall.

St Bartholomew-the-Great   [1]
West Smithfield

This is London's oldest church, founded in 1123 by Rahere, Henry I's court jester, and was once part of a much larger priory. The existing church is approached through the restored 13th-century porch of a 16th-century timbered gatehouse. This used to be the main entrance to the priory which extended from here towards the church. It was pulled down after the Dissolution in 1537.

St Bartholomew-the-Great escaped both the Great Fire and bombing but during the 18th century it was occupied and damaged by industrial workshops. The Lady Chapel was used as a printer's office where in 1725 Benjamin Franklin, the American statesman and scientist, worked. Restoration work was carried out by Sir Aston Webb in the late 19th century. The tower dates from 1628 and contains five medieval bells, claimed to be the oldest complete set in London. The chancel is the finest of any church in London, matched only by the Chapel of St John in the Tower of London, where the structure of

massive Norman piers supporting a gallery is similar.

The unusual and pretty oriel window protruding from the south gallery was built in 1515, perhaps to oversee offerings placed on the tomb of Rahere (built c. 1500) opposite. There are many 16th- and 17th-century monuments around the walls, one of the finest of these is dedicated to Edward Cooke (d 1652) in the south ambulatory. The font dates from the 15th century and is the only medieval example in a City Church. William Hogath was baptized here in 1687.

O ℓ 80%
Note: Closed on Fridays

Nos. 41 and 42 Cloth Fair   [2]

Nos. 41 and 42 Cloth Fair are rare picturesque examples of houses erected shortly

---

Cloth Fair takes its name from Bartholomew Fair, which was held annually at Smithfield from the early 12th century until 1855. It was originally England's premier cloth fair but developed into a lively general entertainment fair in the 17th century and was made famous by Ben Jonson's play of the same name. It was eventually discontinued due to increasing public nuisance and replaced by Smithfield Market.

after the Great Fire (*c.* 1670) (both have been much restored).

St Bartholomew's Hospital   [3]
West Smithfield

This is the oldest hospital in London to occupy its present site. It was founded in 1123 by Rahere (see St Bartholomew-the-Great) who, after surviving a bout of malaria on a pilgrimage, had vowed to build a hospital in London on his return. In 1544 it was refounded by Henry VIII whose statue (1702) stands over the hospital gatehouse. This is London's only outdoor statue of Henry VIII.

The hospital chapel of St Bartholomew-the-Less was founded in 1184 and rebuilt in the 15th century. Much of the tower and the arches below it survive from the 15th century but its unusual octagonal interior is mostly Victorian.

The Great Hall (first door left in court-yard) was built by James Gibbs between 1730 and 1759. Its staircase features two large works by William Hogarth (a hospital governor) dating from 1735 to 1736.

The panelled ceiling and walls are original and there are two excellent 17th-century wooden statues of crippled and wounded servicemen which used to stand at the gate of the hospital. A stained glass window dating *c.* 1664 shows Henry VIII giving the hospital its charter. Portraits of famous surgeons include William Harvey, chief physician in 1609–33 during which time (*c.* 1628) he discovered the nature of blood circulation.

O **Great Hall Mon–Fri 09.00–17.00**

Smithfield Market   [4]

Smithfield Market is the largest dressed-meat market in the world, covering an area of over 10 acres (4 ha). It employs around 3000 people and sells over 350 000 tons of meat every year. It was established in 1638 and despite its insanitary conditions and nuisance to the public, continued as a 'live' mar-

ket until 1855. The majority of the existing building dates from 1868.

Its name derives from the original flat, grassy 'Smoothfield', part of which still remains in front of St Bartholomew's Hospital. It was formerly the site of Bartholomew Fair (see Cloth Fair) and between the 12th and 16th centuries was also one of the principal sites of public executions. The 'speciality' of Smithfield was death by fire. A plaque on the wall of St Bartholomew's Hospital commemorates some of the 200-strong 'noble army of martyrs' who died here during the persecution of Protestants by 'Bloody' Mary Tudor (Mary I). Another plaque commemorates the famous Scottish patriot William Wallace 'put to death near this spot on 23rd August 1305'. Witches and heretics were also burned, roasted or boiled alive at Smithfield (see London Dungeon). These barbaric executions continued here until the mid-17th century.

Smithfield's most historic moment occurred in June 1381 when the 14-year-old Richard II attempted to negotiate personally with Wat Tyler, the leader of the Peasants' Revolt here. Tyler had led a march of some 60 000 men on London and a wake of destruction followed him. Despite this, the boy King had only a handful of bodyguards present. Accounts vary of what exactly happened but as Tyler and the King met, angry words and gestures ensued and Tyler was stabbed by the Lord Mayor. As the peasants prepared to avenge their leader, the alert Richard, now totally at their mercy, saved himself by invoking the prestige of kingship and crying 'Sirs, will you kill your King. I am your captain. I will be your leader. Let him who loves me follow me'. The peasants, convinced the King would grant their reform, dispersed. Richard's promises were later overruled by Parliament and many an execution followed to deter further rebellions.

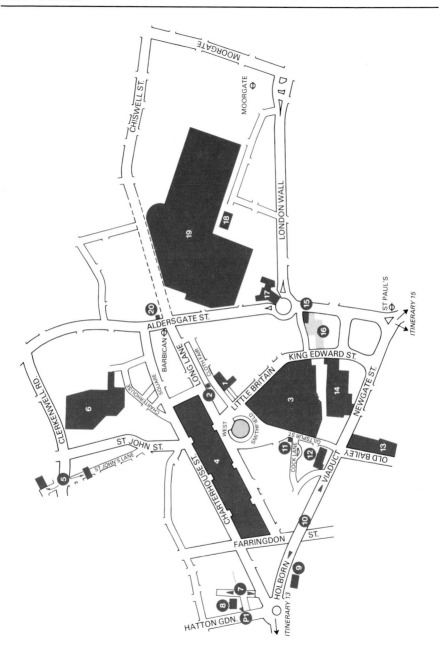

14. CITY—NORTH

Late 19th-century view outside Smithfield meat-market with St Bartholomew's Hospital in the background.

St John's Gate and Priory Church of St John [5]

St John's Gate, St John's Lane

This is one of the oldest surviving gatehouses in London, dating from 1504. It was formerly the entrance to the Priory of the Order of St John (the Priory was burned down by Wat Tyler's peasant army in 1381).

The Order was founded at the beginning of the 12th century in Jerusalem, composed of religious men with a particular duty to care for the sick. The Order soon assumed a military role and the Knights Hospitaller of St John were formed to defend the Crusaders' kingdoms in the Holy Land, Cyprus, Rhodes and Malta. The Order was suppressed in 1540 by Henry VIII but was revived in the late 19th century and led to the formation of today's St John Ambulance Brigade (a voluntary first aid service for the public).

Little remains of the original gatehouse building or its rooms. These consist of

163

the Chapter Hall, the Old Chancery, the Council Chamber, Library and Coin Room, all mostly rebuilt in the late 19th century. A small museum traces the history of the Order, including rare armour used at Rhodes and Malta in the 15th and 16th centuries.

Priory Church of St John, St John's Square

Only the undercroft survived Wat Tyler's destruction of 1381. This is one of London's few Norman buildings still in existence, probably built in the mid-12th century. There is a splendid 16th-century alabaster effigy of Don Juan Ruyz de Vergara, the head of the Castile Order, and an impressive tomb effigy of William Weston, the last prior of the Order. It was said that he died of a broken heart (probably a heart attack) on the day the Act of Dissolution was passed.

The church above was gutted during the war and retains little of historical interest.

O Museum—Tues, Fri, Sat 10.00-18.00; &. 100%;   other rooms and church by tour only (no &.), 11.00 and 14.30;   £ ☎ (01) 253 6644

Charterhouse   [6]
Charterhouse Square

Charterhouse was founded as a Carthusian monastery in 1371, built on a burial ground containing a large number of victims of the Black Death. Its name is a corruption of Chartreuse, the monastery's motherhouse near Grenoble in France.

The rules of the monastery were strict—monks lived and ate alone, except on Sundays, donned hair shirts in penance and had no personal possessions. The most famous member of their community was Sir Thomas More, from 1499-1503. During Henry VIII's Church Supremacy they were persecuted and even infiltrated by Thomas Cromwell's agents. The prior was executed and his arm hung over the priory gate as a grim warning. After the Dissolution the monastery was con-

verted to the private mansion of Sir Edward North who twice entertained Queen Elizabeth and her courtiers lavishly (a dubious privilege of great expense, said to have bankrupted him). In 1611 Charterhouse school was founded and became one of England's chief public schools. John Wesley, the founder of Methodism, and Lord Baden-Powell, the founder of the Boy Scouts Movement, both attended. The school moved away in 1872 and Charterhouse was badly damaged by bombing in 1941. Little remains of the 14th-century buildings but the 16th-century Great Hall and Great Chamber have been restored to almost their original splendour and various contemporary out-buildings survive.

Charterhouse is still a place of residence, with the Hospital of King James, a home for elderly Anglican members, which has existed here since 1611.

O by tour only (1 hour) Apr–July Wed 14.45 (not following PH);   £

Ely Place   [7]

This private road (locked at 22.00 each evening) was originally the site of Ely House, the London residence of the Bishop of Ely from the late 13th century until 1772. (Until the suppression of their powers in 1642, bishops were often powerful statesmen required to attend the king's court and Parliament.)

John of Gaunt moved into Ely House in 1381 and it is from there, according to Shakespeare in *Richard II*, that he delivers his

---

Henry VIII used Ely House for a banquet lasting five days in 1531. The bill of fayre included 100 sheep at 2s 10d (14p) each, 91 pigs at 6d (2½p) each, 24 great beefs at 26s 8d (£1 34p) each, one ox at 24s (£1 20p), 37 dozen pigeons at 10d (4p) a dozen, 340 larks at 5d (2p) a dozen, and 13 dozen swans (no price recorded for these, probably a royal present).

famous speech 'this sceptred isle, this blessed plot, this earth, this realm, this England'. Sir Christopher Hatton, the favourite of Elizabeth I, and from whom Hatton Garden takes its name, was the last distinguished resident of Ely House, from 1576 to 1591. Its only surviving part is its chapel, St Etheldreda.

St Etheldreda [8]
Ely Place

St Etheldreda was the chapel of the Bishops of Ely and is the only surviving part of Ely House (St Etheldreda was a 7th-century Abbess of Ely). It is Britain's oldest existing Catholic church, founded in 1251, and the only church in London (excluding Westminster Abbey) to contain surviving work from the reign of Edward I (1239–1307). It escaped the Great Fire but suffered damage during World War II.

The upper part of the church was probably used as the private chapel of the Bishops. It retains most of its original roof, walls and the intricate tracery of its magnificent windows. The royal coat of arms at the entrance to the chapel dates from the 17th century. The original function of the undercroft is unknown—it may have been the chapel for local worshippers. During the 16th century it was used for offices and for a short period was converted into a tavern. Its walls are 8 ft (2.5 m) thick and may even be of Roman origin.

St Andrew, Holborn [9]
Holborn Circus

St Andrew is the largest of Wren's parish churches, built in 1690 on the site of Saxon and Norman churches. Little remains of Wren's original building due to severe war damage. The large City parish it served in the early 19th century is indicated by the church records for 1820 which include 1552 baptisms, 746 burials and 456 weddings.

The tomb of Thomas Coram (see Thomas Coram Foundation) was removed to here

from the Coram Hospital, together with the 18th-century pulpit, font and organ, the latter being a gift from Handel to the Coram Foundation. Opposite the tomb is a commemorative tablet to hospital pioneer William Marsden.

> ■ *In 1827 Marsden found a young woman dying on the steps of the churchyard and being unable to gain admission for her at any hospital without payment or letters of recommendation from a subscriber, he was moved to found England's first free hospital across the road in Hatton Garden in 1828. It later became the Royal Free Hospital and is now in Hampstead.*

Holborn Viaduct [10]

Holborn Viaduct consists of a series of arches constructed between 1863 and 1869, stretching 1400 ft (427 m) across the old valley of the River Fleet in order to provide flat access east into the City. It was a major feat of engineering in its day, dislodging some 2000 people, but all that is now visible of Holborn Viaduct is the centre span of 120 ft (37 m) which crosses Farringdon Street. The other viaduct sections are hidden by buildings.

> ■ *In 1882 the first electric power station in London was established at 57 Holborn Viaduct by the Edison Electric Company. The nearby City Temple became the first church in Britain to be lit by electricity and the Viaduct Tavern became the first pub so lit.*

Cock Lane [11]

Cock Lane has a colourful history of City low-life. It is thought to have derived its name from a nearby cock-fighting pit and in the 14th century was the only licensed walk for prostitutes in the City.

The corner of the lane with Giltspur Street, known as Pie Corner, is traditionally one of the points where the Great Fire was halted and in grateful memory of this a gilded statue of a cherub (or fat boy as it is also called) was erected here.

Around the turn of the 19th century a pub named the Fortune of War stood on this corner. It was frequented by body snatchers (also known as 'resurrectionists')—men who made money from stealing bodies and selling them to surgeons for research purposes. The 'merchandise' was laid out on the benches around the walls of the pub for inspection and collection by the surgeons of St Bartholomew's Hospital.

St Sepulchre-without-Newgate [12]
Holborn Viaduct

St Sepulchre is the City's largest parish church and was founded by Rahere (see St Bartholomew-the-Great) in 1137 on the site of an old Saxon church. The name is taken from the Holy Sepulchre in Jerusalem and a piece of stone from that building is displayed in the church. St Sepulchre was rebuilt in 1450 and despite Great Fire damage, the fan-vaulted porch and the arches under the tower are original. Wren's master mason, Joshua Marshall, rebuilt the present church in 1670.

St Sepulchre has a close association with the old Newgate prison (see Central Criminal Court) and at midnight, before the next day's execution, a bellman would walk along a tunnel which connected the church to the prison, tolling the bell and shouting into the condemned cell:

'All you that in the condemned hold do lie
Prepare you for tomorrow you shall die
And when St Sepulchre's bell tomorrow tolls
The Lord have mercy on your souls.'

The full text of this final dreadful message, together with the bell, dating from 1605, is displayed in a glass case on the south aisle of the church. The entrance to the old tunnel, now bricked up, is still visible.

Sir Henry Wood (1870-1944) of Albert Hall Promenade Concerts fame, learned to play the organ here and his ashes lie in the Musician's Chapel. Captain John Smith, governor of the first English settlement in Virginia, is buried in the south chapel. A plaque recalls the famous episode of his capture by Red Indians and escape from death due to the pleading of the Chief's daughter, Pocahontas.

Central Criminal Court ('Old Bailey') [13]
Old Bailey

The Central Criminal Court, which exercises criminal jurisdiction over Greater London, takes its more familiar name from the street on which it stands, where a Motte and Bailey, a Norman type of castle is reputed to have once stood. It houses 19 court rooms and 70 cells for prisoners kept in custody. Inscribed above the front entrance is the legend 'Protect the children of the Poor and Punish the wrongdoer'. Its most famous symbol is the bronze lady of Justice standing on the dome, holding a sword in one hand and the scales of justice in the other. This is the only unhooded figure of justice on a courthouse in the world and is also the highest outdoor statue in London, measuring from the ground to the top 212 ft (65 m).

The Court was first built in 1539 as a sessions house of the infamous Newgate Prison which dates back in one form or another to the 11th century. Newgate was the most infamous prison of its day described as 'a prototype of hell' by the famous 18th-century magistrate, Henry Fielding (see Royal Opera House—Bow Street Runners). Amongst its many suffering inmates, probably the most remarkable was the highwayman, Jack Sheppard, who effected two escapes despite being handcuffed, manacled and chained to the floor on the second occasion!

Public executions were transferred to Newgate from Tyburn in 1783 and took place on a scaffold near the corner of Newgate Street. The last beheading in the United Kingdom happened here in 1820 when the Cato Street conspirators, who had planned to murder the cabinet, were first hanged and then decapitated with a surgeon's knife. The last public execution in England took place at Newgate in May 1868, when Michael Barrett was convicted and hanged for the bombing of Clerkenwell Prison in which 12 died. Executions were then carried out inside Newgate's walls and were marked by a black flag and the tolling of the bell of St Sepulchre.

Many did not even survive to stand on the gallows, dying as a result of the insanitary conditions in Newgate, where a virulent form of typhoid, known as gaol fever bred. The appalling stench of the prison used to waft into the adjacent courts and to hide this, judges held posies of sweet smelling flowers, also thought to protect against infection. In recollection of dreadful conditions such as these, judges today still carry posies on ceremonial occasions like the Opening of the Law Courts and the Lord Mayor's Show.

O Mon–Fri 10.30–13.00, 14.00–16.00. Closed Aug and first two weeks in Sept. Note: must be 14+ yrs; expect to queue for important cases

National Postal Museum [14]
London Chief Post Office, King Edward Street

This small museum houses the most important and extensive collection of postage stamps in the world. The Phillips Collection and the Post Office Collection contain virtually every British stamp ever issued and the Berne Collection is the most complete record of stamps issued world-wide since 1878.

The most famous is the Penny Black, the world's first adhesive postage stamp put on sale on 1 May 1840, the proofs of which are held here. The largest stamp ever issued is the Express Delivery of China, 1913, which measures 9.75×2.75 in (247.5×69.8 mm).

O Mon–Thur 10.00–16.30;
Fri 10.00–16.00
☎ (01) 432 3851

St Botolph, Aldersgate [15]
Aldersgate

St Botolph, dedicated to a 7th-century patron saint of travellers, was founded during the 13th century. It was completely rebuilt in 1788–91 and although it looks forbidding from the outside, it holds a rare example of a completely preserved, late 18th-century interior. Its elaborate baroque ceiling and its organ case are particularly attractive. On the east wall is a stone-carved tomb *c.* 1563, the oldest survivor from the previous church.

Postman's Park [16]
Aldersgate

This small tranquil area was opened in 1880, its name derives from the nearby post office. Its principal feature is a unique memorial wall of ceramic tiles, dedicated to ordinary members of the public who all died in heroic acts of self-sacrifice. The youngest of these was 'William Fisher, aged nine, lost his life on Rodney Road, Walworth while trying to save his little brother from being run over, July 12 1886'. The idea of such a national memorial was conceived by the English painter and sculptor, George Frederick Watts and the wall was dedicated in 1900. In all, 53 heroic deeds are commemorated, dating from 1871 to 1927. It is indisputably London's most sentimental memorial site.

O ♿ 1 step

Museum of London [17]
London Wall

The Museum of London opened in 1976 and holds the most complete record of all significant aspects of the capital's history, from prehistoric times to modern day.

Prehistoric (c. 250 000 BC–AD 42) The oldest implement in the Museum is a flint hand-axe (*c.* 250 000 BC) used as an all-purpose tool by a hunter. By 1200 BC London's earliest metal working industry was established; as evidence, amongst other finds, are the bronze swords (*c.* 1000 BC) on display. An iron-age dagger *c.* 550 BC, is one of the earliest pieces of British iron-ware and continues the progress of methods of manufacture.

Roman (AD 43–c. 400) The central feature is a reconstruction of three Roman rooms and the largest and most complete mosaic pavement found in London, dating from the 3rd century. Another great treasure is the collection of sculptures from the Temple of Mithras (see Temple of Mithras) particularly the head of the god Mithras, late 2nd, early 3rd century. Curiosities include a pair of leather bikini-style trunks and fine debris from Boadicea's sack of London in AD 61, including skulls of some of her decapitated victims. Two notable 'first' exhibits are the earliest Christian emblem found in London on a 4th-century bowl, and the earliest known piece of writing containing the name of London (Londini) on a wine jug, AD 70–90.

A vantage window looks on to remains of the Roman fort, built *c.* AD 120–30, which stood at the north west corner of the London Wall. This would have housed the official guard of the Governor of Britain and some 1000 troops.

> ▌ The *Roman London Wall was built between AD 190 and 220. It was thought to be between 15 ft and 20 ft (4–6 m) high, up to 8 ft (2.5 m) thick and encircled 330 acres (133 ha). It was repaired and partly rebuilt in the Middle Ages, the last occasion being in 1476. Notable remains can be seen at 21 sign-posted sites around the City.*

The plain modern exterior of the Museum of London belies the treasure trove contained within.

Medieval (c. 400–1484) Amongst the exhibits from London's early Dark Ages is a large 6th-century silver gilt brooch, the first piece of early Anglo-Saxon jewellery found in the area. Exhibits marking Viking attacks and Danish occupation include weapons dating from *c.* 793–5, a penny coin struck *c.* 886, possibly to commemorate King Alfred's recapture of London from the Vikings, and a carved stone slab from a Danish tomb at St Paul's Cathedral. Moving on, the Museum boasts one of the largest collections of medieval pottery in Europe, dating from the late 13th to early 14th century. Late 14th-century pilgrims' badges are interesting early souvenir items of the London to Canterbury journey to the shrine of St Thomas à Becket.

Tudor (1485–1602) A display of printed works includes the earliest printed view of London from *The Chronicle of England* by

Wynkyn de Worde, 1497, and an engraved copper plate, *c.* 1558, which was a part of the earliest map of London. Exhibits illustrating development of trading include Thomas Gresham's weighing beam, 1572, thought to be from the Royal Exchange. The most colourful collection is the Cheapside Hoard, a goldsmith's stock-in-trade of typical period jewellery, stones and cameos, *c.* 1580–1620. This is a very rare find as, apart from high quality royal jewellery, little else of this period survives.

Early Stuart (1603–66) This represents the most dramatic period of London's history which included the English Civil War, the execution of Charles I, the Restoration, the Great Plague and the Great Fire. The events are recalled by relics of Charles I, the death mask of Oliver Cromwell, a contemporary painting of the coronation procession of Charles II (and the earliest surviving examples of royal souvenir pottery from 1660), a plague bell, rung to announce the corpse collector and 'The Fire Experience'—a model of burning London with readings from the Diary of Samuel Pepys.

Late Stuart (1667–1713) The anti-catholic scapegoat hysteria following the Great Fire is summed up by the 'Papish Plot' slab erected in Pudding Lane in 1681. Clubs and balls used for the game of paille maille (see Pall Mall) and Samuel Pepys' chess set show a lighter side of London. A wealthy room interior is recreated.

Georgian (1718–1800) A section of old Newgate Prison is reconstructed here, including its actual, forbidding iron-clad door (see Central Criminal Court). To add insult to injury, or rather cost to extreme privation, prisoners had to provide their own food and furniture or they could hire a prison bed at 8d (3½p) per week. This is contrasted by London's expanding building programme, its growth as a financial centre and manufactured treasures of this period which include the finest quality Chelsea porcelain (1760s).

19th century (1801–80) Two notable seats are exhibited, a leather chair belonging to Charles Dickens and the 19th-century woolsack from the old House of Lords. A model of the Crystal Palace and relics from the Great Exhibition of 1851 commemorate London's greatest ever show (see Hyde Park).

Imperial (1881–1910) The central feature is a reconstruction of shops (such as tobacconist's, barber's, draper's, tailor's and grocer's), offices (bank manager's, lady telephonist's, etc) and a small pub.

20th century (1911 to date) The most impressive exhibits are the magnificent wrought iron and bronze decorated lifts used by Selfridges during the 1920s. The exhibit with the best story to tell is a small unexploded incendiary bomb. These became commonplace amongst war-hardened Londoners but not everyone was so cool as to take them to the bomb disposal centre by bus, as happened to this one!

Lord Mayor's stage coach This gilded coach took six months to make in 1757 and cost £860. It is used once a year by the newly elected Lord Mayor of London, who will travel in it in a carnival procession known as the Lord Mayor's Show from Mansion House to the Royal Courts of Justice, where he or she will take oaths. This is the most colourful day in London's social calendar and the Gold Coach is the centre piece. It is surrounded by the Lord Mayor's personal bodyguard of pikemen and musketeers and many richly decorated floats.

O Tues–Sat 10.00–18.00; Sun 14.00–18.00; C; ♿ t 100%; H
☎ (01) 600 3699

St Giles without Cripplegate [18]
Fore Street

A church has existed here since at least the 11th century. It was rebuilt in the 17th cen-

On the terrace at the Barbican Centre.

tury and escaped the Great Fire but was gutted in 1940. Its distinctive tower, built in 1682, survived. John Milton (1608–74), the author of *Paradise Lost*, is buried in the chancel. His grave was opened in 1793 and his last five teeth, a rib bone and tufts of his hair were stolen. The coffin was then put on display at sixpence (2½p) per viewing. Oliver Cromwell was married here in 1620 and other famous parishioners have included John Bunyan (*Pilgrim's Progress*) and Daniel Defoe (*Robinson Crusoe*).

> *Cripplegate was the oldest of the eight City Gates, initially built by the Romans, and its name is thought to derive from the old word crepel, meaning covered way, which may have gone from the gate to the watch tower. It was demolished in 1760.*

Barbican Centre   [19]

Barbican means watch-tower or outer defence to a city wall. It is thought that the name was first applied to a medieval watch-tower close by although fortifications were initially built by the Romans (see Museum of London).

The Barbican Arts and Conference Centre is the largest development of its kind in Western Europe. Its buildings cover 20 acres (8 ha) and are on ten levels, the lowest point being 17 ft (5 m) below sea level. It began construction in 1968 and opened in 1982. The initial cost estimate was around £17 million but the major disruption caused by building around the existing residential site resulted in a final cost of £153 million.

The Centre boasts one of London's largest art galleries—constantly changing with the emphasis on 20th-century and contemporary works—and theatre halls purpose-built for the London Symphony Orchestra and the Royal Shakespeare Company—the latter being the largest theatre company in the world. It also comprises a cinema, restaurants, cafés, a pub and shops. In addition, there are daily exhibitions and concerts given free in the foyer.

The Barbican flats is the only residential community in the City, built on land laid waste during 1940, and opened in 1962. The 2011 private flats which make up the largest block in Britain stand on a 40-acre (16 ha) site and accommodate around 6000 people. The tallest of these blocks is the Shakespeare Tower which, at 419 ft 2.5 in (128 m), is the tallest residential building in Great Britain.

O Centre Mon–Sat 09.00–23.00;   Sun and PH 12.00–23.00;   Art Gallery Tues–Sat 12.00–21.00;   Sun and BH Mon 12.00–18.00;   Both よ t 100%;   H ☎ (01) 638 4141

Royal Britain   [20]
Aldersgate Street

Royal Britain is an audio visual exhibition of over 2000 years of royal British history, stretching back in time from today's Royal Family to powerful tribal chiefs such as Queen Boadicea. It features 51 British monarchs and is divided into 25 self-contained areas, each devoted to a specific episode in royal history.

O Daily, 10.00–18.00;   £;   よ t 100% ☎ (01) 588 5858

Ye Olde Mitre Tavern   [P1]
Ely Court

The original Mitre Tavern was built in 1546 for the servants of Ely House (see Ely Place). The present small, cosy pub was rebuilt in the 18th century. It is thought that the mitre attached to the wall on the first floor outside the pub may have come from the Bishop of Ely's gatehouse and in the front bar is the preserved chunk of a cherry tree around which Queen Elizabeth I is said to have danced.

☎ (01) 405 4751

CITY—CENTRAL

This part of the City is dominated by its greatest landmark, St Paul's Cathedral, which looks down on the featureless main thoroughfares of Cheapside, Cannon Street and Queen Victoria Street. There are still bustling alleyways conforming to the old medieval street patterns where pubs, restaurants and small shops abound, but these are increasingly rare. Bow Lane is probably the best surviving example. The most famous street of this area is Fleet Street. Although many of its newspapers have now moved away, the street still retains some of its 'Pen and Ink' atmosphere.

Fleet Street's first newspaper and England's first regular daily paper, The Daily Courant *based at Ludgate Circus, was issued in 1702.*

Guildhall [1]
Guildhall Yard

The first Guildhall, which was the government headquarters of the City, is recorded *c.* 1128 although its earliest courts were held at least a century before then. The City's governing body is the Corporation and its policies are decided by the Court of Common Council, one of England's oldest surviving assemblies, formed in 1295. The Guildhall's most important annual ceremonies are the election of the Head of the Corporation—the Lord Mayor, and the Lord Mayor's Banquet.

Little is known about the ancient Guildhall and the present Guildhall was built 1411–39. It was then the second largest hall in England (after Westminster Hall) at 152×49 ft (46×15 m), and was used for important trials including that of Lady Jane Grey in 1553 (see Tower of London). The building was badly damaged during the Great Fire and the Blitz but the exterior medieval walls have survived and the two outstanding features are its original porch (remodelled) and its crypt covering 4500 sq ft (418 sq m). It is thought that the west side of the crypt even pre-dates the Guildhall, going back to the second half of the 13th century.

Monuments in the Guildhall commemorate some of England's greatest heroes, including Sir Winston Churchill (1955), Lord Nelson (1810) and The Duke of Wellington (1857). The banners around the Hall represent the 12 principal City Livery Companies. These are (clockwise) the Vintners, Salters, Merchant Taylors,

Excavations made next to the Guildhall in February 1988 have discovered the remains of London's Roman amphitheatre. This is thought to have been built between AD 70 and AD 140 and would have been oval-shaped, stretching around 109 yd (100 m) by 87 yd (80 m) with its arena in the space now occupied by Guildhall Yard. It would probably have been used for military weapons training and drill and public spectacles such as animal baiting and possibly gladiatorial combats. (At the time of writing the future of the site is undecided.)

Goldsmiths, Drapers, Mercers, Grocers, Fishmongers, Skinners, Haberdashers, Ironmongers and Clothworkers. The City livery companies were mostly formed between the 12th and 15th century, originally as craft guilds whose members wore a distinctive livery (uniform). There is today a total of 94 companies representing such diverse trades from Air Pilots to Woolmen. Their modern functions are largely educational and charitable.

The two figures at either side of the west gallery are the legendary giants Gog and Magog, who represent the conflict between the ancient Britons and the Trojan invaders, who supposedly founded New Troy 1000 years before the Christian era, on the site where London now stands. These giants are modern, replacing similar 18th-century figures destroyed in 1940.

O **May-Sept daily 10.00-17.00; Oct-Apr Mon-Sat 10.00-17.00;**
& **t 100% (not crypt)**
☎ **(01) 606 3030**

Guildhall Clock Museum [2]
Aldermanbury

This single-room museum contains over 700 clocks, watches and marine chronometers dating back to the 15th century. Some of the more interesting exhibits are a 15th-century German wall clock—a fine example of the earliest type of house clock and a late 16th-century pocket watch said to have been owned by Mary Queen of Scots—in the shape of a skull which has to be flipped open to tell the time.

O **Mon-Fri 09.30-17.00;**
& **access via Guildhall**
☎ **(01) 606 3030 ext 2868**

St Lawrence Jewry [3]
Gresham Street

The first church on this site was built on the edge of the Jewish trading area in 1136. It was destroyed in the Great Fire and rebuilt by Wren in 1671-87. The church was gutted in

Rush hour at the turn of the century, 9am outside Mansion House (left).

15. CITY—CENTRAL

1 Guildhall *
2 Guildhall Clock Museum
3 St Lawrence Jewry
4 Mansion House
5 St Stephen Walbrook *
6 The London Stone
7 St Mary Abchurch
8 St Michael Paternoster Royal
9 St James Garlickhythe
10 Temple of Mithras (remains)
11 St Mary Aldermary

12 St Mary-le-Bow
13 Statue of Queen Anne
14 Paul's Cross
15 St Paul's Cathedral **
16 College of Arms
17 St Benet, Paul's Wharf
18 St Bride

Pubs/Restaurants
P1 The Blackfriar
R1 Sweetings

'Poor Queen Anne' before St Paul's Cathedral.

1940 but sensitive restoration has recaptured the spirit of Wren's church. The Lord Mayor and Corporation have worshipped here since 1820.

O ⚹ (1 step)

Mansion House [4]
Mansion House Street

This is the official residence of the Lord Mayor of London during his year of office. It was designed by George Dance (the Elder) and constructed 1739-52 at a cost of over £70 000.

With the exception of the visiting Sovereign, the Lord Mayor is the single most important person in the City—'the Champion of Civic liberties, seeking always to dignify citizenship and to advance the welfare and status of the City'. He, or she, becomes the head of the City Corporation, the Chief Magistrate of the City and will preside over all the significant meetings of City officers, including the policy body, the Court of Common Council (see Guildhall). An additional office conferred on the Lord Mayor is Admiral of the Port of London. The year of exalted civil and social responsibility will take in, on average, a banquet per day, some of which will be funded personally by the Lord Mayor who will also be expected to make around 1000 speeches.

The office of Lord Mayor dates back to 1192 and was first held by Henry Fitz Ailwyn. The most famous Lord Mayor was Sir Richard ('Dick') Whittington who was elected Lord Mayor on four occasions (see Sir Richard Whittington). The first female Mayor was Lady Donaldson, elected in 1983.

Mansion House is unique in being the only private house in Britain to have its own Court of justice. It also has eleven cells, its most famous former inmate being the suffragette leader Emmeline Pankhurst.

Amongst the many privileges granted to the Lord Mayor is the right to be buried in St Paul's Cathedral (if he or she dies in office) and access to the password of the Tower of London.

O By appointment only
☎ (01) 626 2500

St Stephen Walbrook [5]
Walbrook

Originally founded in the 11th century on the bank of the old Walbrook stream, St Stephen burned down in the Great Fire and was rebuilt by Wren in 1672-9. It has been described as the most majestic of Wren's parish churches due in large part to its excellent dome, which was a 'rehearsal' for the great dome of St Paul's Cathedral. It has been further enhanced by major restoration work (1978-87) and the striking contrast of gleaming white marble floor and columns against 17th-century darkwood fittings is unequalled in London. It also boasts London's most controversial altar-table. This unusual round 8.5-ton block was designed by Henry Moore in 1972 and has been likened to a giant Camembert cheese!

The Samaritans, an organization of anonymous volunteers, created to help the suicidal and desperate, was started in the crypt of St Stephen's in 1953.

The London Stone [6]
Cannon Street

The London Stone is an unmarked piece of limestone set behind an iron grille in the outside wall of the Oversea-Chinese Banking Corporation. Its origin and purpose is unknown but the most popular theory suggests that it was a Roman milestone from which all distances in the Province would be measured. As the Roman Governors' Palace has recently been discovered beneath Can-

> *The London Stone seems to have been an important symbol of the City in the Middle Ages. During the second major Peasants Revolt of 1450, the leader of the Kentish rebels, Jack Cade (calling himself John Mortimer) is said to have struck the Stone with his sword, proclaiming 'Now is Mortimer Lord of the City'.*

non Street railway station (opposite), this theory is quite plausible.

St Mary Abchurch   [7]
Abchurch Yard off Cannon Street

The medieval church of St Mary, dating back to the 12th century, was destroyed in the Great Fire and rebuilt by Wren in 1681–6. Its architectural *tour de force* is its dome, measuring over 40 ft (12 m) across. It was painted in 1708 (by a parishioner who was paid £170) and in the centre is the name of God in Hebrew characters. The church's woodwork has been described as a 'treasury of 17th-century art'. Its unique and finest feature is the carving on the reredos, the only authenticated work by Grinling Gibbons in any City parish church.

St Michael Paternoster Royal   [8]
College Street

The church of St Michael dates back to the 13th century and takes its name from two old thoroughfares, Paternoster Lane and La Riole (corrupted to Royal), a Bordeaux wine centre with which local vintners traded. Sir Richard (Dick) Whittington who lived in College Street rebuilt the church in 1409, possibly intending it to be a burial place for his wife (who died about this time) and himself. Whittington was buried here in 1423 but his tomb perished along with the church in the Great Fire. Wren rebuilt St Michael's in 1686–94 but it was gutted in 1944. A new window on the south side depicts young Dick Whittington and the gold-paved City streets.

Sir Richard (Dick) Whittington

The folk legend of Dick Whittington tells of the poor ill-treated orphan and his faithful cat, making their way to the gold-paved streets of London. In reality, Whittington was never poor. He was born in 1360, the third son of a Gloucestershire knight and made his fortune as a mercer (trading in cloth) before going on to become Lord Mayor for one short term in 1397 (upon the death of the incumbent Lord Mayor) and for three full terms in 1397/8, 1406/7 and 1419/20. He became one of medieval London's greatest benefactors, providing funds for many causes, including old Newgate gaol, St Bartholomew's Hospital, St Thomas's Hospital (a ward for unmarried mothers, so that they could remain anonymous) the Guildhall (especially the Library) and alms houses which still function today. This may explain why his memory has been so fondly, if falsely, perpetuated.

The story of his feline companion, too, is probably just part of old European folk-lore which often featured a cat leading its owner to riches. Other explanations put forward Whittington's trading barges, then commonly nicknamed 'cats', and a 17th-century portrait which initially depicted Whittington holding a small skull which was later painted over to become a small cat in order to give the picture more sentiment. (See also the Whittington Stone, Highgate.)

St James Garlickhythe   [9]
Garlick Hill

The church is first mentioned *c.* 1170 and takes its name from the dock (hythe) close by where garlic was unloaded and sold. It was destroyed in the Great Fire and rebuilt by Wren 1676–83. The church's registers survived the Fire, however, and are claimed to be the oldest in England, dating back to 1535. Its interior is the tallest of any of the City parish churches and is splendidly filled at its west end by an original 1697 organ built by Father Smith—one of the great 17th-century organ makers.

Temple of Mithras (remains) [10]
Temple Court, Queen Victoria Street

In 1954 building excavation a few yards from the present site uncovered the remains of the first and only Roman building in London of which there is a complete plan. The discovery of the marble head of Mithras—the Persian sun-god—was conclusive evidence that here was a Mithraic Temple dating from the late 2nd century. The cult of Mithraism which survived until the late 4th century valued strength, courage and action and was popular amongst the Roman legions. The excavated Temple attracted an estimated 100 000 visitors within five days of its discovery. It was then moved the short distance to where it is now, in order to allow new building work to go ahead on the original site. The Museum of London houses its finds.

Cockney flower seller within easy earshot of Bow Bells.

St Mary Aldermary [11]
Queen Victoria Street

The 16th-century church of St Mary burned down in the Great Fire and only the bottom section of its tower remains. It was rebuilt by Wren in 1682, unusually for him, in Gothic style with high arches and plaster-cast fanvaulting. It was damaged in World War II but has been restored. Impressive furnishings include the door cases, the prettily decorated organ and a rare wooden sword-rest dating from 1682.

St Mary-le-Bow [12]
Cheapside

The original Saxon church on this site was replaced by a Norman church *c.* 1090. The Norman crypt is the oldest ecclesiastic structure in the City and its bowed arches are thought to have given the church its name. The church's most famous feature is its bells, one of which has tolled to mark curfew within the City since the Middle Ages. This probably accounts for the notion that in order to qualify as a Cockney (i.e. a true Londoner) a person must be born within the sound of Bow Bells. The Norman church burned down in the Great Fire and Wren rebuilt the present church in 1670–83. Its 217 ft (66 m) high spire was described in its day as the finest in Europe. The church was gutted in 1941 and the interior is completely modern.

The term cockney derives from the old English coke-ney meaning a cock's egg (i.e. a mis-shapen egg) and applied to people, it meant an effeminate or simple person. In time it was applied specifically to mean a Londoner, usually pejoratively, but nowadays is commonly used, without disrespect, to describe both Londoners and their accent.

The Tijou Gates and the top of the High Altar in St Paul's Cathedral.

Statue of Queen Anne   [13]
Front of St Paul's Cathedral

This is an 1886 replica of Francis Bird's original statue, erected in 1712. Bird's monument was vandalized on several occasions and a contemporary satirist, referring to the Queen's drinking habits and the fact that the statue faced away from the church, wrote 'Brandy Nan, Brandy Nan, you're left in the lurch. Your face to a gin shop, your back to the church'.

> *'Poor Queen Anne' had 17 pregnancies, more than any other British monarch, yet produced only five live births and none of the children lived to adulthood to survive her. She was consequently the last Stuart monarch.*

Paul's Cross   [14]
St Paul's Cathedral Churchyard

The site of the original Paul's Cross, which was a wooden pulpit, is marked close by the existing Cross that was erected as a memorial in 1910. Up until the early 14th century it was compulsory for citizens of the City to meet there quarterly to discuss City affairs. It remained an important medieval meeting place where proclamations were made and politics discussed. The historian Thomas Carlyle described it as, 'the *Times* newspaper of the Middle Ages'.

St Paul's Cathedral   [15]

A church dedicated to St Paul has existed here since AD 604. The first St Paul's was a small circular wooden church built by England's first Christian king, Ethelbert. It burnt down and was rebuilt in stone, AD 675-85. This second church was destroyed by the Vikings in AD 961. Its successor, too, burnt down and the construction of 'Old St Paul's' began in AD 1087. On completion it was the longest cathedral in England at 600 ft (183 m)

and its roof covered an area of 9 acres (4 ha). After the destruction of the central tower of Lincoln Cathedral in 1548 it became the world's tallest structure thanks to its 489 ft (149 m) high spire built in 1315. This was destroyed by lightning in 1561 and not replaced. Old St Paul's became the focus of City life and as a holy building was much abused. John Evelyn, the 17th-century diarist, records that the nave ('Paul's Walk') was ankle deep in horse manure from 'men leading mules, horses and other beasts' through it as a shortcut from Ludgate into the City. Business transactions were conducted on top of the tombs and font, and during the Civil War Cromwell's troops used the nave as a cavalry barracks.

In 1663 Christopher Wren was asked to effect repairs to Old St Paul's. He recommended that it should be completely remodelled but this was rejected. Three years later it burned down completely in the Great Fire and so paved the way for Wren's design. It was not until nine years later, however, that Wren's plans were finally accepted and the foundation stone was laid in 1675. Although Wren's only engineering resources were manpower and pulleys, Parliament became exasperated by the slow rate of progress of St Paul's and halved Wren's meagre salary of £200 per annum. After 35 years the final (and highest) stone was put into position in the lantern by Wren's son in 1710. The first English cathedral to be built under the supervision of a single architect was complete.

St Paul's exterior length is 515 ft (157 m) and in total it covers 87 400 sq ft (8119 sq m). The west front of St Paul's is probably the most familiar cathedral face in the world. It is 180 ft (55 m) wide, the lower portico columns are 40 ft (12 m) high and the upper are 32 ft 6 in (9.91 m). St Paul stands on the apex with St Peter to the left and St James to the right. The towers are 212 ft (65 m) high and in the right hand tower hangs Great Paul, the heaviest hung bell in Great Britain at 16 tons 14 cwt (17 002 kg). It was installed in 1882

St Paul's Cathedral

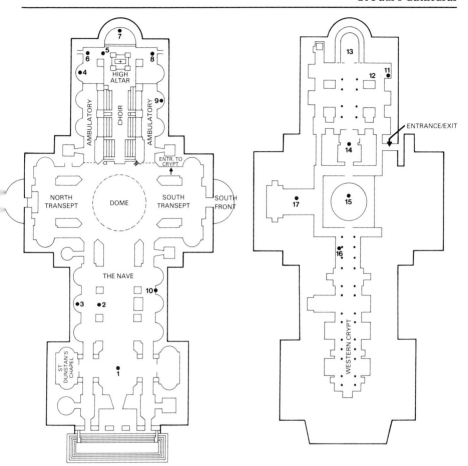

St Paul's Cathedral

1 St Paul's Watch Memorial Stone
2 The Wellington Monument
3 Memorial to General Charles Gordon
4 Statue of Mother and Child by Henry Moore
5 Sanctuary Screen
6 Chapel of Modern Martyrs
7 American Memorial Chapel
8 Lady Chapel
9 Statue of John Donne
10 The Light of the World

St Paul's Cathedral Crypt

11 Tomb of Sir Christopher Wren
12 Painters' Corner
13 Chapel of the Order of the British Empire
14 Tomb of the Duke of Wellington
15 Tomb of Admiral Lord Nelson
16 Tombs of Admiral Beatty and Admiral Jellicoe
17 Treasury

and since then has been ringing every week-day at one o'clock for five minutes (originally to call the apprentices from the fields for their lunch).

Nave

St Paul's Watch Memorial Stone [15.1]
The St Paul's Watch was a group of around 100 volunteer fire-fighters who 'by the grace of God saved this Cathedral from destruction in war, 1939–45'. The worst night was 29 December 1940, when 28 incendiary bombs had to be dealt with. (A famous photograph of St Paul's surrounded by the burning City on three sides is displayed next to St Dunstan's Chapel.) St Paul's was said 'to ride the sea of flames like a great ship' and became a symbol of the survival of London during the War.

The Wellington Monument [15.2] This huge monument to Victorian England's greatest soldier is the largest in the Cathedral and it took Alfred Stevens from 1855 to 1875 to complete it. The equestrian statue of the Duke atop the monument was added in 1912 (see Crypt)—a somewhat late addition as a previous Dean would not give permission for a statue including a horse, however heroic, to be in 'his church'!.

Memorial to General Charles Gordon (1833-85) [15.3] The epitaph to one of England's great generals, 'he saved an empire by his warlike genius', is ironic. A hero of the Chinese campaign and ex-governor of Sudan, Gordon was sent out of retirement back to Sudan to evacuate the British garrison. He chose instead to stay and fight and was killed on the steps of Khartoum Palace—just two days before the relief column arrived.

Dome

St Paul's boasts the second largest dome of any church or cathedral in the world (after St Peter's, Rome). The inner diameter of St Paul's dome (within the Whispering Gallery)

is 107 ft (33 m) and the total exterior height from the church pavement to the top of the cross surmounting the dome is 365 ft (111 m). The concept of a dome, instead of the more usual steeple, was at the time revolutionary—St Paul's is still the only English cathedral with a dome. It also gave Wren a major design problem. He had observed that domes which looked good from the outside looked too tall when viewed from within and that, conversely, domes which looked good from within looked flat and uninteresting on the outside. Therefore, in order to meet his objectives both inside and outside, Wren constructed an interior as well as exterior dome and in between a third conical shaped brick dome to support the weight of the 700-ton stone lantern, golden ball and cross. As the dome was nearing completion, Wren was precariously hauled up inside a basket to make regular inspections. The monochrome frescoes depict events in the life of St Paul and were painted in 1715 by James Thornhill.

During the painting Thornhill was inches away from falling to his death when absent-mindedly stepping backward from his platform to view the work on the 218 ft (66 m) high dome. His quick-thinking assistant saw the danger and, rather than risk calling to him, he started to daub over Thornhill's masterpiece. Enraged, the artist sprang forward, and so to safety!

There are 627 steps to the top of St Paul's, passing through four galleries. At 100 ft (30 m) is the Whispering Gallery, so named because of its remarkable acoustics which will transfer a whisper from one side quite audibly to the other. In ascending order follow the Stone Gallery, the Inner Golden Gallery and the Outer Golden Gallery from which a marvellous City panorama can be enjoyed. Immediately beneath the centre of the dome on the Cathedral floor a compass design adorns a grille containing Wren's epitaph. It may be translated as:

'Beneath lies buried the founder of this church and city, Christopher Wren, who lived more than ninety years not for himself but for the public good. Reader, if you seek his monument, look around you.'

(Immediately beneath this is Nelson's tomb —see Crypt.)

North Transept

The North Transept Chapel is dedicated to the Middlesex Regiment and contains various military memorials, including a huge font, sculpted by Francis Bird in 1726. The North Transept was bombed during the war and the balcony above the doorway was destroyed. In order to serve as a reminder of St Paul's darkest days it was never rebuilt and Wren's perfect symmetry is therefore broken. The memorial to Sir Joshua Reynolds (1813) commemorates the 'Prince of the painters of his age', buried in the Crypt below.

Choir and High Altar (View from Nave)

Close to the choir steps a floor tablet marks the place where Sir Winston Churchill's catafalque stood on 30 January 1965, the Cathedral's most distinguished funeral service this century.

The brilliant mosaic work on the saucer domes was carried out in 1891–1912 and depicts (from foreground to background) the beasts of the field, including tigers and elephants; the creatures of the sea; the birds of the air; Christ in Majesty.

The choir stalls and organ case are two of the greatest works of the master-carver Grinling Gibbons.

The organ, originally built in 1695 (rebuilt 1973–7), is reckoned to be one of the finest in the world—even though Wren once referred to it as 'a box of whistles'!

In 1940 the high altar area was destroyed by a bomb but the present baldachino (canopy) over the altar (with its massive twisted oak pillars) is as Wren would have wished. The Cathedral's most famous recent celebration on this spot was the wedding of Prince Charles to Lady Diana Spencer on 29 July 1981.

Behind the high altar may be seen the only stained glass in the upper part of the Cathedral (in the American Memorial Chapel).

Wren originally planned for plain glass to be used throughout St Paul's. Victorian restoration taste, however, dictated stained glass. This was blown out during the War and replaced with plain glass, thus allowing a clear view of its architecture as Wren wished.

Ambulatory

Statue of Mother and Child by Henry Moore [15.4]   This is one of the last great

George Swan Nottage, Lord Mayor of London, d 1885—the final privilege of office.

achievements of the best known 20th-century English sculptor. A modern rendition of motherhood and compassion, it was installed in 1984.

Sanctuary Screen [15.5]   The ornamental ironwork by the French mastercraftsman Jean Tijou is considered to be his finest work in England. The 'Tijou Gates' were made at his Hampton Court workshop *c.* 1695-7.

Chapel of Modern Martyrs [15.6]   The most famous of the recent martyrs commemorated in this chapel is Stephen Biko (d 1977). The figure of Christ at the altar was saved from the bombed Victorian reredos.

American Memorial Chapel [15.7] The roll of honour lists the names of some 28 000 Americans based in Britain who lost their lives in World War II. It was presented by General Dwight D Eisenhower in 1951. The oak stalls on either side of the altar contain medallion portraits of Eisenhower and Queen Elizabeth II. The beautifully-carved limewood garlands include birds, fruits and flowers of the United States (and hidden in between even a rocket!).

Lady Chapel [15.8]   Although the Chapel is modern, the table is the Cathedral's original high altar and the statue of the Virgin and Child was part of the Victorian reredos.

Statue of John Donne (1572-1631) **[15.9]** This statue, by Nicholas Stone, was the only figure to survive intact from Old St Paul's and is one of the Cathedral's greatest treasures. Donne, one of St Paul's most celebrated Deans, posed for the statue which is wrapped in a sheet to represent his funeral shroud.

▌*Passing along the Ambulatory is the Prebendaries' Vestry. Fixed on either side of the wall are two holy relics—a piece of stone from Solomon's Temple and a fragment of Herod's Temple brought here from Jerusalem in 1886.*

The scorch-mark on the urn below is a rare tangible survivor of the Great Fire of 1666.

South Transept
England's greatest naval hero, Admiral Lord Nelson, is commemorated here by a statue of Britannia pointing him out to two young boys as a model for emulation. His three greatest victories, the Nile, Copenhagen and Trafalgar are named on the monument. It was at Copenhagen in 1801 that Nelson passed into folklore by deliberately disobeying his Admiral's signal to withdraw from his assault on the Danish Fleet in 1801: 'I have only one eye—I have a right to be blind sometimes . . . I really do not see the signal'.

A huge monument to Nelson's contemporary, Lord Cornwallis (1738–1805), represents him as Governor General of Bengal. He is more famous in American history books as the General who surrendered the final battle of the War of Independence at Yorktown in 1781.

The Light of the World [15.10]   Painted by William Holman Hunt in 1904, this is the third and largest version of one of the world's most celebrated religious pictures. It shows Jesus bringing a light (i.e. his love) to a door that has been long shut—as can be seen by the creepers and brambles around it. Hunt's message is therefore that the door to 'The Light of the World' can only be opened from the inside.

The Crypt
Corresponding in floor size with the church above, the crypt is the largest in Great Britain. It contains over 350 memorials and over one hundred tombs.

Tomb of Sir Christopher Wren (1632–1723) **[15.11]**   Appropriately Wren was one of the first to be buried in the Crypt. His tomb is marked by a plain black marble slab adjacent to the Cathedral foundation stone. The epitaph echoes that above (see the Dome); family members are buried around him.

Painters' Corner [15.12] The most famous of the many English painters buried here are:
Joseph Mallord William Turner (1775–1851), probably England's greatest artist (see Tate Gallery).
Sir Joshua Reynolds (1723–92), first President of the Royal Academy of Art (see Burlington House) and the leading portrait artist of his day.
Sir John Everett Millais (1829–96), a founder of the Pre-Raphaelite school of art (see Tate Gallery). Millais' most famous work is *Bubbles*—the picture of the young girl immortalized by Pears soap advertising.
William Holman Hunt (1827–1918), another founder of the Pre-Raphaelite school; he will be forever remembered for his *Light of the World*.
Other famous artists and sculptors buried here include Lord Frederic Leighton (1830–96) (see Leighton House) and Sir Edwin Landseer (1802–73).

Chapel of the Order of the British Empire [15.13] This chapel is dedicated to members of the Order of the British Empire. One of its most famous recent members is Bob Geldof, made a Knight Commander in 1986.

Tomb of the Duke of Wellington (1769–1852) [15.14] Around 18 000 people attended the funeral of the Duke in 1852 (an invitation is displayed in the Wellcome Institution at the Science Museum). The huge sarcophagus was not completed until six years after his death.

Tomb of Admiral Lord Nelson (1758–1805) [15.15] The Crypt's grandest tomb stands directly beneath the 'eye' of the Dome. The sarcophagus was originally designed for the tomb of Cardinal Wolsey but it was seized by Henry VIII when the Cardinal fell out of favour and it was never used. The coffin was made from the main mast of the French Flagship *L'Orient*, destroyed at Nelson's victorious Battle of the Nile. The floor mosaic includes Nelson's immortal signal to the fleet on 21 October 1805 before the Battle of Trafalgar: 'England expects every man to do his duty'.

> *Nelson actually expected to be buried in Westminster Abbey, remarking before the Battle of Cape St Vincent in 1797 'Westminster Abbey or victory', and making a similar statement before the Battle of the Nile.*

Tombs of Admiral Beatty (1871-1936) and Admiral Jellicoe (1859-1935) [15.16] Britain's two World War I naval leaders lie here. Beatty succeeded Jellicoe as Commander-in-Chief of the Grand Fleet in 1916 and received the surrender of the German fleet in the Firth of Forth in November 1918. His was the last body to be buried in the Crypt, thereafter only ashes have been accepted.

Treasury [15.17] The carpeted entrance area includes a model of Old St Paul's, fire damaged effigies from the same, the death mask of Sir Christopher Wren and some of his work implements. Vestments on display include Order of the British Empire robes and the splendid Jubilee Cope made in 1977.

Western Crypt
The most valuable item here is Wren's Great Model built 1673–4, an accurate 1:24 scale model of his favourite second design for St Paul's. Its importance to Wren as a presentation piece (to secure approval of his plans) may be judged by its cost of around £600, which was equivalent to three years of his salary or the cost of a three-storey house! Despite this and Wren's tearful appeals to the King, the design was rejected. His fourth plan was accepted, however, and (as may be seen from the pictures around which tell the story of St Paul's) Wren took his 'designers

licence' to include elements of his favourite design anyway!

Two 'unique' graves in the Western Crypt include: Pilot Officer Fiske—the first US citizen to be killed in World War II (ironically he is not honoured in the American Memorial Chapel above as it was illegal for a US citizen to join the RAF); George Swan Nottage (1822–85), one of only two Lord Mayors of London to die in office and the only one to exercise his right of burial in the present Cathedral.

The Lecture Room contains an audio visual display on the history of St Paul's and changing exhibitions.

O Daily 07.30–18.00 (Nov–Mar to 17.00); T Mon–Sat 11.00, 11.30, 14.00, 14.30; £ Ambulatory, Galleries, Crypt Easter–Sept Mon–Fri 10.00–17.00; Oct–Easter 10.00–16.00; Sat 11.00–16.45; £;
♿ t (in crypt) enquire about entry, 1+2 steps to lift, 80%
☎ (01) 248 2705

Sir Christopher Wren (1632–1723)

Wren began his career as an astronomer and mathematician and rose to become Professor of Astronomy at Oxford. He turned to architecture, however, and in 1667 was appointed Surveyor of Rebuilding after the Great Fire. His plans for a 'new London' foundered on the complex network and politics of land ownership. Instead, as Surveyor General, he turned his immense design talents and energy to City churches and St Paul's Cathedral. Between 1670 and 1686 he designed or rebuilt 51 City churches (23 are still complete) whilst working concurrently on St Paul's Cathedral, the Royal Hospital at Chelsea, The Monument, and the churches of St Clement Dane and St James', Piccadilly. He also worked on the Royal Palaces of Hampton Court and St James's and designed the Royal Naval Hospital at Greenwich. The tireless Wren continued work into his eighties, by which time he had created a classical style of English architecture that profoundly affected his contemporaries and successors.

St Paul's Cathedral South Front

In the pediment of the transept there is the motto 'RESURGAM'. The story behind this is explained by Sir Christopher's son (also Christopher) in his book *Parentalia*:

'In the beginning of the new Works of St Paul's an Incident was taken as a memorable Omen, when a Labourer was ordered to bring flat stone from the Heaps of Rubbish . . . to be laid for a Mark and Direction to the Masons, the Stone which was immediately brought and laid down for that Purpose happened to be a Piece of Grave-stone with nothing remaining of the Inscription but this single word in large capitals RESURGAM'. Resurgam (translated from Latin) means 'I will rise again' and above this is a sculpture of the Phoenix bird, a symbol of the new Cathedral rising from the ashes of the old.

College of Arms [16]
Queen Victoria Street

This is the home of the royal heralds whose principal function is to identify, authenticate and grant coats of arms. Historically, this was a vital task as on the battlefield this was often the only means of identification. The heralds are also responsible for organizing great state banquets.

Their first charter was granted in 1484 by Richard III, although the college was probably established during the late 12th to early 13th century. The building dates from 1688. It is one of the few remaining heraldic courts in Western Europe and is the oldest existing heraldic college in the world. The Earl Marshal's Court-Room where armorial disputes used to be resolved is original and the Commonwealth flags around the room are from the 1953 coronation of Queen Elizabeth II.

O Court-Room Mon–Fri 10.00–16.00
☎ (01) 248 0911

St Benet, Paul's Wharf [17]
Upper Thames Street

This is one of the most attractive of Wren's churches, built in 1683 to replace the old church of 1111 destroyed in the Great Fire. The famous architect Inigo Jones was buried here and is commemorated by a monument.

Note: Often closed to the public

> *The neighbouring institution of ecclesiastical lawyers known as Doctor's Commons (demolished 1867) had a special agreement with St Benet's to provide hasty marriages. Between 1708 and 1731 the church claims to have held 13 423 weddings i.e. an average of over eleven per week every week for 23 years!*

St Bride [18]
Fleet Street

This is one of London's most historic religious sites, having housed eight different churches dating from the original 6th-century St Bridget's which marks the first Irish settlement in London, to Wren's famous landmark built in 1671-8. It was an important medieval meeting place and in 1210 was the setting for at least one of King John's Councils. In 1500 the Dutch printing pioneer Wynkyn de Worde (apprentice to William Caxton) set up the first press just across the road in Fleet Street and since then St Bride's has always been linked with the printing and publishing industry. The Dutchman was buried here in 1535 and another man of letters, Samuel Pepys, was baptized here in 1633. The interior is modern, as St Bride's was gutted in 1940. The most famous aspect of St Bride's is its splendid spire—'a madrigal in stone', rising 226 ft (69 m). It is the tallest of any spire or steeple by Wren and is the model for the traditional wedding cake, first made famous by a local baker, Mr Rich, around the turn of the 19th century. The crypt has been turned into a museum largely devoted to the earlier churches on the site and reaching beyond that to the remains of a Roman house and pavement. Other exhibits include an iron coffin made in 1818 to frustrate body snatchers.

O **Daily 09.00-17.00;** ⅃ **1 step, via Salisbury Court side entrance** ☎ **(01) 353 1301**

The Blackfriar [P1]
174 Queen Street

The Blackfriar is London's only example of a pub decorated in Art Nouveau fashion and boasts one of the richest and strangest bar interiors in London. Dating from 1875, it features bronze reliefs of friars going about their daily business, arched mosaic ceilings and marble columns.

Note: Cold buffet only in evening ☎ **(01) 236 5650**

> *The pub stands on the site of the Blackfriars monastery, a community of Dominican monks whose lands included this area in 1294. It was dissolved in 1538 and destroyed in the Great Fire. The only surviving fragment of wall can be seen in Ireland Yard (off Blackfriars Lane behind the pub).*

Sweetings [R1]
39 Queen Victoria Street

Sweetings began business as fishmongers in 1830. This branch, built in 1906, is the best known and one of the oldest surviving fish and oyster restaurants in London. From the street it looks unremarkable but its high ceilinged interior, complete with original marble and mahogany fittings, affords a grand Edwardian atmosphere.

☎ **(01) 248 3062**

This is the very heart of the business City, containing the greatest concentration of financial and commercial services in the world. Not only is this the hub of the British money-go-round but, within a few hundred yards of the Bank of England, there are over 460 branches and offices of overseas banks represented in the City.

The area is characterized by the ancient thoroughfare of Fenchurch Street. The first City skyscraper, 14 storeys high, was erected on this street between 1954 and 1957, yet beneath its pavements Celtic cinerary urns some 3000 years old have been discovered. A few yards away the space-age Lloyd's building looks down on the medieval church of St Andrew Undershaft and elsewhere Wren churches are dwarfed by burgeoning office developments. Nowhere else in London is the contrast of ancient elegance and modern efficiency so sharply thrown into relief.

The eastern end of Lombard Street and western part of Fenchurch Street overlie the site of the oldest street in London, known to have been established by the Romans before AD 60.

Bank of England   [1]
Threadneedle Street

The Bank of England was established in 1694 to hold government funds raised to finance war with France. It was England's first joint-stock bank and in 1695 it issued the first bank notes in England: £10, £20, £30, £40, £50 and £100. The Bank moved to Threadneedle Street in 1734 and was rebuilt as a master-piece of architecture by Sir John Soane between 1788 and 1808. It was controversially rebuilt in 1921–37 and all that remains of Soane's work is the windowless wall (so designed for security reasons) on the south and west sides. It covers some three acres and includes ten storeys, seven above ground and three below.

The Bank has long since ceased dealing directly with the general public and today its functions are to issue notes, to act as the government's and bankers' bank, to execute monetary policy and to hold the nation's gold reserves.

The doormen of the Bank wear a distinctive uniform, dating back to 1694, with pink tailcoat, red waistcoat and gold trimmed top hat.

A small museum, covering both the history and everyday aspects of today's Bank of England, has recently opened.

O Mon–Fri 10.00–18.00; After 30 Sept 1989 also Sat 10.00–18.00, Sun 14.00–18.00; ♿ ring for special arrangements; Museum entrance at side of building in Bartholomew Lane.
☎ (01) 601 4878

The Bank's nickname 'The Old Lady of Threadneedle Street' was coined after the playwright Richard Brinsley Sheridan (speaking in his capacity as a Member of Parliament in 1797) referred to 'an elderly lady in the City of great credit and long standing'. A statue of the 'Old Lady' sits below the pediment high on the south façade of the building.

St Margaret Lothbury [2]
Lothbury

The first church dedicated to St Margaret of Antioch was established here c. 1181. It was destroyed by the Great Fire and the present church was rebuilt by Wren in 1686–90.

The interior of St Margaret's is one of the most picturesque of the City churches, featuring superb 17th-century woodwork which was gleaned from other old City churches (demolished in the 18th and 19th centuries). The chancel screen, dating c. 1689, is its most impressive item. The paintings of Moses and Aaron date c. 1700.

O ⛔ **1 step**

Stock Exchange [3]
Threadneedle Street

The origins of the Stock Exchange lie in nearby Change Alley where in the late 17th century brokers (responsible for buying and selling stock for their clients) and jobbers (acting as middle-men between brokers as well as trading on their own account) met in Jonathan's and Garraway's Coffee Houses. Jonathan's burned down in 1778 and the 550 brokers and jobbers who constituted membership of the first Stock Exchange moved to the present site in May 1801.

By 1905 membership had reached an all-time high of 5567. The present modern building was opened in 1972 and accommodates around 4000 members. As a reminder of the old Coffee House days the attendants are still called waiters and wear traditional blue coats with red collars.

The Stock Exchange is the central market place for over 7000 securities—the largest number listed in the world. The public are not allowed on the 'floor' of the Exchange but may view from above where an exhibition area explains its workings. There are 15 hexagonal stations or 'pitches' around which trading nominally takes place. However, the auction-like hustle and bustle of 'open-out-cry' dealing which was once the norm on the

floor is now the exception, as 95 per cent of business is conducted via computerized links. Despite the modern technology, the Stock Exchange's motto 'My word is my bond' is adhered to today as strictly as it was in the days of the Coffee Houses.

O **Mon–Fri 09.45–1515;** ⛔ **100% (ask for alternative entry)**
☎ **(01) 588 2355**

> *There were around 500 Coffee Houses in London by the early 18th century. They were used as social as well as business meeting places and were the forerunners of gentlemen's clubs (see Jamaica Wine House).*

Royal Exchange [4]
Threadneedle Street, Cornhill

The original Royal Exchange was built on this site in 1566–7 by the wealthy City merchant Sir Thomas Gresham (1519–79), as the first covered meeting place for traders in London. It was destroyed in the Great Fire and rebuilt in 1667. This second Exchange is depicted in relief on a water pump, erected in 1799, at the south-east corner of the building in Cornhill. It, too, burned down in 1838 and the existing building was opened in 1844.

Its bell tower, 177 ft (54 m) high, supports the crest of Sir Thomas Gresham, a gilded grasshopper, 11 ft (3 m) long, which acts as a

> *Britain's first municipal public lavatory was sited outside the Royal Exchange in 1855. Initially it was 'Gents' only and the charge was one old penny (hence the expression 'to spend a penny'). The original lavatories were destroyed in World War II but their successors (in the Bank Underground subway) held the charge of one old penny for over 115 years, until the introduction of decimalization in 1971. This is thought to be a price maintenance record for any London municipal service!*

weather-vane. A statue of London's most famous City merchant, Dick Whittington, stands on the Threadneedle Street side. The Royal Exchange ceased to function in 1939 and is now occupied by the London International Financial Futures Exchange (LIFFE) where trading 'pits' deal in currency and government securities in the lively traditional manner of open outcry. The traditional sombre City suit is eschewed here in favour of brightly coloured jackets, so that members of the same trading firms may easily be distinguished on the busy Exchange floor.

O Visiting Gallery: Mon–Fri 11.00–14.00 Note: Gallery sometimes closed to the public ☎ (01) 623 0444

16. CITY—EAST

1 Bank of England *
2 St Margaret Lothbury
3 Stock Exchange
4 Royal Exchange
5 St Michael, Cornhill
6 St Peter, Cornhill
7 St Ethelburga
8 National Westminster Tower
9 St Helen, Bishopsgate *
10 Lloyd's *
11 Leadenhall Market
12 St Andrew Undershaft

13 St Katharine Cree
14 St Mary-at-Hill
15 St Magnus the Martyr
16 The Monument
17 St Clement Eastcheap
18 St Edmund King and Martyr
19 St Mary Woolnoth

Pubs/Restaurants
P1 Jamaica Wine House
P2 The Olde Wine Shades
R1 George and Vulture

* Specially recommended by author

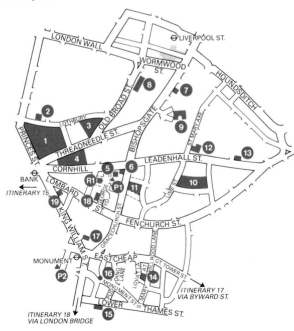

St Michael, Cornhill [5]
Cornhill

The original church first mentioned in 1055 was destroyed in the Great Fire and rebuilt by Wren in 1672. The impressive pinnacled 130 ft (40 m) high tower was completed by his pupil Nicholas Hawksmoor in 1722. Extensive restoration work was undertaken in 1857–60 by Sir George Gilbert Scott who added the richly carved entrance porch where a bronze statuette of St Michael commemorates the dead of World War I. The large wooden pelican in the vestibule was formerly an altarpiece and dates from 1775. The pelican is a symbol of Christian piety and is often shown, as here, pecking her own breast in order that her offspring may feed off her

High and mighty—The National Westminster Tower at 600 ft 4 in (183 m).

blood. Scott's marble reredos features 17th-century paintings of Moses and Aaron.

St Peter, Cornhill   [6]
Cornhill

This is traditionally the earliest Christian church in London, founded on the site of the Roman Basilica (see Leadenhall Market) in AD 179. During the 15th century it was the most venerated church in the City—then much larger than it is today. St Peter's was virtually destroyed in the Great Fire and rebuilt by Wren 1679-82. It features much original woodwork, the most impressive being the intricately carved chancel screen.

Mendelssohn played the organ here in 1840 and 1842 and displayed in the vestry is a letter of thanks from him together with the original 17th-century tortoise-shell encrusted organ keyboard. Also displayed are a 17th-century breadshelf on which food would be left for the poor of the parish and an engraved 14th-century plaque from the old church referring to its ancient origins.

O ♿ 1+1 step, rear entry

St Ethelburga   [7]
Bishopsgate

St Ethelburga is the smallest church in the City and also one of the oldest, dating from the 13th century (rebuilt in the 15th century). It is dedicated to the daughter of Ethelbert, King of Kent 860-66. Its picturesque ragstone front has a late 14th-century doorway and a 15th-century window. It is surmounted by an elaborate weather-vane of 1671. Many of the interior fittings are modern, although on the north wall hangs a 16th-century Flemish painting of Christ. Three windows commemorate Henry Hudson, who discovered Hudson's Bay in 1609. He took communion here before setting off on his last voyage to try to discover the North West Passage. The stained glass depicts the

mutiny of his crew who cast him adrift on 22 June 1611, never to be seen again.

O ♿ 1 step

National Westminster Tower   [8]
25 Old Broad Street

This is the tallest building in Britain and the tallest cantilevered building in the world at a height of 600 ft 4 in (183 m) (see Greenwich). Its 52 floors are supported on foundations extending 60 ft (18 m) below ground and 375 piles driven down a further 80 ft (24 m).

O National Westminster Bank account holders only, contact local Branch Manager for details

St Helen, Bishopsgate   [9]
Great St Helen's

St Helen's dates back to the 12th century and is an unusual internal arrangement of two churches, side by side. A nunnery was built c. 1210 with the nuns' own church built adjacent to the existing parish church. The two churches were then divided by the four late 15th-century arches that still stand and a wooden screen. The nunnery was dissolved in 1538 and the screen has since gone, leaving St Helen's with London's only surviving 'Nuns' church' in addition to its parish church. The Nuns' church entrance dates from c. 1500 and the parish church entrance from c. 1300.

There are two visible reminders of the old nunnery on the north wall. The tiny steps up the narrow passageway set into the wall is the 'Night Staircase' (c. 1500) which led to the

The nuns of Bishopsgate had quite a riotous reputation. In 1385 they were reprimanded by their prioress for 'kissing secular persons' and in 1432 parishioners complained that services were being shortened in order that the nuns could devote their time to 'dancing and revelling'.

nuns' dormitory and the Nuns' Squint (1525), a grill of stone bars angled towards the altar which gave those nuns unable to come into the church a view of proceedings from outside.

The memorial window (1884) to William Shakespeare commemorates the church's most famous parishioner, his name appearing in the records of 1597.

St Helen's boasts more monuments than any other City church. The most impressive are those to: Sir Thomas Gresham (d 1579)—founder of the Royal Exchange, Sir William Pickering (d 1542)—Elizabeth I's Ambassador to Spain, and Sir John Crosby (d 1475)—a wealthy merchant (see Crosby Hall, Chelsea) and church benefactor.

In the chancel is a very rare wooden sword-rest, dating from 1665.

The south doorway, dating from 1633, is the most impressive of the three entrances and should also be viewed from the outside. A rare surviving Poor Box effigy (17th century) of a bearded beggar holding out his hat stands by the west door.

Lloyd's [10]
Leadenhall Street

Lloyd's of London is the world's most famous society of underwriters who accept insurance risks for profit and also the traditional obligation of unlimited liability. Lloyd's claim to insure almost anything but they are best known for marine insurance, dating back to the original Edward Lloyd's Coffee House, opened in 1688, where ship's captains, owners and merchants would gather to exchange shipping news. *Lloyd's News*—the first published provision of reliable shipping intelligence—appeared in 1696. It lasted only four months but was revived in 1734 as *Lloyd's List* which has appeared ever since. Lloyd's officially began trading with 79 members in 1774 in the Royal Exchange. Now, the society numbers around 30 000 who deal with around £25 million in premiums every working day. They moved to their present site in

1928 and to the new 'space-age' structure in 1986. Designed by Richard Rogers (of Georges Pompidou Centre fame) at a cost of £163 million, it is one of London's most talked-about buildings and has been described as resembling 'a post-modern oil refinery'!

An exhibition area which traces the history of Lloyd's, how it works and its many famous and unusual policies, is located on the fourth floor. From here a viewing gallery looks down on to the Underwriting Room where the daily business is conducted, and up to the impressive 200 ft (61 m) high glass atrium. In total 120 000 sq ft (11 148 sq m) is spread over the four floors of what has been termed the largest open-plan office in Europe. The wooden rostrum on the ground floor contains the famous Lutine Bell. Originally from the French frigate *La Lutine*, it was transferred to HMS *Lutine* which was lost with all hands. The bell was salvaged and is rung for important announcements, once for bad news, twice for good news. A single toll marked the loss of the 'unsinkable' *Titanic* on 16 April 1912 and again on 19 January 1976 when the Supertanker *Berge Istra* at 227 556 tons (nearly five times bigger than the *Titanic*) became the largest ship ever shipwrecked.

Some of the more unusual insurance policies taken out with Lloyd's have protected the legs of Rudolph Nureyev and Marlene Dietrich, a £1 million reward for the capture of the Loch Ness monster and a miniscule portrait of Queen Elizabeth II and the Duke of Edinburgh on a grain of rice.

O **Mon–Fri 10.00–14.30;**
& **100% (alternative entry)**
☎ **(01) 623 7100**

Leadenhall Market [11]
Gracechurch Street

This classic Victorian edifice of glass and iron, built in 1881, is the most attractive 'street market' in the city.

Lloyd's of London, started in a humble coffee house three centuries ago.

First established in the 14th century, it takes its name from a mansion with a lead roof which stood on the site.

It now caters mostly for City lunchtime workers and tourists in place of the indigenous population but retains a lively atmosphere.

O Mon–Fri 07.00–15.00

Leadenhall Market stands on the site of the Basilica—the first Roman administrative centre in Great Britain. Built in the late first century, it was around 500 ft (152 m) long and combined the functions of town hall and law courts.

St Andrew Undershaft [12]
Leadenhall Street, St Mary Axe

Originally dating back to the 12th century, the present church was constructed in 1512–32. It survived both the Great Fire and World War II and despite restoration work remains one of the City's most attractive medieval church exteriors. John Stow, author of the *Survey of London* and the City's first real historian, was buried here in 1605 (his present monument dates from 1905). Poor Stow spent so much time on his writing that his tailor's business collapsed and he had to become a licensed beggar in order to continue his work. Every April, a service of commemoration is held in his honour and a new quill pen is placed in the effigy's hand. The old one, and a copy of Stow's Survey, are given to the child who has written the year's best London essay.

Note: Often closed to the public

> *The church takes its strange name from the shaft of a giant maypole, which was erected annually in the 15th century, next to it.*
>
> *The equally curious street name of St Mary Axe derives from a church which once stood here. The story behind the dedication comes from an axe which the church possessed, said to be one of the three used in the 5th century by Attila the Hun, to slaughter the daughter of the king of England and her eleven thousand hand-maidens while they were journeying in the Rhineland!*

St Katharine Cree   [13]
Leadenhall Street

Originally built in 1280, the existing church dates from 1630, having survived both the Great Fire and the Blitz. The name Cree is thought to be an abbreviation of Christ Church. The stained glass in the east window is original and is a symbol of the wheel on which St Katharine (or St Catherine of Alexandria) was supposed to have been tortured in AD 307 for her beliefs. (This is where the catherine wheel firework derives its name from.) An alabaster figure commemorates Sir Nicholas Throckmorton, Ambassador to Queen Elizabeth I, who is buried here (d 1570) and after whom Throgmorton Street in the City is named.

St Mary-at-Hill   [14]
Lovat Lane

St Mary-at-Hill is hidden away among some of the few remaining cobbled alleys left in the

City. It was founded in the 12th century and rebuilt by Wren in 1670-6. It has been described as the least spoiled and the most gorgeous church interior in the City. Much of its woodwork was replaced in 1840 but it is so true to the original 17th-century work that it is almost indistinguishable from it.

St Magnus the Martyr   [15]
Lower Thames Street

St Magnus was founded in the mid-11th century and was an important meeting place and forum for medieval London. It was destroyed in the Great Fire and rebuilt by Wren in 1671-6. The interior was described by T S Eliot in 'The Waste Land' (1922) as an 'inexplicable splendour of Ionian white and gold' (referring to its Ionic columns). Although this description may be a little grandiose, the church is richly furnished with a fine reredos and much original woodwork.

O &

> *Stones from Old London Bridge (which then ran next to St Magnus) and a timber post from one of London's earliest Roman wharves stand in the churchyard.*

The Monument   [16]
Monument Street

The Monument was commissioned by order of King Charles II in 1666, following the Great Fire 'to preserve the memory of this dreadful Visitation'. Sir Christopher Wren joined forces with City Surveyor Robert Hooke to design a fluted Doric column surmounted by a 42-ft (13 m) high gilded urn of flames. It was constructed between 1671 and 1677 at a cost of £13 450. When built, The Monument was the world's highest freestanding column at 202 ft (62 m), this being equal to the distance due east to the site of the bakery in Pudding Lane where the fire began.

It is a sad irony that nearly as many lives have been lost from the top of The Monument as during the Great Fire. One person fell accidentally in 1750, and between 1788 and 1842 six committed suicide. To prevent further jumps, an iron cage was erected. It is also curious that of the six suicides two were bakers and one a baker's daughter. (The Fire started in the King's baker's shop.) As if to expatiate any residual feelings of guilt, a ceremony was enacted at The Monument on 2 September 1986 (the 320th anniversary of the Great Fire) whereby the Worshipful Company of Bakers made a formal apology for the first time in 320 years to the Lord Mayor regarding the Great Fire!

The Latin inscription on the north panel of the pedestal records the City's destruction and its final sentence, which accused Papists of having started the fire, has been amended three times to suit the prevailing religious view. Charles II originally ordered the inscription, then it was removed after the Catholic accession of James II, William III restored it and in 1830 it was finally removed by the Court of Common Council. The sculpture on the west panel represents Charles II giving protection to the ruined City and directing its rebuilding.

The Monument may be ascended by a spiral staircase which, after 311 steps, opens to a public balcony affording one of the finest views over the City.

O **Apr–Sept, Mon–Fri 09.00–18.00; Sat, Sun 14.00–18.00; Oct–Mar, Mon–Sat 09.00–16.00; p**

St Clement Eastcheap [17]
Clements Lane

The original 11th-century St Clement burned down in the Great Fire. Wren rebuilt it in 1683–7 and received as thanks from the parishioners a 17.5-gallon (79.5 litre) barrel of wine! St Clement has been renovated internally but still retains much of its original woodwork including an excellent pulpit, some finely carved bread shelves for the poor of the parish and its reredos.

This church of St Clement has a better claim than St Clement Dane to be the 'Oranges and Lemons' church as Mediterranean citrus fruit used to be unloaded at Old London Bridge close to here.

St Edmund King and Martyr [18]
Lombard Street

The original church on this site was founded *c.* 1000 and is dedicated to Edmund, King of East Anglia, who was martyred by the Danes. It was destroyed in the Great Fire and rebuilt in 1670–9. The design is generally attributed

The Monument—recording London's most catastrophic accident.

to Wren but may have been that of the City Surveyor, Robert Hooke.

The interior was renovated in the late 19th century but it retains many fine examples of 17th-century woodwork, including its impressive reredos.

St Mary Woolnoth [19]
Lombard Street

The present church is believed to be the fifth place of worship on this site and was designed by Wren's pupil, Nicholas Hawksmoor, in 1716-27. During excavation work a Roman pavement was found which it is believed may have been part of a temple. Norman, Saxon and medieval churches have also occupied the site.

The interior is small but spacious due to its cubic design. Its excellent furnishings include an original reredos and pulpit. The church's most colourful character was ex-slave trader turned reformer, John Newton, who became the rector here in 1780. His preaching inspired William Wilberforce, a church parishioner, to develop his Abolition Bill which was passed in 1801, thus ending the British slave trade. Newton's most lasting memorial is the hymn 'Amazing Grace' which he co-wrote. Another famous parishioner was Edward Lloyd, founder of Lloyd's of London, buried here in 1713.

Jamaica Wine House [P1]
15 St Michael's Alley, Cornhill

The Jamaica was established as a Coffee House sometime between 1674 and 1680. It acquired its name from its early clientele, many of whom had business interests in Jamaica and used the Wine House as their business address and as a meeting place for exchange of trade information and underwriting. In 1869 it began trading as the Jamaica Wine House.

☎ (01) 626 9496

The Jamaica is built on or close to the site of London's first Coffee House. Differing authorities claim this was established either first in 1652, by Christopher Bowman as Bowman's Coffee House, or in 1652 or 1657 by a young Turk, Pasqua Rosee, who sold coffee 'at the sign of Pasqua Rosee's Head'. Neither premises survived the Great Fire. The advent of Coffee Houses was vehemently attacked by the brewers who described the new fashionable beverage as 'syrup of soot' and claimed it caused sterility!

The Olde Wine Shades [P2]
6 Martin Lane

This claims to be the oldest wine house in the City, dating back to 1663. It did not survive the Great Fire completely but enough of the building may have survived for it to have been built on its original foundations. Its front is early Victorian.

Note: Jacket and tie must be worn at all times
☎ (01) 626 6876

George and Vulture [R1]
3 Castle Court

A George Inn has existed on this site since the 12th century. It became a coaching inn, burned down in the Great Fire and was rebuilt soon afterwards. Much of the present building survives from this time. When and how it acquired its unusual 'Vulture' appendage is unknown.

The George and Vulture is one of the City's best known traditional 'steak and chop houses', the meat being grilled on an early 19th-century range. It was made famous by Charles Dickens as a hostelry in *The Pickwick Papers* (1836-7), but now only functions as a restaurant.

☎ (01) 626 9710

TOWER OF LONDON AND ENVIRONS

The Tower of London is the capital's greatest historical sight. It was begun over 900 years ago by William the Conqueror in order to intimidate the people of London against uprising. William Shakespeare wrongly attributed the foundation of the Tower to Julius Caesar but at least his Roman connection was correct, as the Tower was built on the site of the old Roman wall, of which part remains on Tower Hill. The area's history to the Saxon period may be followed in the crypt museum in the church of All Hallows by the Tower.

Inside the walls of the Tower, the awesome central keep, the White Tower, still casts a menacing spell. Outside its confines the atmosphere is dissipated amongst the surrounding featureless modern streets and precincts. The recently redeveloped St Katharine's Dock is an honourable exception, bringing a splash of colour to the area, and close above soars Tower Bridge, the greatest engineering legacy of London's golden Victorian age.

Port of London Authority Building and Trinity House [1]
Trinity Square

The huge tiered building overlooking Tower Hill was constructed between 1912 and 1922 for the Port of London Authority which

The Tower of power—its awesome majesty undiminished after 900 years.

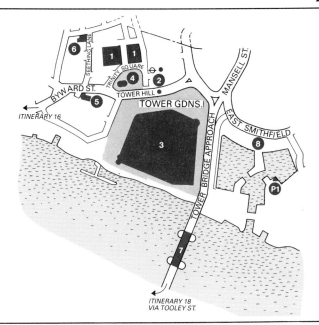

17. TOWER OF LONDON AND ENVIRONS

1 Port of London Authority Building and Trinity House
2 London Wall (sections)
3 Tower of London **
4 Tower Hill Scaffold Memorial
5 All Hallows (Barking) by the Tower *

6 St Olave *
7 Tower Bridge (Museum) *
8 St Katharine's Dock

Pubs
P1 Dickens Inn

* Specially recommended by author
** Highly recommended by author

moved away in 1971. Known locally as the 'Wedding Cake' its giant statue, often thought to be Neptune, represents 'Old Father Thames'. The adjacent Trinity House was built between 1792 and 1794. Although severely damaged during World War II its elegant frontage has been restored. Trinity House has been the lighthouse authority for England and Wales since 1565 and is responsible for the largest fleet of light vessels in the world. (One of its oldest surviving lightships, the *Nore*, lies only a few yards away in St Katharine's Dock.)

London Wall (sections) [2]
Tower Hill

Section No 1 This is the only surviving example of a large medieval gate tower in the City Wall. It was probably built *c.* 1270.

Section No 2 This 35 ft (11 m) section of wall is Roman from its base up to 14 ft (4 m) and then medieval above. The inscription on display is a replica of part of the inscription from the tomb of Julius Classicianus, Roman Procurator of Britain (d *c.* AD 61), discovered here in 1935 (the original is in the British

Museum). This is the earliest monument to have been found in London dedicated to a person known from historical accounts.

Tower of London   [3]

The official name of this world-famous institution is Her Majesty's Fortress and Palace—The Tower of London. This accurately describes its principal original and medieval functions. There is a total of 20 towers (19 bastions plus the White Tower) within its 18-acre (7 ha) complex and throughout its 900-year history it has housed the Royal Palace (1140–1625), the Royal Mint (1300–1810), the Royal Menagerie (1235–1834) and the Crown Jewels (1303–present). It is the oldest continuously occupied fortress in Europe.

The oldest and original part is the dominating central Norman keep, The White Tower, which gives the Tower its name. William the Conqueror began its construction in 1078 in order to defend the City against any possible uprising by his new subjects. It was

> *The gentleman who will take your ticket as you enter the Tower is one of the 41 Yeomen Warders of the Tower. Their day-to-day wear is a blue uniform with red facings (introduced in 1858), and their famous picture-postcard scarlet uniforms (dating from the 16th century) are only worn on ceremonial occasions. Their function is to guard the Tower and they also give guided tours to visitors. They are popularly known as 'Beefeaters' which may derive either from their old function of attending the king's table (buffetiers) or from the meat allowance they used to receive from the Crown. They are also popularly called 'Yeomen of the Guard' but this is one of London's most common misnomers. The culprits for spreading this were Gilbert and Sullivan! The Yeomen of the Guard are a separate bodyguard for the Sovereign.*

during the reigns of Henry III and his son Edward I (1272–1307) that the Tower took its present form—the White Tower being encircled by two heavily fortified walls and a formidable moat. Between 1275 and 1285 Edward spent the huge sum of £20 000 on the Tower's defences making it the most expensive castle of its time.

O Mar–Oct, Mon–Sat 09.30–17.00;   Sun 14.00–17.00;   Nov–Feb, Mon–Sat 09.30–16.00;   Closed Thursday before Easter; Bastion Towers not open unless stated; T (continuous) Accompany Yeomen Warders;   & t 25% (Most of Crown Jewels and most interiors inaccessible but still worth a visit—despite fiendish cobbles!) ☎ (01) 709 0765 Note: Long queues in summer and on Sundays (particularly for Crown Jewels)

The Moat   [3.1]

The present moat which is about 120 ft (37 m) wide was dug during Edward I's reign but has been dry since 1843 (excluding a freak flood tide of 1938 which filled it). It was drained by the Duke of Wellington, then Constable of the Tower, due to its insanitary stagnant condition.

Middle Tower   [3.2]

Middle Tower was built in 1280 and rebuilt in the early 18th century. An outer moat, filled in the 17th century, once guarded its approach.

Byward Tower   [3.3]

The Byward Tower began construction in 1280 and takes its name from its position by the ward—the term given to an administrative division of the City—the boundary of which passes through the Tower of London here. It contains one of the two portcullises in the Tower of London.

Bell Tower   [3.4]

The Bell Tower was built c. 1200 and houses London's oldest curfew bell, which dates

Close to the Middle Tower was the Royal Menagerie, started in 1235 by a present of three leopards to Henry III. Around 1252 a polar bear arrived at the menagerie and Londoners were treated to the bizarre sight of the chained bear, taken fishing in the Thames! The animals were on view to the public and it was the earliest exhibition of its kind in Great Britain. It was one of the country's great tourist attractions and became even more popular when the first elephant in Great Britain was introduced to the menagerie in 1255. When it died it was buried in the Tower and it may therefore claim another record—that of the largest grave in the Tower!

from the early 17th century. It has held many prominent prisoners, the most famous being Sir Thomas More in 1535, and Princess Elizabeth (later Queen Elizabeth I) in 1554. She was allowed to take exercise, for the sake of her health, on the ramparts between here and the Beauchamp Tower, hence its name Elizabeth Walk. She was released in May 1555, after 14 months.

Traitors' Gate [3.5]

Traitors' Gate, dating from Edward I's reign, was the river entrance to the Tower of London before the Thames was moved back and was barred by a portcullis. 'Traitors' were brought through the gate by boat, usually on their last journey.

'Abandon hope all ye who enter here'—but how many were really traitors?

Tower of London

1 The Moat
2 Middle Tower
3 Byward Tower
4 Bell Tower
5 Traitors' Gate
6 St Thomas's Tower
7 Wakefield Tower
8 Bloody Tower
9 White Tower
10 Ravens' Cages
11 Tower Green (site of execution block)
12 Queen's House and Yeoman Gaoler's House
13 St Peter ad Vincula
14 Beauchamp Tower
15 Oriental Armoury
16 Jewel House
17 Bowyer Tower
18 Royal Fusiliers Museum
19 New Armouries

Although the Tower of London was a 'one-way ticket' for many prisoners it was not escape-proof. Ironically its very first prisoner in 1100, Ranulf Flambard, Bishop of Durham, got his guards drunk and escaped from his cell window by rope. The most colourful escape was made by Lord Nithsdale in 1716. A daring plot was hatched by his wife to smuggle him out from under the guards' noses, dressed as a woman. She enlisted the regular visiting help of two lady friends and on the eve of his execution, while she chatted with the guards, her friends dressed him up in clothes they had managed to take in. As three 'ladies' left the cell, Lady Nithsdale bought time for them by 'last goodbyes' to her husband. By the time the pretence was discovered their escapes had been made good.

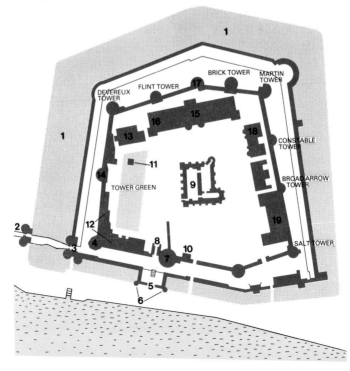

St Thomas's Tower   [3.6]

St Thomas's Tower was built by Henry III (rebuilt in 1866) and is dedicated to Thomas à Becket who had been Constable of the Tower of London in 1161, prior to his appointment as Archbishop of Canterbury.

Wakefield Tower   [3.7]

The Wakefield Tower is the largest of the bastion towers, and is the only survivor of the Royal Palace of Henry III, built in 1225.

Henry VI was murdered here on 21 May 1471 whilst at prayer, an event commemorated annually by his two most famous foundations, Eton College and King's College, Cambridge. The Wakefield Tower held the Crown Jewels from 1869 until 1967.

Leading from the Wakefield Tower is a wall walk with excellent views that runs along the inner wall to the Martin Tower and allows access to the interiors of the Lanthorn, Salt, Broad Arrow and Constable Towers respectively.

The Crown Jewels were kept in the Martin Tower until 1869 and in 1671 they were stolen for the first and only time. The culprits, led by a colourful character named Colonel Blood, only got as far as Tower Wharf, however, and Blood was brought before Charles II. To everyone's astonishment he was pardoned, leading to rumours that the impecunious King was in league with him and had intended to share in the spoils. Another explanation is that the King, impressed by his ingenuity and daring, employed him as a spy.

Close by the Martin Tower was the firing range where eleven spies were shot during World War I. The last execution at the Tower of London was that of a German spy, Josef Jacob, shot on 14 August 1941.

Open

Bloody Tower   [3.8]

The lower level of this most infamous of towers was built by Henry III and the first floor was added in the 14th century. Its original name was the Garden Tower but it was rechristened during the reign of Queen Elizabeth I when the 8th Earl of Northumberland shot himself here. It may already have had this name due to the alleged murder here in 1483 of the captive Little Princes, the 12-year-old boy King Edward V and his 10-year-old brother, the Duke of York. The chief suspect was their uncle, Richard, Duke of Gloucester, who usurped Edward's crown as Richard III. The case against Richard has never been proven, however, and it remains one of the great mysteries of English history.

The top floor (best entered off Tower Green) was built c. 1600 and was home to Sir Walter Raleigh from 1603 to 1616. The furniture (excluding the bed) in Raleigh's room is from this period. Charged with treason, Raleigh had already survived one death sentence, commuted (whilst he was on the scaffold) to life imprisonment. He was the most popular prisoner the Tower of London had ever held and crowds waved and cheered to him as he took his daily walk. Often his confinement was comparatively comfortable. His wife lived with him and his second son was born here. He occupied his time by writing a massive five-volume *Histories of the World* (see also Old Palace Yard).

The portcullis of the Bloody Tower is the only one in England in working order. It weighs two tons and before it became mechanized, it used to require 30 men to raise it.

Open

White Tower (exterior view)   [3.9]

This is the second largest Norman keep in Britain (next to Colchester Castle) measuring 107×118 ft (33×36 m) and towering 90 ft (27 m) high. It was built c. 1078–97 with its distinctive ogee (onion shaped) caps added in the late 14th century. Designed to withstand siege, its walls vary in thickness between 12 ft (4 m) at the top, and 15 ft (5 m) at the base. The base is finished with inclined batteroned walls in order to bounce off missiles such as boulders, hurled from the top, towards attackers. The original entrance may be seen at first floor (Guard-Room) level and would have been accessible only by wooden steps which would have been destroyed in case of siege. In 1674, below the steps were discovered the bones of two children, which may well be the remains of the Little Princes. They were transferred to Westminster Abbey.

Ravens' Cages [3.10]

There is always a minimum complement of six 'official' ravens at the Tower of London plus one kept in reserve. Their origin is unclear but they may have been part of the Royal Menagerie. There is a legend that if the ravens ever leave, then both the Tower and England will fall. It is unlikely that the present ravens will leave, however, as their wings are clipped!

The oldest Tower raven was James Crow, who died in 1927 aged 44 years.

Tower Green (site of execution block) [3.11]

A paved square marks the private execution site where six noble persons are known to have lost their heads. A seventh to die on Tower Green was Lord Hastings, chamberlain to Richard III. His execution was the least judicial of all and the exact site is unknown. He was rounded upon by the King at a council meeting in 1483, pronounced a traitor, dragged outside and beheaded.

The first and probably most famous 'official' victim on Tower Green was Henry VIII's second wife, Anne Boleyn. Condemned on charges of adultery, she requested death by the sword in preference to the (often clumsier) axe, and a master sword executioner was brought from France for the fateful day on 1 June 1536. Henry's fifth wife, Catherine Howard, was the next to die on Tower Green on 13 February 1542, another victim of alleged adultery. She had prepared to conduct herself with dignity for the event

Lady Jane Grey holds the British monarchy record for the shortest reign of 13 days between 6–19 July 1553 (she was proclaimed on 10 July so is often referred to as the '9-day Queen').

by macabre rehearsals of laying her neck on the actual block. She was immediately followed by Lady Rochford (sister-in-law to Anne Boleyn) who was implicated in the charges. The oldest to die was the Countess of Salisbury. Although in her seventies, she too was executed by Henry.

The youngest victim of Tower Green was Lady Jane Grey, executed on 12 February 1554. Her scheming father-in-law, the Duke of Northumberland, put the teenage girl (born 1537) on to the throne in front of the rightful successor, Mary I, but reckoned without Mary's popular support. Lady Jane was actually pleased to relinquish the Crown and was allowed to live in imprisonment but a subsequent rebellion against Mary meant that politically it was too dangerous to let her live. The final execution here was in 1601 of Queen Elizabeth's ex-favourite, Robert Devereux (Earl of Essex) for his part in a rebellion against the Queen.

Queen's House and Yeoman Gaoler's House [3.12]

The Queen's House is the L shaped building in the corner of the Tower. It dates c. 1530 and is now the residence of the governor of the Tower. Anne Boleyn stayed here before her coronation and execution. All state prisoners were taken to the Queen's House to be registered and searched on arrival. The last famous 'guest' of this house was Rudolph Hess, the former deputy Nazi leader briefly imprisoned here in 1941.

Lady Jane Grey was kept in the adjacent Yeoman Gaoler's House in 1554.

St Peter ad Vincula [3.13]

The original chapel on this site was built in

the early 12th century and rebuilt in the late 13th century. It burned down and the present building was completed in 1520. Originally built for prisoners of the Tower, it is appropriately dedicated to St Peter in chains ('ad Vincula').

Within the altar rail are buried Anne Boleyn, Catherine Howard, Lady Jane Grey, Robert Devereux (Earl of Essex) and James Scott (Duke of Monmouth). Elsewhere in the chapel an estimated total of 1500 bodies have been laid to rest throughout the centuries. During restoration work in the 1870s, these were exhumed and removed to the crypt. As many were headless, it was impossible to identify all but 34, and these are named on a brass plate near the chapel entrance. Amongst the famous names are Henry VIII's chamberlain, Thomas Cromwell (d 1540) and Sir Thomas More (d 1535).

Note: Admission only with Yeoman Warder tour party; closes 16.00.

Beauchamp Tower   [3.14]

Built between 1275 and 1285, this tower was used to house prisoners of noble rank. Its most famous captive was Lady Jane Grey's teenage husband, Lord Guildford Dudley, executed just a few hours before the '9-day Queen' on Tower Hill. Four of Guildford Dudley's brothers were also imprisoned here and a craftsman is thought to have been hired to carve their coat of arms in the Beauchamp Tower—the most splendid example of many similar 'memorials' to be found here and in the other towers.

Open

The White Tower (interior)   [3.9]

The White Tower is devoted to the Chapel of St John and the Royal Armouries. This is claimed to be Britain's oldest national and first public museum recording its first visitor in 1489 (see St Mary at Lambeth, Museum of Garden History). Henry VIII founded the Armouries in their present form and the collection is as valuable as the Crown Jewels.

(The following floor order is an obligatory 'one-way system' and a few highlights are picked out below.)

First floor

Sporting and Tournament Armouries
The collection of 'Guns as works of art' (17th and 18th centuries) includes some of the Armouries' most ornamental weapons. The joust armour from the Court of the Emperor Maximilian I (c. 1490) is a notable early tournament example.

Second floor

Chapel of St John   This is the original 11th-century chapel of the Tower of London. It is one of the best preserved examples of Norman architecture in England and is the oldest complete ecclesiastic building in London. Below the Chapel (where the shop now stands) was thought to be the smallest of the dungeons in the Tower of London. Measuring only 4 ft (1 m) square it was aptly nicknamed 'Little Ease', with no room to stand or lie comfortably, no light and no ventilation. Guy Fawkes was confined here for his part in the Gunpowder Plot of 1605.

Medieval and Renaissance Armouries
The Medieval section features a colourful collection of late 15th-century painted shields (pavises) and a rare complete set of German horse armour, c. 1480, as well as the earliest known English cannon, the Boxted Bombard c. 1450. The 16th-century Renaissance Gallery holds the tallest suit of man's armour in the Tower of London. The giant who wore this measured 6 ft 10 in (2.08 m).

Third floor

Tudor and Stuart Armouries   The most popular Tudor items are the four suits of armour (and horse armour) of Henry VIII. The suit designed by Hans Holbein in 1540 was to fit the King at his most obese. Henry's 'walking staff', a combination of mace, bayoneted battle club and pistol, is one of the strangest weapons in the collection. The gilded armour of Charles I in the Stuart Armoury is positively svelte by comparison to Henry's and the smallest armour is a suit made for a 37-in (94 cm) tall midget of Charles' court.

Basement

Mortar Room, Cannon room and Old Armoury The basement was used as the torture chamber—the most feared place in England. The dreaded rack was introduced in 1446 and here it forced Guy Fawkes to confess his guilt and betray his fellow conspirators' names in 1605. Included amongst the mortar collection is the nine-barrelled mortar used for Handel's *Firework Music*, performed in Green Park in 1749. It was held to celebrate the peace treaty of Aix-la-Chapelle in 1748 and was the greatest firework display of its day, firing over 10 000 rockets into the sky.

Oriental Armoury (Waterloo Barracks) [3.15] This colourful and striking display includes exhibits from Turkey, Persia, China, Japan, India, North Africa and the Balkans. It contains what is claimed to be the largest suit of armour in the world, a complete set made for an elephant (late 17th century, early 18th century) probably captured by General Clive of India in 1757. Next to it is a fearsome 18th-century Indian executioner's processional sword weighing 68 lb (31 kg). The Japanese collection is particularly impressive and contains one of the first Japanese suits of armour (16th century) to come to the West, arriving here in 1613.

The adjoining Herald's Museum illustrates heraldry in British history.

Open Apr–Sept

Jewel House (Waterloo Barracks) [3.16] The Jewel House contains the world's best known jewel collection. The old regalia was largely destroyed in 1649, after the Civil War, by Cromwell's Republican government who had the gold melted down and sold along with the jewels. It fetched just £2647. The

cost of Charles II's new regalia 12 years later (which forms the basis of the existing collection) was nearly £32 000. Although the Crown Jewels are the ornaments of English monarchy, they do, however, belong to the state.

The most valuable and interesting items are as follows:

CASE 5

The Delhi Durbar Crown: This was created in 1911 for George V to wear in India (English law prohibits either of the two coronation crowns from leaving the country) and contains over 6000 diamonds.

The Crown of Queen Elizabeth, The Queen Mother: The largest diamond in the crown is the famous 106.5 carat Koh-i-noor ('Mountain of Light') which dates back to the 13th century. It is believed to bring ill-luck to a man and therefore has always been kept in a queen's crown.

Queen Victoria's 'small' crown: This was made in 1870 as a comfortable alternative to the heavier Imperial State Crown.

Queen Mary's Crown: Mary was consort to George V and this crown was made for her in 1911. It holds the Third Star of Africa (95 carats) in the mould and the Fourth star of Africa (64 carats) in the cross at the top.

CASE 11
(Right-hand side of case)
St Edward's Crown: This has been worn for the actual ceremony of coronation since 1661, although it is so heavy (about 5 lb/2 kg)

The Four Stars of Africa were cut from the world's largest ever diamond, the Cullinan, weighing 3106 metric carats (over 1.25 lb/567 g). It was presented to Edward VII in 1907. The first cut became the First Star of Africa, the world's largest cut diamond at 530 metric carats with 74 facets. The Second Star of Africa is second in the world ranking at 317 metric carats.

that it is replaced during the service by the Imperial State Crown. It is thought to contain gold from the original crown of Edward the Confessor, as there are no records of this having been melted down.

Imperial State Crown: This is the most famous of the crowns and is used at major official functions. It was made for the coronation of Queen Victoria and contains 3250 jewels of which the most important are:

— The sapphire in the top cross which belonged to Edward the Confessor (removed from his dead body in the 12th century).

— The Black Prince's balas ruby. This was given to the Black Prince (the heroic son of Edward III) by the King of Castile in 1367. It was worn by Henry V in his battle helmet at Agincourt in 1415 and again by Richard III at Bosworth in 1485 where the King literally lost both crown and life. It is said that the crown was pulled out from a bush to be put on the head of the victorious Henry VII.

— The Second Star of Africa (see above) sits below the Black Prince's ruby.

Orb: This golden globe surmounted by the cross is placed in the monarch's left hand to symbolize that Christ rules the world. It was made in 1661.

(Left-hand side of case)

Ampulla and Spoon: The Golden Eagle (Ampulla) carries holy oil which is poured from its beak on to the Spoon at the coronation service. The archbishop then touches the monarch's hands, breast, and head with it. Records of this ceremony, the most sacred part of the service, date back to AD 785. These are the only items to have definitely escaped Cromwell's destruction, probably because they are not specifically royal ornaments. The Ampulla is thought to have been first used in 1399 and the Spoon dates from the late 12th century.

Sceptre with Cross: This symbolizes the monarch's power as the ruler of the people and is surmounted by the prize jewel of the collection, the First Star of Africa (see above).

Closed Feb (reduced entry charge to Tower)

Bowyer Tower   [3.17]

The Bowyer Tower was built in the 13th century and it is said that the Duke of Clarence, brother of Edward IV and a thorn in the side of the King, was drowned in a barrel of Malmsey wine here in 1478—if true, surely the Tower of London's strangest demise! The Bowyer Tower now displays a small collection of torture instruments and the executioner's block and 16th-century axe last used for the execution of Lord Lovat in 1747.

Open

Royal Fusiliers Museum   [3.18]

The Royal Fusiliers were founded in 1685 to guard the royal guns kept at the Tower and this museum traces their history. It includes the original Victoria Cross (VC)—the highest British award for valour—struck in 1856.

Additonal charge (p)

New Armouries   [3.19]

This display of the British Military Armoury contains examples of almost every weapon designed in the Tower of London and supplied to the British Forces from *c.* 1600–1855.

Tower Hill Scaffold Memorial   [4]

Tower Hill was the principal place of execution for traitors imprisoned in the Tower (excluding royalty—see Tower Green). Between 1381 and 1780 over 300 people were executed here—most of them beheaded. The first important person to die here was Simon de Burley of Sudbury, Archbishop of Canterbury and the last executions were of two prostitutes and a one-armed soldier for their part in the Gordon Riots of 1780. The most famous was Sir Thomas More in 1535. One of the bloodiest and most bungled executions was that of the Duke of Monmouth in 1685, condemned as a leader of the failed Jacobite rebellion. He was reportedly hacked at five

On 9 April 1747 the 80-year-old Lord Lovat was taken to Tower Hill scaffold for his part in the Jacobite uprising. The spectators' stands were so overladen that they collapsed, killing 12 people. Lord Lovat did not miss the irony, murmuring 'the more mischief, the better sport'. This was the last public execution by beheading in Great Britain.

times by the notorious axeman Jack Ketch who finally decapitated him with a knife. The barbarity of the incompetent butchery was often painfully counterpoised by the victim's serenity. Of the many who died with dignity at Tower Hill none was more composed than Sir Thomas More or the elderly Scottish Lord Lovat (see above).

Crowds flocked to the executions in their thousands (estimates of the largest crowds are 200 000) and would climb frantically over each other in order to dip their handkerchiefs or rags in the spilt blood, believing it to be a miracle cure for all ills.

All Hallows (Barking) by the Tower [5]
Byward Street

All Hallows was initially founded from the great Abbey of Barking—hence its unusual name. It boasts the oldest complete arch of any City church. This may be seen in its 7th-century Saxon wall beneath the organ. The semicircle of the arch itself appears to be made of even older materials—Roman tiles. Beneath this, in the undercroft are more Saxon walls and a Roman tessellated pavement (*c.* AD 45). The church itself almost went up in the Great Fire of 1666. Indeed, it got so close that the clock face melted. After the Great Fire had been stopped just short of

the church on 6 September 1666, Samuel Pepys climbed the tower to record 'the saddest sight of desolation that I ever saw'.

Sadly, it did not escape World War II and was virtually gutted by bombing.

The church's greatest treasure is its intricately carved limewood font cover, attributed to Grinling Gibbons, 1682, kept behind a protective screen. It was believed that the holy water in fonts had magical properties and was often stolen, so lockable covers, such as this one, were made. The covers were sometimes carved so elaborately, however, that they, too, became valuable items and were stolen!

O Mon–Fri 09.00–17.30; &
Undercroft—must be accompanied by church Guide (not always available); £;
(no &); Sat–Sun closed during services
☎ (01) 481 2928

In the late 12th century Richard I ('the Lionheart') built a Lady Chapel at All Hallows and by tradition his heart is buried in the church. An altar from a Crusader castle in Palestine may be seen in the undercroft.

St Olave [6]
Seething Lane/Hart Street

The churchyard's splendidly macabre skull-decorated entrance dates from 1658. It obviously impressed Charles Dickens as he referred to it as 'The church of St Ghastly Grim'. This is the third church on the site dedicated to Saint Olave (formerly King Olaf—see London Bridge), and was begun *c.* 1450. It escaped the Great Fire but was badly damaged during the Blitz. Fortunately, its many impressive 17th-century monuments survived and excellent interior restoration has provided a rare example of a 'medieval' City church. On the south wall is a memorial to the diarist Samuel Pepys who worshipped

Official fatality records of plague deaths were compiled by the clerks of the 109 parishes in and around London. They were then centrally counted and publicized as official Bills of Mortality, the records of 'London's Dreadful Visitation'. However, these were often gravely understated in order to allay public alarm. The clerk of St Olave's admitted to Pepys that he recorded only six deaths due to plague in one week when in fact there had been nine. The other causes of death were accounted for by such vague reasons as 'frighted', 'lethargy', 'winde' etc.! The total plague deaths recorded in the Bills of Mortality from 27 December 1664 to 19 December 1665 were 68 596. In reality it would probably have been around 110 000 (see the Great Plague).

in this church and was buried here in June 1703 in a vault below the communion table. His wife Elizabeth (d 1669) lies with him and her memorial is above the table. The burial register records that 'Mother Goose' was buried here on 14 September 1586. It is thought that this Mother Goose was a local character rather than the pantomime bird! There are also 365 plague victims' names in the register for 1665.

Samuel Pepys (1633–1703)

The world's most famous diarist was born just off Fleet Street and educated at St Paul's school. He became a Navy clerk and lived and worked in Seething Lane opposite St Olave. He later progressed to become secretary to the Admiralty, a post he filled with distinction. His Diary, an invaluable historical and social reference, began on 1 January 1660 and continued until 31 May 1669. During this period, arguably the most eventful decade in London's history, he noted the Restoration of the Monarchy, bravely stayed in London to record the Plague, and witnessed the Great Fire at close quarters.

The Diary was written in shorthand in six notebooks and lay undeciphered for over 150 years. It took four years to decode Pepys' 1.25 million words and was first (part) published in 1825.

Tower Bridge (Museum) [7]

Tower Bridge is one of London's most famous landmarks and is the most famous drawbridge in the world. It was the final major Thames road bridge to be built in London and is the last bridge before the Thames makes its way 42 miles (68 km) to the North Sea. It was built 1886–94 and was hailed as one of the great engineering wonders of the day, although one critic described it as 'the most monumental example of extravagance in bridge construction in the world'. It consists basically of two skeletons of iron and steel, clothed in some 50 000 tons of cement and stone. It contains over 27 000 tons of brickwork, enough to build around 350 detached houses. An average of 432 men worked 2896 days on it and the final cost was £1 184 000. The bridge is 880 ft (268 m) long from shore to shore. Its bascules (the drawbridges operated by a counterpoise see-saw action) each measure 170 ft (52 m) in length and weigh 1000 tons. Their function was to allow large ships into the Upper Pool of London beyond the bridge, and at the peak of the Thames' traffic they used to open up to 50 times per day. Nowadays they open on average four to five times per week.

The walkways which span the top of the bridge were designed to allow pedestrians to cross when the bascules were raised. They provide magnificent views up and down the

The most dramatic moment Tower Bridge has witnessed occurred in December 1952 when a London double-decker bus accidentally entered the bridge whilst it was opening and, reaching the point of no return, jumped the gap between the bascules!

river from their vantage height of 140 ft (43 m) above high water.

The exhibition areas inside the towers describe the history of the bridge, working models demonstrating the bridge's operation, and below in the engine rooms, is the original hydraulic machinery which powered Tower Bridge prior to the installation of electrical equipment in 1976.

O Daily 10.00–17.45 (Nov–Mar closes 16.00); £; & t 100%
☎ (01) 407 0922

St Katharine's Dock [8]

St Katharine's Dock was built in 1825–8, brusquely sweeping aside a community of over 11 000 protesting inhabitants. Its huge warehouses provided around 100 000 tons of cargo capacity and specialized in valuable commodities such as ostrich feathers, drugs, spices, special teas, turtles and ivory. The latter is recalled by Ivory House, the Dock's dominant building, which dates from 1854 and at its peak stored around 22 000 tusks in a year. Despite its excellent warehousing facilities, St Katharine's was never a commercial success, primarily because its river lock could not admit large ships, and after years of loss the Dock closed in 1968. It has been attractively redeveloped into offices, flats, shops and a yacht marina where elegant early 20th-century Thames sailing barges are moored.

Dickens Inn [P1]

This picturesque pub was formerly a brewery and a warehouse standing just outside St Katharine's Dock. It was moved to its present site and refurbished as the Dickens Inn, incorporating 17th-century timbers into its galleried frontage.

☎ (01) 488 2208 or (01) 488 9932

Defending the bridge—Tower Bridge from Tower Wharf.

SOUTHWARK

Southwark begins at the south end of London Bridge and, due to its riverside location, was part of the first Roman settlement built up on the north bank. However, Roman remains pre-dating the main invasion have been found around the City and Southwark, giving rise to the theory that a wharf and warehouse settlement was built by a few Roman prospectors a decade or so before AD 43.

Southwark derives its name from its original function, as a stronghold with fortifications or 'works', to protect the river crossing, south of the City (South-works). It continued to be the main entry to London from the south, and until London Bridge was widened to allow coaches across, it was the terminus for travellers wishing to enter the City. The combination of both Londoners and travellers seeking local entertainment and the fact that Southwark lay just outside the jurisdiction of the puritanical City authorities, meant the early development of the area was

Borough High Street is one of the oldest parts of Southwark and was once lined with inns to accommodate travellers. The most famous of these was The Tabard, formerly in Talbot Yard, where in the 14th century pilgrims would gather before setting off to visit the shrine of St Thomas à Becket in Canterbury Cathedral. Chaucer mentions the Inn in the prologue to his Canterbury Tales *(1383). Charles Dickens and William Shakespeare also wrote of the Borough inns. The White Hart, formerly in White Hart Yard, was featured in both* Pickwick Papers *(1836-7) and in* Henry VI *(1594-5).*

notable for its 'houses of pleasure' and inns. Not surprisingly, there was also an abundance of prisons—no less than seven in Southwark by the early 17th century. However, not all the entertainment was of a dubious nature and in the late 16th century the Elizabethan theatrical fraternity established England's first theatre-land on Bankside.

London Bridge [1]

The original London Bridge was a wooden structure built by the Romans c. AD 43. After the Romans left London, the bridge was destroyed and rebuilt several times. The most famous occasion was in 1014, when according to the Norse Sagas, King Ethelred II sailed up the Thames with his ally King Olaf, in order to reclaim London from the occupying Vikings. They were attacked from the heavily-defended bridge, however, so they fastened ropes around the bridge piles and then rowed upstream, pulling it asunder. The event was commemorated by a Norse poet who wrote the original version of 'London Bridge is broken down' and this was revived as a nursery rhyme in the mid-17th century. The first stone bridge, 'Old London Bridge', comprising 20 piers was built 1176–1209 by Peter de Colechurch and is held to be one of the greatest engineering feats of medieval Europe. By 1358 it was crowded with 138 separate buildings, some up to seven storeys high.

Inevitably, a major fire broke out on the bridge, c. 1212 and with both ends burning and rescuing ships in confusion, the historian John Stow records that 'through fire and shipwreck three thousand people were killed'—the worst ever river or fire disaster in this country.

Heads of traitors displayed on poles above the southern gatehouse ('Traitors' Gate') were a common sight on the bridge from 1305 onwards. The first head was that of the Scots patriot William Wallace and the most famous that of Sir Thomas More (later retrieved by his daughter to be buried at Canterbury). In 1589 over 30 heads were counted on the bridge. This gruesome custom was discontinued in 1678. In 1581 two waterwheels were built on the bridge to harness the energy of the river at this point. It therefore became the world's first pumping station in the modern sense and piped water to private houses for the first time in Britain since the Roman occupation. London Bridge continued to be the only bridge in London until 1750 when Westminster Bridge was built.

By 1762 all the houses had been removed and in 1823–31 a new bridge was built by Sir John Rennie. This bridge in turn was replaced by the present bridge in 1967–72 and in March 1968 the second 'Old London Bridge' was sold for £1 029 000 to the McCulloch Oil Corporation of Los Angeles, USA. At 10 000 tons (of façade stonework) it is the largest antique ever sold. It was reassembled at Lake Havasu City, Arizona where it stands as a tourist attraction.

During a particularly cold winter the Thames would freeze over completely due to the 20 piers of Old London Bridge impeding the river flow. 'Frost Fairs' with all kinds of entertainment would then take place. The first of these is recorded in 1564–5 and included archery and dancing. The most severe frost occurred in 1683–4 when the ice was so thick as to allow an ox-roast. Other Frost Fair events included bull-baiting, horse racing and football. The last of these took place in 1813–14, after which the new bridge allowed the river to flow freely.

HMS *Belfast* [2]
Symons Wharf

HMS *Belfast* is the last survivor of the Royal Navy's big gun ships from World War II and is permanently moored by Tower Bridge. It was built 1936–8 with a displacement of 10 553 tons and measures 613 ft (187 m) long by 66 ft (20 m) wide. Its first involvement was at the Battle of North Cape in the Arctic in 1943. In 1944 it supported the D-Day landings at Normandy and last saw action in the Korean War during 1950–2. HMS *Belfast* was turned into a museum in 1971, the first warship since HMS *Victory* to be preserved for the nation. It gives an excellent insight into the conditions of war and peace at sea and includes naval exhibitions and paintings. (A clearly marked numbered route for touring the ship is laid out.)

The following areas are of particular interest:

'A' turret This is one of the four turrets which comprise the ship's main armament. It has three 6-in (15 cm) guns, each with a maximum range of 14.1 miles (22.7 km). From its present mooring it could therefore destroy Hampton Court Palace!

Compass Platform (Bridge) The view from here, originally an open bridge, gives an idea of what it would have been like to have captained HMS *Belfast* by sole reliance on visual observation.

Galley and Food Areas With a total complement of between 750–800 men, over 2100 meals were served per day in temperatures above 104°F (40°C) when in the tropics. Daily consumption included 1200 lb (544 kg) of fresh baked bread, 1100 lb (500 kg) of potatoes and 330 lb (150 kg) of fresh vegetables.

Boiler Room and Engine Room This is the heart of the ship where superheated steam at 350 lb per sq in (2413 kPa) is produced to drive turbines which in turn drive the propellers. An idea of the propeller size may be gauged from the largest spanner on board (near the 4-in guns on deck—signposted No. 2) which is used to tighten the propeller securing nut. It stands some 3 ft 10 in (1.17 m) high and has an inside diameter of 15.75 in (40 cm).

O **Daily 20 Mar-31 Oct 11.00-17.20, 11 Nov-19 Mar 11.00-16.00; C; £**
☎ **(01) 407 6434**
Note: Confined spaces and steep ladders involved.

Space Adventure [3]
64-6 Tooley Street

Space Adventure claims to recreate the sensation of space travel, taking some 80 people at a time on board Europe's largest 'space-flight simulator' on a 'journey' to Mars. This type of simulator is similar to that used to train airline pilots and the impression of the 20-minute 'ride' is considerably more intercontinental than inter-planetary.

O **Daily except 25 Dec 10.00-18.00; C; £;** ♿
☎ **(01) 378 1405**

London Dungeon [4]
Tooley Street

The world's first and only medieval horror museum was founded in 1975 by Annabel Gedes, a Chelsea housewife whose children were bitterly disappointed by the lack of 'blood and thunder' at the Tower of London. Set in dark atmospheric vaults beneath London Bridge station, it consists of a series of life-size tableaux portraying the macabre and dark side of British history.

Above the Dungeon are 878 arches built for the London and Greenwich railway in 1836. Still in use, it is Britain's longest railway viaduct and the world's longest brick structure at 3.75 miles (6 km).

The martyrdom of St George, the patron saint of England, illustrates perhaps the Dungeon's hardiest victim. He was tied to a cross, his flesh scraped with sharp irons, then nailed to a table and poisoned. Still refusing to die he was sawn asunder by sharp wheels, boiled in a cauldron of molten lead and finally beheaded! (If St George did exist, he was probably a Christian soldier martyred in Palestine c. 300 and later adopted as a soldier saint by the Crusaders.)

Some barbaric methods of 'rough justice' doled out in London in particular are reconstructed. One of the worst fates was to suffer death by being boiled in a cauldron of water. Henry VIII sanctioned this method of execution by an Act in 1531 and it is recorded that a cook named Richard Roose, who accidentally poisoned to death two of the household of the Bishop of Rochester, suffered this fate at Smithfield. The Act was repealed in 1547.

In an age when 300 crimes were punishable by death (including such heinous acts as damage to fish ponds!) London's most infamous execution site was Tyburn Gallows (reconstructed here), upon which some 50 000 people were hanged between 1196 and 1783 (see Tyburn Gallows site).

Two exhibits for the strong-stomached include:

Hanging, drawing and quartering. (The victim was strangled, but not killed, by hanging, disembowelled whilst alive and cut into four pieces.) David, Prince of Wales, was the first victim of this 'Godly Butchery' at the hands of Edward I in 1282.

Death by beheading—the headless Mary Queen of Scots is shown here, losing several gallons of blood a day! Beheading was apparently introduced to England by William the Conqueror for execution of 'high society' criminals. It was first carried out in England in 1076 and finally in 1747 at Tower Hill.

The final horror before leaving the Dungeon is the 'Fire of London' exhibition which features a life-size reconstruction of Pudding Lane. The smell of flaming timbers and other

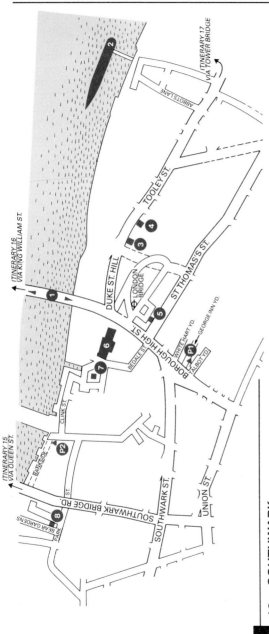

18. SOUTHWARK

1 London Bridge
2 HMS *Belfast*
3 Space Adventure
4 London Dungeon
5 Operating Theatre of Old St Thomas's Hospital
6 Southwark Cathedral *
7 Winchester Palace (Winchester House)
8 Shakespeare Globe Museum

Pubs
P1 The George Inn
P2 The Anchor

* Specially recommended by author

Gunboat diplomacy—inside 'A' turret of HMS Belfast, *last of the Navy's big gun ships.*

atmospheric effects create the illusion of burning London on 2 Sept 1666 (see The Monument).

O Daily 10.00–17.30; £; ⅍ t (ladies only) 100%
☎ **(01) 403 0606**

Operating Theatre of Old St Thomas's Hospital [5]
St Thomas's Street

In 1957 the only surviving example of an early 19th-century British operating theatre was discovered in the attic of St Thomas's Church. The church had been adjacent to the old hospital which moved away in the late 1860s. This theatre, solely for female patients, was built in 1821 and was in use until 1862. It has been restored to its original form and consists of a 45 ft (14 m) wide, semicircular auditorium, flanked by five terraced rows, from which students could observe early surgical practices. (Anaesthesia was not used in London during a surgical operation until 1846.) During the operation patients would be propped up on the wooden table, able to watch if they could stand the pain! If students were present the patients were blindfolded to preserve anonymity. Below the table is a box filled with sawdust which the doctor would have moved into position with his foot to catch the blood.

A hospital was founded on this site in 1106 and therefore St Thomas's may claim to be the oldest surviving hospital in London. It was probably then part of the Priory of St Mary Overie (see Southwark Cathedral) and was not founded as St Thomas's until 1213.

The rest of the loft has been reconstructed to resemble its original use as a drying-room and store for herbs and medicines. There is also a contemporary collection of medical memorabilia, including saws, knives, bullets and shrapnel extracted from British soldiers of the day.

O **Mon, Wed, Fri, 12.30–16.00;** £
☎ (01) 407 7600

Southwark Cathedral [6]

The first church on this site is said to have been built in the 7th century. It was named St Mary Overie, meaning over the water (i.e. the Thames). It was rebuilt in 1106 and destroyed by fire. Its successor, the first major Gothic church in London, began construction in 1220. It was not completed until about 200 years later, however, interrupted by lack of funds and fire. The pinnacled tower was added in 1689 but like most of its external features was extensively renovated in the 19th century. The church had become known as St Saviour's since 1539 and in 1905 it became Southwark Cathedral.

The Nave   The present nave was rebuilt in 1890–7, although immediately to the left of the entrance door are remains of 13th-century arcading. The late 15th-century wooden roof was taken down in 1831 and 13 of its finely-carved bosses are displayed—the most interesting of these depicts the devil swallowing Judas Iscariot. The round arch nearby in the north wall dates from the 12th-century Norman church, which was some 2 ft (60 cm) lower than the present church. The elaborate colourful tomb of John Gower (d 1408), poet and friend of Chaucer, commemorates 'the first English poet', so called because he was the first literary man to break the tradition of writing in French or Latin.

North Transept   There are several grand monuments here. The most bizarre recalls Lionel Lockyer (d 1672), who was one of the greatest charlatans of his day. 'His virtue and

his PILLS are soe well known. That envy can't confine them under stone.' Lockyer claimed his pills could cure 'a regiment of diseases' and achieved fame and some fortune by selling them to credulous Londoners at the exorbitant price of four shillings (20p) per box.

The Harvard Chapel is dedicated to John Harvard (1607–38) who was baptized in St Saviour's and lived in Southwark. He emigrated to Massachusetts and by his will became the major benefactor of Harvard University, the senior university and oldest educational institution of the USA.

North Choir Aisle   The highly coloured life-like monument to John Trehearne and his wife is dedicated to one of the four parishioners who purchased the church in 1614, thereby saving it from demolition. Next to this is a sombre stone effigy of an emaciated corpse in a shroud (probably 16th century). The adjacent figure of a knight (1280–1300) is one of the earliest surviving wooden monuments in England. The magnificent wooden inlaid and carved Nonesuch Chest in the retrochoir pre-dates 1588 and is regarded as one of the finest cabinets of its kind in England. It was used to hold parish records.

South Choir Aisle   This area contains the tombs of Edward Talbot, who became the first Bishop of Southwark in 1905 and Lancelot Andrewes (d 1626), the last Bishop of Winchester to live at the neighbouring Winchester Palace.

High Altar   The splendid stone screen dates from 1520 although the present statues were not added until 1905, possibly replacing figures destroyed at the Reformation.

South Transept   The coat of arms of Cardinal Beaufort, Bishop of Winchester in the late 14th century, are displayed on the wall. A cousin of Richard II and half-brother to Henry IV, he sat in the trial of Joan of Arc in 1430.

South Aisle   The Shakespeare memorial,

featuring 'The Bard' recumbent, was dedicated in 1911 to Southwark's most famous parishioner who lived in the area from 1599 to 1611 and was a partner in the local Globe Theatre (see Shakespeare Globe Museum). His brother Edmund (d 1607) and some of his fellow dramatists are buried in the Cathedral. The site of Edmund's grave is unknown, although a floor stone in the choir is dedicated to him.

Winchester Palace (Winchester House) [7]
Clink Street

All that remains of the Palace of Winchester is the west wall of the 14th-century Great Hall with its elaborate rose window tracery. The Palace was the London residence of the bishops of Winchester from 1109 to 1626. In an age when bishops were often statesmen as well as churchmen this was a convenient location for the king's court at Westminster. It is reputed that Henry VIII first met his fifth wife Catherine Howard here in 1540. When the bishops' powers were suppressed in 1642 the Palace was converted to a prison for Civil War Royalists.

Clink Street takes its name from the 'Clink' prison of the bishops of Winchester who had jurisdiction of the local area. This was a particularly feared, damp and squalid gaol, situated between the river, the common sewer and the bishop's fishponds. It was destroyed in 1780 but lives on in the English language—to be 'in the clink' (to be in prison).

Many of the brothels on old Bankside stood on land owned by the bishops of Winchester and contributed a sizeable income to the estate (the high class brothels charged up to £5 per visit). They were known as 'stews', the old word for a fish-pond, after the bishop's fish-ponds, and their women were nicknamed 'Winchester Geese'.

Shakespeare Globe Museum [8]
Bear Gardens

This museum traces the history of the Elizabethan and Jacobean theatre, with particular reference to its development in the local area from 1576 to 1642. There is a full-size replica of a small theatre, based on an Inigo Jones design of 1616, which is used to present workshop performances of Elizabethan drama.

O Mon–Sat 10.00–17.00; Sun 13.30–17.30; £; ♿ Museum only, 1 large step
☎ (01) 620 0202

The site of the museum formerly held the Davies Amphitheatre—the last bear-baiting ring of Bankside—closed in 1682. This dubious popular pastime, first mentioned locally in 1546, involved betting on the outcome of bloody battles between bears and dogs and was patronized by Henry VIII and Elizabeth I. Bear-baiting was outlawed in 1835.

A few yards away from the museum, work is underway to reconstruct the Globe Theatre on its original site. Built in 1599, this was London's first great popular theatre. Shakespeare was a part owner and saw the first performance of many of his plays there including *Hamlet*, *Othello* and *King Lear*. The first Globe burned down in 1613 and the second was demolished in 1644. It is hoped that the third will be completed by 1992.

The George Inn [P1]
Borough High Street

The present building dates from 1676 and is the only galleried inn left in London. When strolling actors (amongst them Shakespeare) came on to the scene around the turn of the 17th century, inns added theatrical entertainment to their services and performances would take place in the courtyard while drinkers would watch from the galleries. (In the summer performances of Shakespeare's plays are still staged here.) Before the first train service to Southwark in 1836, the George was the major coaching terminus for south east England. It is mentioned by Charles Dickens in *Little Dorrit* (1855–7) and it is likely that Dr Johnson would also have used the inn.

A rare 'Act of Parliament Clock' from 1797 hangs on the wall in the first bar. A tax of five shillings (25p) was imposed that year on every personal timepiece. Not surprisingly most people had to sell their watches and clocks and so communal clocks were made for public places such as inns. This unpopular Act was repealed the following year.

☎ **(01) 407 2056**

The Anchor [P2]
Bankside

The original Anchor dates back to the 15th century and entertained some of the very worst of Southwark—smugglers, press-gangs and warders from the Clink Prison (see Winchester Palace). The present pub, built 1770–5, still has small hide holes for fugitives from the Clink and more cheerfully a minstrels' gallery. It was probably from here that Samuel Pepys 'staid till it was dark and saw the fire grow' on 2 September 1666.

☎ **(01) 407 1577**

Southwark Cathedral—one of London's finest Gothic buildings.

GREENWICH AND THE THAMES BARRIER

Greenwich takes its name from either the Anglo-Saxon for 'green village' or Scandinavian for 'green reach'. It lies less than 5 miles (3 km) downriver from the City and has always been regarded as an important strategic passing point.

In 1427 Greenwich Palace was built by Humphrey, Duke of Gloucester, the brother of Henry V. It changed royal hands many times and eventually became a favourite residence of the Tudor monarchs. Henry VIII was born here in 1491 and his daughters,

19. GREENWICH AND THE THAMES BARRIER

1 *Cutty Sark*
2 *Gipsy Moth IV*
3 Royal Naval College
4 National Maritime Museum *
5 Greenwich Park
6 Old Royal Observatory
7 Ranger's House
8 Thames Barrier *

Pubs
P1 Trafalgar Tavern

* Specially recommended by author

Mary and Elizabeth, two future Queens, were born to him in 1516 and 1533 respectively. Henry hunted in the parkland and found Greenwich a convenient site from which to visit his newly established docks and armouries at Deptford and Woolwich.

Greenwich declined in popularity as a royal residence after the Restoration but in 1675 Charles II founded the Royal Observatory in Greenwich Park.

This established Greenwich as England's most important naval observation site and ultimately led to the universal acceptance of Greenwich for the world's zero or prime meridian of longitude in 1884.

The river view towards Greenwich has remained virtually unchanged for over two centuries since Canaletto painted it and is one of London's most elegant vistas. The area has been popular as a countrified day out for Londoners since the Greenwich Fairs described by Dickens in 1837. It now includes the excellent National Maritime Museum, whilst just down river the ultra-modern Thames Barrier at Woolwich provides a striking contrast to the antiquity of maritime Greenwich.

Note: The most pleasant way of getting to Greenwich in the summer is by one of the many river boat services, usually with guided

▐ *A much closer modern contrast will be provided in the 1990s with the development of Canary Wharf on 71 acres (29 ha) of the Isle of Dogs facing Greenwich. This will be one of the biggest building projects that Europe has ever seen at a cost in excess of £4 billion. It will include Britain's tallest building, the Canary Wharf Tower which, at 800 ft (244 m), will be one third as tall again as the tallest existing building, the National Westminster Tower.*

The Isle of Dogs is popularly thought to derive its name from the Royal Kennels, somewhat smaller structures that originally occupied the site in the 16th century.

commentaries, that run regularly from Charing Cross Pier (by Embankment underground station), Westminster Pier (below Westminster Bridge) and Tower Pier (by the Tower of London). An interesting alternative is to take London's newest rail link, the Docklands Light Railway (D.L.R.), which runs on a high level track giving excellent views over the old Docklands. This runs from Tower Gateway D.L.R. station (Mansell St, a few yards from Tower Hill underground station) to Island Gardens station on the Isle of Dogs. Greenwich is then reached by a foot tunnel under the Thames.

Cutty Sark [1]
King William Walk

The *Cutty Sark* is the most famous and the last surviving British sailing clipper. She takes her name from Robert Burns' poem 'Tam O'Shanter' in which a cutty sark (a short skirt) is worn by the witch Nannie, who is represented here on the ship's figurehead. Launched in 1869 she originally shipped tea from China before making regular voyages in the Australian wool trade. She was restored in 1922 and used as a training ship before arriving at dry dock in Greenwich in 1954. Her dimensions are: length 212 ft (65 m), beam 36 ft (11 m), depth 21 ft (6 m), tonnage 921. Her maximum crew was 28.

Below deck is a display of the ship's history and the world's largest collection of 40 ships' figureheads.

O Apr–Oct Mon–Sat 11.00–18.00; Sun 14.30–18.00; Oct–Mar closes 17.00; £; ⅗ 40%
☎ (01) 858 3445

Gipsy Moth IV [2]
King William Walk

On 28 May 1967 Francis Chichester stepped on to Plymouth harbour after spending 226 days alone across 29 677 miles (47 750 km) of ocean. He had become the first Englishman to sail single-handed around the world and was knighted by Elizabeth II, using the same sword that Elizabeth I had used to knight Sir Francis Drake in 1581. Drake was the first British marine circumnavigator, although his journey aboard the *Golden Hind* was somewhat more leisurely at 1017 days. He was also a mere youngster at 41 years of age, compared to the amazing 66-year-old Chichester (who in 1957 had successfully fought off lung cancer).

Gipsy Moth IV is 54 ft (16 m) long and 15.75 tons gross.

O Apr–Oct, Mon–Sat 11.00–18.00;   Sun 14.30–18.00;   Oct–Mar closes 17.00;   p ☎ (01) 858 3445

Royal Naval College [3]
King William Walk

The Royal Naval College comprises four separate buildings, the King Charles block and Queen Anne block, fronting the river and behind them, respectively, the domed King William and Queen Mary blocks. The blocks on the river frontage are separated by a 115 ft (35 m) wide gap in order that the Queen's House, set back on the hill, should have an uninterrupted view of the Thames.

The College stands on the site of the old Greenwich Palace which, by 1660, had fallen into disuse. Charles II decided to rebuild it and in 1629 the first stage, the King Charles Block, was completed. It never progressed any further as both interest and funds in the project ran out. In 1694 Sir Christopher Wren was commissioned to build a Royal Naval Hospital on the site (a marine version of the Royal Hospital, Chelsea) and the remainder of old Greenwich Palace was demolished. The King Charles Block was enlarged and the King William finished in 1708, the Queen Anne in 1731 and the Queen Mary in 1745. The first elderly and infirm Royal Naval pensioners arrived in 1705 and by 1814 they numbered over 2700. By the mid-19th century, however, the number of pensioners had declined and allegations of cruelty and corruption levelled at the hospital's administrators had soured the atmosphere. The buildings were vacated in 1869 and occupied in 1873 by the present Royal Naval College, which provides officer training for the Royal Navy.

The ceiling of the Grand Hall features the largest painting in Great Britain, the *Triumph of Peace and Liberty* (a tribute to King William and Queen Mary) by Sir James Thornhill. It measures 106×51 ft (32×15 m) and has been described as the finest example of English baroque decorative painting. The rate of pay was £3 per square yard for the ceiling and £1 per square yard for the walls. Thornhill and his assistants worked on it between 1707 and 1727 and received a total of £6685, a sum then in excess of that paid for the world's highest priced painting. The Upper Hall ceiling painting, also by Thornhill, features George I and includes a self-portrait of the artist beckoning to the onlooker. The Grand Hall is used as the dining hall of the Royal Naval College.

The Chapel—Queen Mary Block This bright, spacious chapel was built by James 'Athenian' Stuart in neo-Grecian style, 1779–89. It features an unusual pulpit supported on columns and a fine altarpiece painting by Benjamin West of St Paul shipwrecked off Malta.

O Chapel and Painted Hall only buildings open Fri–Wed 14.30–17.00 ☎ (01) 858 2154

National Maritime Museum [4]
Romney Road

The National Maritime is the world's largest and most comprehensive museum of its kind, housing some of the world's finest and oldest collections of ship models, maritime paintings and navigational aids. Its major themes are the history of wooden ships up to the 20th century, the development of steamships and the story of maritime Britain.

In architectural terms this is the most out-standing museum complex in Britain and, with the Royal Naval College, is arguably the greatest set of period buildings in the country. The central building is the Queen's House, begun in 1616 by Inigo Jones as the first Palladian style building in England. The wings were built 1807–16 and formerly housed the Royal Hospital School for sailors' orphans. The Queen's House is unfortunately closed for refurbishment until late 1989. The main galleries are in the west wing whilst the east wing is devoted to temporary exhibitions.

The following is a selection of the most popular and outstanding exhibits.

Home for tea—Cutty Sark *in dry dock as she might have appeared after racing back from China with the first of the new season's crop.*

West Wing

LOWER GROUND FLOOR

Wooden Shipbuilding and Archaeology
This includes full size models of the Ferriby Boats, found on Humberside, dating from *c.* 1500 BC—the oldest boats found anywhere in the world outside Egypt, and the 7th-century Sutton Hoo burial ship (see British Museum).

Barge House The magnificent carved and gilded state barge of Frederick, Prince of Wales, made in 1732, is the most elaborately decorated full-size vessel in the museum.

Neptune Hall This illustrates the development of ship building and is dominated by the steam-paddle boat *Reliant*, built in 1907. At 106 ft (32 m) long and a gross displacement of 156 tons, it is thought to be the largest single exhibit of industrial history under cover in any museum in Europe. When the boat was installed in the Hall, the curved glass roof had to be removed to drop it in and it was therefore dubbed 'the world's largest ship in a bottle'.

FIRST FLOOR

Room 3 This traces the development of Britain as a world sea-power during the Tudor and Stuart periods.

Room 6 This is devoted to Britain's greatest naval explorer, Captain Cook, and the exploration of the Pacific. His portrait by Nathaniel Dance (1776) is considered to be an excellent likeness.

Room 9-10 Amongst the many museum relics of Admiral Lord Nelson, the most popular is the uniform coat he was wearing on 21 October 1805 at the Battle of Trafalgar, when mortally wounded. The fatal bullet hole may be clearly seen in the left shoulder. J M W Turner's *Battle of Trafalgar* (1824) is one of the museum's most valuable paintings.

Navigation Room This holds the world's finest collection of globes, dating back to the 16th century, and many early charts and instruments. These include the world's first accurate marine time-keepers (chronometers) made by John Harrison between 1735-60, two of which were used by Captain Bligh and Captain Cook.

Second Floor The collection of ship models features some of the world's finest and oldest miniature prototypes of ships under construction. The *St Michael* of 1669 is a particularly fine example.

Queen's House

This beautiful miniature palace was originally designed for Anne of Denmark, wife of James I. She died in 1619 during its construction and it was not completed until *c.* 1635 for Henrietta Maria, wife of Charles I. The most important and best preserved rooms are the hall and the Queen's bedroom. The hall is a

Green and pleasant Greenwich—National Maritime Museum colonnades with Old Royal Observatory beyond.

perfect 40-ft (12m) cube and features the first cantilevered spiral staircase in England.

When the House reopens in late 1989 it will contain 16th- and 17th-century portraits, early marine paintings and ship models.

O **Summer Mon–Sat 10.00–18.00; Sun 14.00–18.00; winter closes 17.00; £;** ⓑ **t 20%;** ☎ **(01) 858 4422**

> *Beneath the Queen's House is the site of the old Deptford to Woolwich Road. It was here that Sir Walter Raleigh is supposed to have made the gallant gesture of laying his cloak over a puddle to save Queen Elizabeth I's feet from getting wet.*

Greenwich Park [5]

In 1433, Humphrey, Duke of Gloucester, marked off the present 200-acre (81 ha) site of Greenwich Park. It was taken over in 1447 by Henry VI and may therefore claim to be the oldest of London's royal parks. It was used by the Tudors for hunting and sport and relaid by Charles II at the Restoration. It rises steeply from the river and gives a magnificent panoramic view over to London.

Old Royal Observatory [6]
Greenwich Park

The foundation stone of the first purpose-built observatory in Great Britain was laid in August 1675. It was founded by Charles II in order to develop nautical astronomy for the purpose of accurate navigation and has been called Britain's first scientific institution. In 1767 the first standard navigation almanac was produced, and with the coming of the railways, Greenwich time became British Standard Time (until then communities kept their own local times). In 1884 an international conference agreed that the meridian passing through the centre of the Transit

instrument (observation telescope) at Greenwich should be the zero for world longitude and therefore the world's standard time reference, since referred to as Greenwich Mean Time.

By the 1930s the ever-increasing smoke and street lighting of London meant that Greenwich Park was no longer the best place for the Royal Observatory and so, after the War, it was moved to Herstmonceux in Sussex. The Old Royal Observatory is now a museum.

Flamsteed House This is the oldest part of the Observatory, built in 1675 and named after the first Astronomer Royal, John Flamsteed. It was designed by Sir Christopher Wren, himself an expert astronomer, and retains many of its original features, particularly the excellent Octagon Room which was used as an observation room. Flamsteed House is generally concerned with the development of precision time-keeping and contains some of the finest and oldest time measurement instruments in the world. The building is surmounted by a large orange ball on a pole. The ball is hoisted to the top of the pole at 2 minutes before 1 pm each day and dropped at precisely 1 pm (13.00). This was erected in 1833 as the world's first accurate visual time signal. It enabled ships in the river below to set their time-pieces accurately, consequently aiding navigation precision.

Meridian Building This building dates from the mid-18th century and early 19th century and is concerned with astronomy and the development of telescopes as measuring instruments. At the rear is Flamsteed's original observatory, built in 1675. The Airy transit instrument (telescope) defines the east–west meridian and its axis line is marked by an inlaid brass rail outside the building. It is a popular source of tourist amusement to stand astride it with one foot in each hemisphere.

Great Equatorial Building This was

built in 1857 to house the Observatory's first large telescope of 12.75-in (32.38cm) aperture. It now holds Britain's largest telescope of 28-in (71cm) aperture. Further up the hill is the Altazimuth Pavilion (named after a telescopic instrument) built in 1898, and the splendid contemporary South Building which holds a planetarium.

O Part of National Maritime Museum—details same, combined ticket;
& (unsuitable for wider wheelchairs)
50%;   South Building planetarium
shows, ring for details.
☎ (01) 858 4422

Ranger's House   [7]
Chesterfield Walk

This handsome red-brick villa began construction in 1688 and became the residence of the Greenwich Park Ranger in 1815. It holds the 53 paintings of the Suffolk Collection—one of the finest collections of English 17th-century portrait paintings—and the Dolmetsch Collection of historical musical instruments.

O Daily 10.00–17.00 (Nov–Jan closes 16.00)
☎ (01) 853 0035

Thames Barrier   [8]

The Thames Barrier is the world's largest movable flood barrier and is one of the most remarkable pieces of modern engineering in Britain. It consists of ten steel gates which, in the lowered position, lie flat against a concrete sill on the river bed (i.e. most of the time they are submerged and therefore invisible).

London has recorded many floods, the worst of modern times being in 1928 when 14 people drowned in the basements of Westminster and in 1953 when the Thames Estuary flooded and over 300 lives were lost.

When a flood-tide threatens, they are pivoted up through 90° to a vertical position. There are six gates 200 ft (61 m) wide and four gates 103 ft 4 in (31.5 m) wide. Each measures 65 ft 7 in (20 m) high (the height of a five-storey house). Each of the larger gates weighs 3700 tons and takes 30 minutes to erect fully.

Between each gate are the huge concrete piers which support the gates and house the operating machinery. The distinctive stainless steel roofs over the machinery on the piers (resembling a disjointed version of the Sydney Opera House), are said to have been inspired by the shape of a ship's bow. Each of the main central piers penetrates around 56 ft (17 m) below the river bed and together with the concrete sills they contain around 500 000 tons of concrete—enough to build 9 miles (14 km) of six-lane motorway. Construction began in 1975 and was completed in 1982. The final cost of the whole scheme was £550 million, of which the Barrier cost £450 million. There is an audio-visual presentation of the Barrier in the adjacent Visitors Centre and regular cruises around the Barrier leave from its pier.

O Mon–Fri 10.30–17.00 Sat, Sun 10.30–17.30;   & t 100%
☎ (01) 854 1373
Note: The best way of getting to the Thames Barrier is by boat, direct from Westminster Pier or from Greenwich Pier.

Trafalgar Tavern   [P1]
Park Row

This inn was originally built in 1837 and became famous for the annual Cabinet Ministers' dinners of locally-caught whitebait. River pollution killed off the tradition and the Tavern closed in 1915. It was restored and reopened in 1968, once again serving whitebait, although no longer fresh from the Thames.

O &
☎ (01) 858 2437

HAMPSTEAD AND HIGHGATE

These are two of London's loveliest villages, meeting each other on Hampstead Heath. Hampstead is the older, first mentioned in the late 10th century, its name deriving from the Saxon for homestead. During the Great Plague it became a sanctuary from the City and the law courts were transferred here, as recalled by Judges Walk next to Whitestone Pond. This enforced taste of Hampstead as a healthy retreat developed during the early 18th century when the village discovered spring waters which were reputed to possess medicinal properties.

Hampstead has long been known as a 'select, respectable and opulent neighbourhood' particularly favoured by writers including Lord Byron, John Keats, H G Wells, R L Stevenson and D H Lawrence. The great landscape artist, John Constable, had several Hampstead homes, and his paintings of the area may be seen in the Tate Gallery and the Victoria & Albert Museum. He is buried at St John's church, Hampstead.

A hamlet is known to have existed at Highgate since the 13th century and its name derives from a 14th-century toll gate erected on the site where Ye Olde Gate House Inn on North Road now stands. This was the highest toll gate in London at 400 ft (122 m) above sea level. (It was demolished in 1769.)

Highgate, like Hampstead, became an aristocratic retreat and also attracted literary people, including Samuel Taylor Coleridge (of 'Ancient Mariner' and 'Kubla Khan' fame), who lived at No. 3 The Grove from 1823 to 1834 and is buried in St Michael's church. Highgate still retains its village charm, although its most famous feature since Victorian times has been its cemetery.

Due to the steep hill which is a feature of both villages, Hampstead boasts London's deepest underground station at 192 ft (58 m) below ground level, whilst less than half a mile away a white marker stone at Whitestone Pond records London's highest ground at 443 ft (135 m) above sea level.

20. HAMPSTEAD AND HIGHGATE

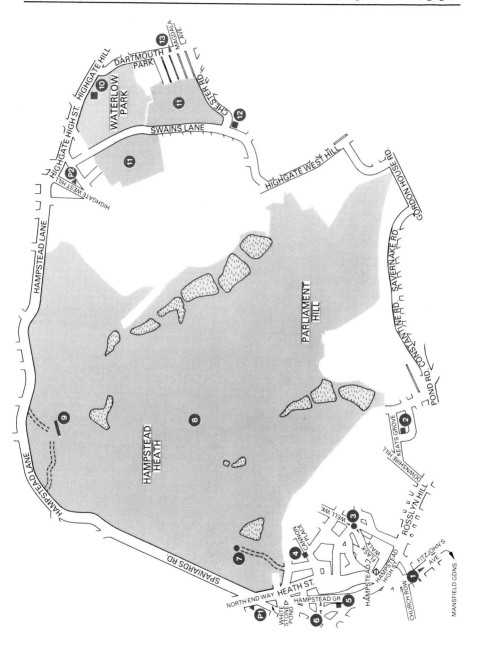

Freud Museum [1]
20 Maresfield Gardens

Sigmund Freud (1856–1939), the father of psychoanalysis, moved to his last home in Hampstead in September 1938 as a refugee from Nazi-occupied Austria. His library/study room contains his original Viennese furnishings, books and the famous couch which became *de rigueur* for all subsequent psychoanalysts, as well as his collection of over 1800 Greek, Roman, Oriental and Egyptian antiquities.

O Wed–Sun 12.00–17.00;   T (ring for times);   £;   ⅊ 40%
☎ (01) 435 2002

Keats House [2]
Keats Grove

Keats House was built in 1815–16 as Wentworth Place, then a pair of semi-detached houses. John Keats (1795–1821) lived there from December 1818 until September 1820. In 1819 Fanny Brawne (aged 18) came to live next door and they soon became engaged; but Keats died from tuberculosis, aged 25. The house is now a single unit but is preserved virtually in its original state and has been a memorial to Keats since 1925. It was here that he wrote many of his finest poems including (in the garden) his most famous 'Ode to a Nightingale'.

O Mon–Sat 10.00–13.00, 14.00–18.00; Sun, spring BH, late summer BH 14.00–17.00
☎ (01) 435 2062

Flask Walk, Well Walk [3]

Hampstead's spring waters were bottled here around the turn of the 18th century and sold at 3d (just over 1p) per flask. (By comparison, Hogarth's Londoners were 'drunk for a penny' (1d) on gin in the mid-18th century.) A memorial fountain outside No. 13 Well Walk marks the site where the springs were first discovered in *c*. 1700.

Burgh House which stands back off Well Walk was built in 1703 and is now a local museum and gallery.

O Wed–Sun 12.00–17.00

Cannon Place [4]

This takes its name from the early 18th-century Cannon Hall, presumably named after the two cannons embedded in the footpath outside the Hall, formerly used as hitching posts. The Hall was used as a local magistrates court and in the garden wall remains one of London's few surviving parish lock-ups. This grim temporary tiny prison cell was in use from 1730 onwards.

Fenton House [5]
Hampstead Grove

Fenton House is the oldest building in Hampstead and is one of London's best preserved late 17th-century houses. It dates from 1693 but the architect is unknown and the house name is taken from an 18th-century resident. On display are pieces of 18th-century furniture and English and Chinese porcelain, as well as pictures by G F Watts and Brueghel the Elder and a large collection of early musical instruments, including a 1612 harpsichord. These are kept in playing order for use by students and for occasional musical recitals. When in use, they bring a splendid evocative atmosphere to the house. Works by Shakespeare are also performed here in the summer.

O Apr–Oct, Sat–Wed (inc BH Mons) 11.00–17.00; Mar, Sat and Sun only 14.00–18.00;   £
☎ (01) 435 3471

Admiral's Walk [6]

Admiral's Walk and Admiral's House both take their name from Admiral Barton, an

18th-century Hampstead resident who, until recently, was erroneously thought to have lived here. The large white Admiral's House, built c. 1700, was the home of the architect Sir George Gilbert Scott. Close by is Grove Lodge where John Galsworthy lived from 1918 to 1935 and wrote most of the *Forsyte Saga*—the epic story of a London merchant family. It was adapted for television in 1967 and became one of the most celebrated British television serials ever made.

Vale of Health   [7]

This small settlement is the only village on Hampstead Heath and has probably been inhabited since the 10th century. It was developed from a paupers' marsh in the late 18th century and given its poetic name to attract new residents. These have included the poet Leigh Hunt and D H Lawrence.

Hampstead Heath   [8]

London's largest and most famous heathland covers around 800 acres (324 ha), much of it undeveloped woods and parkland. It has attracted Londoners since the 16th century when washerwomen came here for its soft waters.

One of the most popular parts of the Heath is Parliament Hill which covers 270 acres (109 ha) and rises to a height of 319 ft (97 m). Its name is thought to derive from the Gunpowder Plotters who intended to meet here to watch the Houses of Parliament burning on 5 November 1605.

Note: If you plan to roam across the Heath it is advisable to buy a local map to avoid getting lost.

Kenwood House (The Iveagh Bequest)   [9]
Kenwood, Hampstead Lane

Kenwood is one of the most important country houses open to the public in London. It was remodelled from an existing 17th-century house in 1764 by Robert Adam for the 1st Earl of Mansfield. It remained in the family until bought by Edward Cecil Guinness, first Earl of Iveagh, in 1925. He refurnished it and brought here his valuable collection of paintings. On his death in 1927 he bequeathed the House and contents to the nation.

The Dining Room   Here are some of the most important pictures, including *The Guitar Player* by Jan Vermeer (probably 1670s), *Portrait of the Artist* by Rembrandt (late 1660s) and *Pieter van den Broecke* (The Man with the Cane) by Frans Hals (1633).

The Library   With its elaborately decorated curved ceiling and Corinthian columns, this is the finest room in the house and is regarded as one of Adam's best interiors. It was intended to be a reception room as well as housing the collection of books.

Lord Mansfield's Dressing Room   English artists represented here include Sir Joshua Reynolds and Thomas Gainsborough.

Parlour   The 'Iveagh sea-piece' by J M W Turner (1802) is one of the earliest of his important sea-scapes; *Old London Bridge* (1630) by Claude de Jongh is one of the oldest pictures in the house and is a valuable reference work.

Orangery, Music Room and Lobby   These three rooms are all devoted to British portrait-painters, including George Romney, Sir Thomas Lawrence, Sir Joshua Reynolds and Thomas Gainsborough. There is a portrait of Henrietta of Lorraine (1634) by Van Dyck in the Orangery.

The portrait of John Joseph Merlin by Gainsborough (1781) shows one of the 18th century's great eccentric inventors. Merlin is claimed to have invented the first roller skates and chose to demonstrate them by making a grand entrance at a masquerade at Carlisle House in Soho Square in 1760. He skated into the ballroom playing a violin, but was unable to stop himself and hurtled into a large mirror, smashing it to pieces and injuring himself in the process! On show in the Music Room are two other interesting works by Merlin—a skeleton table clock made in 1776 probably as an exhibition piece, and an early type of modern invalid chair dating from the early 19th century.

The house looks on to 74 acres (30 ha) of beautiful wooded estate, first landscaped in the late 18th century. It contains a small wooden summer house which belonged to Dr Johnson (brought here from Streatham Park). Summer concerts are given in the idyllic setting by the lake.

O Daily Apr–Sept 10.00–19.00; Oct, Feb, Mar closes 17.00, Nov, Dec, Jan closes 16.00, Open BH; ᵬ t 60%
☎ (01) 348 1286

Lauderdale House   [10]
Waterlow Park

Lauderdale House is one of the original mansions to have been built in Highgate by aristocrats moving out of the crowded City. It takes its name from the Earl of Lauderdale, Scottish Secretary to Charles II. Originally built c. 1580, the House was remodelled c. 1800 and restored recently. It now holds a local museum and tea-house.

O Tue–Fri 11.00–16.00;   Sun 12.00–17.00; ᵬ t 20%

Charles II is reputed to have borrowed the House as a summer residence for his mistress Nell Gwyn. Nell had at least one son by Charles but he refused to give him a title and it was supposedly here that Nell greeted the returning King, dangling their son from a first floor window and threatening to drop him. Charles is said to have called to her 'So be it, pray spare the Earl of Burford'.

Highgate Cemetery   [11]

This 'Victorian Valhalla' is London's most famous cemetery. Around 51 000 tombs lie within its 37 acres (15 ha) accommodating 166 000 people. The west section contains the finest collection of Victorian necrobilia in the country. It was opened in 1839 and became an immediate attraction. At its heart is a magnificent cedar tree around which winds a circular passageway, lined with catacombs. This 'Circle of Lebanon' is approached through an arch flanked by Egyptian columns and obelisks and here the most interesting and unusual memorials as well as the largest monument in the cemetery can be found. The funereal folly of the millionaire newspaper proprietor Julius Beer (d 1880) was commissioned at a cost of £5000 and is based on the Mausoleum at Halicarnassus.

Elsewhere amongst the overgrown vegetation two of Highgate's most popular memorials are the sleeping stone lion on the tomb of George Wombwell (d 1850), a famous menagerie owner, and the huge stone dog on the tomb of Tom Sayers (d 1865), the last of the barefist prizefighters. Sayers was an enormously popular figure of his day and his funeral attracted 100 000 people. Pride of place in the procession went to his favourite companion, his pet dog, immortalized with him.

The most famous grave in the east section is that of Karl Marx (d 1883), the father of modern Communism. A huge bust, added in 1956, stands above the grave on which is inscribed Marx's famous rallying call from the Communist manifesto 'Workers of the World unite'. Other famous names buried in this part of the cemetery include the author Mary Ann Evans (d 1880)—better known by her pen-name of George Eliot (see Cheyne Walk, Chelsea), child prodigy actor William Betty (d 1874) (see theatre Royal, Drury Lane) and the great modern actor Sir Ralph Richardson (d 1983).

O East section daily 10.00–16.45 (15.45 winter) except during funerals;   West

section T only on hour Apr–Oct Daily
10.00–16.00; Nov–Mar Sat, Sun 10.00–
15.00 (Mon–Fri ring for details);
& paths very steep
☎ (01) 340 1834

Holly Village   [12]

This mini-estate of eight 'Hansel and Gretel'
Victorian Gothic revival cottages was built in
1865 by Henry Darbishire who did much
work for the charitable banking heiress, Bar-
oness Angela Burdett-Coutts. Her name is
engraved above the gateway entrance but in
this case the cottages were built as a simple
business venture.

Whittington Stone   [13]
Highgate Hill

This small stone traditionally marks the
spot where the runaway apprentice Richard
(Dick) Whittington heard Bow Bells, some
4 miles (6 km) away, chiming 'Turn again,
Whittington, thrice Lord Mayor of London'.

The stone's inscription 'Sir Richard
Whittington Thrice Lord Mayor of London,
1397, 1406, 1420' is much debated. He was
Lord Mayor four times (1397, 1397/8,
1406/7, 1419/20) although the first period in
1397 was an interim term following the death
in office of the previous incumbent. It is also
argued that the term Lord Mayor came into
use only after 1414, or even later in 1545, and
therefore Whittington could only ever have
been Lord Mayor once, if at all. However, the
earliest records of the term Lord Mayor,
'domino Majori', occur in 1283. Finally,

there is no record of him ever having been
knighted.

On top of the stone is a small cat, Dick
Whittington's legendary companion, which
probably never existed. This was added in
1964. (See Sir Richard Whittington—City
Central.)

Jack Straw's Castle   [P1]
North End Way

This famous weatherboarded coaching inn is
said to have taken its name from one of the
lieutenants of Wat Tyler's Peasant Army
who attempted to seek refuge near here but
was caught and executed outside where the
pub now stands. The present pub is a modern
rebuild of the original, destroyed in World
War II. It is the highest pub in London at 443
ft (135 m) above sea level. Dickens and
Thackeray both patronized Jack Straw's
Castle.

☎ (01) 435 8885

The Flask   [P2]
77 Highgate West Hill

This pub, like its namesake in Hampstead,
took its name from the flasks which people
used to buy to fill with water at the
Hampstead springs. It was originally built in
1663, rebuilt in 1767 and renovated in 1910.
It is said that Dick Turpin once hid in the cellars here (many pubs in the area claim similar
associations!). It was, however, a definite
haunt of William Hogarth and Karl Marx.

☎ (01) 340 3969

OUTER LONDON

It is beyond the scope of this Guide to go into detail on the major attractions in outer London. However, no visitor to the capital should miss the world-famous Royal Botanic Gardens at Kew or the magnificent Tudor Palace of Hampton Court.

The Royal Botanic Gardens, Kew

This world-famous institution is a combination of research centre and public gardens, containing over 25 000 plant species and varieties and covering 288 acres (116 ha). The Royal Botanic Gardens were founded in 1759 by Princess Augusta, the mother of George III, and laid out by Lancelot 'Capability' Brown, around 1770. It now comprises several glasshouses, museums and exhibition areas, a former royal palace and gardens of over 50 000 species of living plants and trees. Check on the notice-board at the gate for which areas are in season to appreciate the gardens at their best.

The following are its most popular buildings (suggested route from main gate):

The Orangery Designed in 1761 by Sir William Chambers, this is one of the finest buildings at Kew and is now an exhibition and history gallery.

Kew Palace This is the smallest royal palace in England at only 70×50 ft (21×15 m). Originally built for a Dutch merchant in 1631, it was acquired by George II in 1728 and was used as a summer home by George III and Queen Charlotte from 1802 to 1818. (In the north-west corner of the park is Queen Charlotte's quaint cottage retreat, built about 1772.)

Temporary Palm House Until the main Palm House is re-opened this holds some of the most popular specimens including banana, cocoa, pawpaw and rubber plants.

Princess of Wales Conservatory This latest conservatory opened in 1987 boasts a computer-controlled climate, and includes ten different habitats from desert and mangrove swamp to cloud forest and tropical pools. Its collection includes Giant Water-lilies which grow up to 6 ft (2 m) in diameter in 7–10 days and the ever popular carnivorous plants.

Palm House This, the Garden's most impressive glasshouse, was designed by Decimus Burton and built between 1844 and 1848. It is unfortunately closed to the public, for restoration work, until 1990.

Temperate House The largest of the glasshouses, this covers just over one acre (5209 sq m). Designed by Decimus Burton, it was completed in 1899 and was then the world's largest greenhouse. In the centre of the house is a huge Chilean Wine Palm, believed to be the world's tallest glasshouse plant. Raised here in 1846 from a seed it is now over 58 ft (18 m) tall.

Close by is the tallest flagstaff in Great Britain. It towers 225 ft (69 m) and was made from a single trunk of a 371-year-old Douglas Fir.

Pagoda This is the most famous of several follies once built in the gardens. It towers 163 ft (50 m) high and was erected in 1761. (Not open to the public.) Close by is another oriental folly, the Japanese Gateway brought here in 1910.

O Gardens: Daily summer 10.00–20.00,
winter 10.00–16.00; £
Museums: Mon–Sat 10.00–16.50
(latest); Sun 10.00–17.50 (latest)
Glasshouses: Mon–Sat 11.00–16.50
(latest); Sun 11.00–17.50 (latest);
& t 90% (long distances)
Kew Palace: daily Apr–Mid-Oct 11.00–
17.30; p
Queen Charlotte's Cottage: summer
weekends and BH; p
☎ (01) 940 1171

**Kew is seven miles (11 km) west of
central London. It can be reached by
underground (Kew Gardens—District
Line), British Rail, bus or boat (summer
only) from Westminster Pier (1½ hours).**

Hampton Court Palace

The Palace was originally built in 1514 by
Henry VIII's Lord Chancellor, Cardinal
Wolsey. Henry acquired Hampton Court
Palace in 1525 for his own royal residence,
enlarging the buildings and developing the
gardens. He spent five of his six honeymoons
here and his son Edward was born at the Palace. In 1559 Elizabeth I moved in. She was a
keen gardener and in 1586 Hampton Court
was allegedly the first place in England where
the newly introduced crops of tobacco and
potatoes were planted. The early Stuarts and
Oliver Cromwell all spent time at Hampton
Court until James II broke the tradition of
royal residence. William III re-established it
and appointed Sir Christopher Wren to re-
design the apartments. Queen Anne and
George I, successively, found Hampton
Court a pleasant country refuge and George
II became the last resident monarch. 'Grace
and Favour' apartments for retired members
of the royal household were instituted by
George III and are still in use.

The Palace is entered across the dry moat
via the Great Gatehouse built by Wolsey and
added to by Henry VIII in the late 1530s. On
the inside of the inner gateway is one of the
most impressive and oldest outdoor clocks in
England, an astronomical clock made for
Henry VIII in 1540 that shows the hour, day,
month, phases of the Moon and even information on the tides.

The State Apartments These are some
of the most sumptuous of any royal palace,
featuring work by such craftsmen and artists
as Grinling Gibbons, Antonio Verrio and
Jean Tijou and by designers William Kent
and Sir John Vanbrugh. The apartments
hold a collection of 500 paintings, many from
the 16th- and 17th-century Italian schools.
The most valuable works (displayed in the
Lower Orangery) are the nine paintings, *The
Triumphs of Julius Caesar* (completed *c.*
1490s) by Andrea Mantegna. Charles I paid
the royal sum of £10 500 for these in 1629,
making them then probably the world's most
valuable set of paintings.

The highlights of the apartments are the
Great Hall and the Chapel Royal. The
Chapel was built by Wolsey and embellished
by Henry VIII who added a magnificent
fan-vaulted ceiling which 100 men worked on
for over nine months. The Great Hall 106 ft
(32 m) long and 60 ft (18 m) high, built by
Henry VIII in 1531–6, possesses one of the
finest examples of a hammerbeam roof in
existence.

Grounds and Outbuildings

The Royal Tennis Court This court was
built for James I in 1626, probably on the site
of an open court built by Henry VIII *c.* 1530,
when the game of royal (corrupted to real),
tennis was in its heyday amongst the European aristocracy. The court was remodelled
and refitted in 1661–2 for Charles II. It is still
in frequent use and games may be watched on
it.

The Great Vine This is England's largest
vine, planted in 1768. Its girth is 85 in
(215 cm) with branches up to 114 ft (35 m)
long and an average yield of 703 lb (319 kg)
or around 600 bunches of the finest Black
Hamburgh grapes every year.

Hampton Court's Sunken Garden laid out in formal 17th-century style.

The Maze The most famous maze in the country was originally laid out for William III but replaced by the present shape in 1714. Its yew hedge 'walls' are around 7 ft (2 m) high and 2–3 ft (60–90 cm) wide. The paths within the maze extend for just over ½ mile (836 m).

O State Apartments and Vine: May–Sept, Mon–Sat 09.30–18.00; Sun 11.00–18.00; Mar, Apr, Oct, Mon–Sat 09.30–17.00, Sun 14.00–17.00; (Nov–Feb closes 16.00); £; T 11.15, 14.15 Mon–Fri during summer;
 ♿ t 90% (long distances)
Royal Tennis Court, other outbuildings, hours as above, closed Oct–Mar
Grounds 08.00–dusk
Maze 10.00–17.00 (no ♿)
☎ (01) 977 8441

Hampton Court is 15 miles (24 km) west of central London. There is no direct underground link. Public transport is either by British Rail from Waterloo to Hampton Court station, bus, Green Line coach, or boat (summer only) from Westminster Pier (up to 4 hours).

Major Museums and Galleries

Bethnal Green Museum of Childhood
Cambridge Heath Rd, Bethnal Green

A branch of the Victoria & Albert Museum, the Museum of Childhood was deliberately located in the poorer East End in 1872. It claims to be the largest public collection of toys, dolls houses, games and puppets on view anywhere in the world.

O Mon–Thur and Sat 10.00–17.50; Sun 14.30–17.50; C; ♿ t 75%; Short walk from Bethnal Green underground station
☎ (01) 980 2415

Dulwich Picture Gallery
College Rd, Dulwich

This is Britain's oldest purpose-built picture gallery, built 1811–13 by Sir John Soane. It is one of the most important galleries in London and is strangely unique in incorporating a mausoleum for its benefactors. Dulwich boasts around 300 Old Master paintings, the largest private collection on permanent view in the country, including excellent works by Rembrandt, Van Dyck, Rubens, Canaletto and Gainsborough. Amongst these is London's most stolen picture, *Jacob III de Gheyn* by Rembrandt. Valued at around £10 million, it has been stolen from Dulwich and recovered four times between 1967 and 1986.

O Tues–Sat 10.00–13.00, 14.00–17.00; Sun 14.00–17.00; £; ♿ t 100%; Short walk from either West Dulwich or North Dulwich (British Rail) stations
☎ (01) 693 5254

Horniman Museum
London Rd, Forest Hill

This small museum is devoted mainly to ethnography, natural history and early musical instruments. It boasts one of London's most eclectic and eccentric collections where live piranhas can be found next to a Spanish Inquisition torture chair.

O Mon–Sat 10.30–18.00; Sun 14.00–18.00; C; ♿ t 70%; H; Short walk from Forest Hill (British Rail) station
☎ (01) 699 2339

RAF Museum
Grahame Park Way, Hendon

This large museum is devoted to the history of aviation and Britain's military air-power with special emphasis on the Battle of Britain and Bomber Command (the World War II allied bomber force). It is specially notable for its unique collection of some 60 complete historic aircraft.

O Mon–Sat 10.00–18.00; Sun 14.00–18.00; C; ♿ t 100%; 15-minute walk from Colindale underground station
☎ (01) 205 2266

Outstanding Country houses

Chiswick House
London's finest Palladian revival villa, built in 1729.

O Mar–15 Oct Daily 09.30–18.00 (may close 13.00–14.00); 16 Oct–end Feb 10.00–16.00 (may close 13.00–14.00); £; Turnham Green underground station then E3 bus
☎ (01) 995 0508

Ham House
The most perfectly-preserved 17th-century furnishings in the country are held here.

O Tues–Sun and BH Mons 11.00–17.00; £; Richmond underground station then No. 65 or 71 bus
☎ (01) 940 1950

Osterley Park House and Syon House
Both houses are renowned for their late 18th-century Robert Adam interiors and stand in extensive parkland. Syon Park is particularly attractive and contains The London Butterfly House, and the British Motor Museum.

Osterley Park House O Tues–Sun 11.00–17.00; £; Short walk from Osterley underground station
☎ (01) 560 3918
Syon House O Easter–end Sept Sun–Thur 12.00–16.15; Oct Sun only 12.00–16.15; closed Nov–Easter; £
Syon Park O Daily 10.00–17.00 or dusk; £ summer, p winter; ♿ t Gardens, Butterfly House, Motor Museum; Gunnersbury underground station then 237 or 267 bus
☎ (01) 560 0881

PERFORMING ARTS AND SPECTATOR SPORTS

Theatre

There are 51 functioning mainstream theatres in central London, more within the space of two square miles than in any other capital city. Most of these are to be found in the West End, the top quality exceptions being the National Theatre on the South Bank, the Old Vic (next to Waterloo Station) and the Royal Shakespeare Company at the Barbican. In addition, there are many excellent suburban playhouses, summer outdoor theatre is performed in Holland Park, Regent's Park and Covent Garden and there is a large and proliferating number of 'fringe' venues.

The most famous modern play in London, if not the world, is The Mousetrap *by Agatha Christie. It opened in 1952 at the Ambassadors Theatre and transferred to St Martin's Theatre in 1974. It boasts the longest continuous run of any show in the world with the 35th anniversary performance on 25 Nov 1987, bringing the total to 14 566. It is predicted to run and run!*

Classical Music, Opera and Dance

The South Bank and the Barbican are the most important centres for these activities, although the popular highlight of the musical year is the 'Proms' at the Royal Albert Hall (see entry). Smaller, more intimate concert-hall venues include St John's, Smith Square, the Wigmore Hall and St Martin-in-the-Fields. The Royal Opera House at Covent Garden is the home of the Royal Opera and the Royal Ballet companies. The English National Opera perform operas in English at the West End's largest theatre, the Coliseum, seating 2358 people. The leading theatre for contemporary dance is Sadler's Wells Theatre.

Rock and Pop Music

London has been the innovative centre of the 'industry' since the early 1960s, with its most recent phenomenon being the 'Punk' explosion of the late 1970s. 'Up and coming' groups can be found in pubs and clubs whereas established stars will play in the larger venues such as Hammersmith Odeon, Earls Court etc. The most famous local London-boys 'made good' are the Rolling Stones and David Bowie.

Jazz

The best known clubs are Ronnie Scott's in Frith Street, Soho and the 100 Club, 100 Oxford Street. As with rock and pop many pubs and clubs feature jazz musicians.

Spectator Sports

The main spectator sport in the capital is the national game of football (soccer). London boasts 12 football league clubs, at least half of which will be playing in the premier First Division over the next few seasons. The 'glamour' clubs are Arsenal and Tottenham

Murder in The Mousetrap—*over 15 000 performances and still going strong.*

Hotspur (visitors are recommended to book seats rather than stand on the terraces). The two other regular popular sports in London are rugby union and cricket. There are ten first-class rugby union clubs, of whom the most successful in recent years are Wasps (who play at Sudbury) and Harlequins (who play at Twickenham, close to the National stadium). There are two first-class County Cricket Clubs. Surrey play at the Oval in Kennington and Middlesex play at Lord's in St John's Wood—the most hallowed sporting turf in England to devotees of the game. (The Cricket Memorial Gallery, a museum of the game, is open on matchdays at Lord's where the rare game of 'real' tennis, dating back to

the 11th century is also played. ☎ (01) 289 1611.)

The major set-piece sporting events are the FA Cup Final (the world's most televised annual soccer match), the world-famous Wimbledon Tennis Championships, the University Boat Race and the London Marathon—see Calendar of Events for dates.

For details of all performing arts and spectator sports in the London area, consult the following information sources: Tourist Information Centres, local press (*London Evening Standard*), the 'quality' daily press and especially the London listings magazines (*City Limits, Time Out, What's On*).

BIBLIOGRAPHY

I would like to acknowledge the invaluable help which the following books have provided in the course of my research:

The London Encyclopedia—Ben Weinreb and Christopher Hibbert
London 2000 Years of a City and its People—Felix Barker and Peter Jackson
The Shell Book of Firsts—Patrick Robertson
The Buildings of England (London volumes)—Nikolaus Pevsner
Readers Digest Book of Facts
also
Highgate Cemetery—Victorian Valhalla—John Gay and Felix Barker
Chelsea—Thea Holme
St Paul's and the City—Frank Atkinson

Recommended Reading for London Visitors
Shopping—*Time Out, Shopping in London*
Pubs and bars—*Nicholson's London Pub Guide*
Restaurants—*Time Out, Eating Out in London*

UNDERGROUND

Registered User No. 88/930

Colour Key to lines

Bakerloo
Central
Circle
District
East London
Jubilee
Metropolitan
Northern
Piccadilly
Victoria
British Rail
Docklands Light Railway

○ Interchange stations
Connections with British Rail
Connections within walking distance
* Closed Sundays
* Closed Saturdays and Sundays
▲ Served by Piccadilly line early mornings and late evenings Mondays to Saturdays and all day Sundays
† See poster maps at Underground stations for opening and closing times of these stations

RIVER THAMES

CALENDAR OF SELECTED LONDON EVENTS OPEN TO THE GENERAL PUBLIC

Date	Event and Venue	Notes/refer to entry for details
January (last Sunday)	Charles I Commemoration, St James's Palace to Banqueting House	Statue of Charles I and Banqueting House
February (late Jan early Feb)	Chinese New Year, Soho	Soho (introduction)
Late March/ Early April	Oxford v. Cambridge University Boat Race, Putney to Mortlake	
Easter Sunday	Easter Parade, Battersea Park	
March/April	London Marathon, Greenwich to Westminster Bridge	Europe's largest marathon (22 469 runners in 1988)
May (second Sunday)	Punch and Judy Festival, Covent Garden Piazza	Covent Garden
Late May	Chelsea Flower Show, Royal Hospital Chelsea	Royal Hospital, Chelsea (admission charge)
June (second Saturday)	Trooping the Colour, Horse Guards Parade	Horse Guards Parade (apply for tickets well in advance)
Last week June first week July	All England Lawn Tennis Championships, Wimbledon	Queue for early rounds. Very difficult to obtain tickets for later rounds
July	Doggett's Coat and Badge Race, London Bridge to Chelsea	Chelsea
July–September	Henry Wood Promenade Concerts, Albert Hall	Albert Hall (admission charge)
Late August	Notting Hill Carnival, Notting Hill and Ladbroke Grove	Europe's largest street carnival

Date	Event and Venue	Notes/refer to entry for details
Last Sunday September, first Sunday October	Punch and Judy Festival, Covent Garden Piazza	Covent Garden
October (first Sunday)	Pearly Kings and Queens Harvest Festival Service, St Martin-in-the-Fields	St Martin-in-the-Fields
November	London to Brighton Veteran Car Run, Hyde Park	Hyde Park
November (second Saturday)	Lord Mayor's Show, Mansion House to Royal Courts of Justice	Mansion House Museum of London, Royal Courts of Justice
November (second Sunday)	Remembrance Sunday, Cenotaph	Cenotaph
Mid-November	Christmas Lights, Regent Street and Oxford Street	
Mid-December	Christmas Trees, Trafalgar Square	Trafalgar Square

A complete calendar of all London's traditional events is available free from the London Tourist Board (see General Information). For additional information on the above, telephone (01) 730 3488.

Slowly does it—the London to Brighton Veteran Car Run. All vehicles must be built between 1895 and 1905.

INDEXES

Places and Attractions Index

Subject Index

Entries for people with more than five references have, where possible, been broken into sub-entries. This does not mean that there are no statues or portraits of people with five or less entries. Sub-entries have been kept to a minimum to allow as many references as possible to be included.

INDEX

Superlatives Index